INTERPRETING THE NUCLEAR NON-PROLIFERATION TREATY

Interpreting the Nuclear Non-Proliferation Treaty

DANIEL H. JOYNER

OXFORD
UNIVERSITY PRESS

OXFORD
UNIVERSITY PRESS

Great Clarendon Street, Oxford OX2 6DP

Oxford University Press is a department of the University of Oxford.
It furthers the University's objective of excellence in research, scholarship,
and education by publishing worldwide in

Oxford New York

Auckland Cape Town Dar es Salaam Hong Kong Karachi
Kuala Lumpur Madrid Melbourne Mexico City Nairobi
New Delhi Shanghai Taipei Toronto

With offices in

Argentina Austria Brazil Chile Czech Republic France Greece
Guatemala Hungary Italy Japan Poland Portugal Singapore
South Korea Switzerland Thailand Turkey Ukraine Vietnam

Oxford is a registered trade mark of Oxford University Press
in the UK and in certain other countries

Published in the United States
by Oxford University Press Inc., New York

© Daniel H. Joyner, 2011

British Library Cataloguing in Publication Data
Data available

Library of Congress Cataloging-in-Publication Data

Joyner, Daniel.
Interpreting the Nuclear Non-proliferation Treaty / Daniel H. Joyner.
p. cm.
ISBN 978–0–19–922735–8 (hardback)
1. Treaty on the Non-proliferation of Nuclear Weapons (1968) 2. Nuclear
nonproliferation. 3. Nuclear arms control. 4. Nuclear energy—Law and
legislation. I. Title.
KZ5670.J69 2011
341.7'34—dc22

2011013773

Typeset by SPI Publisher Services, Pondicherry, India
Printed in Great Britain
on acid-free paper by
CPI Antony Rowe, Chippenham, Wiltshire

ISBN 978–0–19–922735–8

10 9 8 7 6 5 4 3 2 1

To Jaeden, Merigan, and Rhiannon.
Our jewels.

Foreword

This study is a remarkable one and is greatly welcomed at an important juncture and after a successful NPT Review Conference in 2010. Daniel H. Joyner has relied on solid grounds in interpreting the Treaty not relying entirely on statements made by certain officials and personalities involved in negotiating the Treaty. Since my book was published more than 30 years ago, it is a great source of comfort to find such a new and remarkable study that greatly enhances our understanding of the NPT and which can be considered as an inescapable companion to my study of the NPT negotiations.

This new study should be required reading for anyone who would wish to deal with nonproliferation. I am grateful to the author for having resorted to my book frequently in which I do not pretend to have an answer to all questions raised or still to be raised in the future. Congratulations for a well-thought-out study which is original and faithful to the tradition of meticulous interpretation.

Congratulations!

Mohamed I. Shaker
Chairman of the Egyptian
Council for Foreign Affairs
and author of *The Nuclear
Nonproliferation Treaty: Origin
and Implementation
1959–1979* (1980)

Contents

Table of Cases

Table of Instruments

Introduction

This book was not originally meant to take the form that it has. When I first considered writing a book on the 1968 Nuclear Non-proliferation Treaty (NPT), I intended it to take the form of a legal commentary on the NPT. I began my planning for this project while I was still writing my first book, *International Law and the Proliferation of Weapons of Mass Destruction*, which is a broad treatment of international law relating to the proliferation of weapons of mass destruction, including both non-proliferation law and counterproliferation policy. In that book, I wrote a chapter on the NPT and the various hard and soft law normative regimes associated with it. That chapter eventually grew to become by far the longest chapter in the book, covering every legal question that I could come across that was associated with the NPT. In a sense, that chapter became the NPT legal commentary that I had separately planned to write.

At the same time, however, while writing that chapter on the NPT, I began to see that there were problems of legal interpretation of the NPT in the international community which struck at an even more fundamental level than I had been able to address systematically in my first book, which again was of broad scope and which had its own overarching thesis. These were problems which went to the very essence of the treaty's content, meaning, and structure, and which were a challenge to the basic rules of treaty interpretation in international law. They were problems which had produced distorted and unsustainable policy positions, particularly among Western, nuclear-weapon-possessing states. I decided not to try to revise the NPT chapter in my first book, as it covered the questions necessary to that volume's scope of inquiry, but resolved instead to follow up that book with a stand-alone volume on the NPT containing the more fundamental analysis that I could see was needed to address the remaining problems of interpretation.

The current volume, therefore, is not a legal commentary on the NPT. To the extent that such a thing can be written about a treaty as controversial as the NPT, that more comprehensive analysis of legal questions relating to the NPT is contained in my first book, *International Law and the Proliferation of Weapons of Mass Destruction*. The current volume is, rather, a thesis-driven monograph which will apply the rules of treaty interpretation in international law to produce what I will term a 'holistic interpretation' of the NPT. More on exactly what this means shortly. Through the application of these interpretive methods, I will hope to demonstrate that a number of the legal interpretive positions on the NPT, maintained particularly by nuclear-weapon-possessing governments, are legally incorrect.

When I read a thesis-driven book, I appreciate it when the author provides a summary of the thesis in the introduction. I think this straightforward approach firstly helps the reader to know if they want to continue reading the book or not, i.e. whether the book is addressing the questions the reader wants to read about. Secondly, I think it helps to lay the author's cards on the table from the beginning, so that the reader can more clearly understand the structure and intent of the work. So, for these reasons I will proceed to give a summary of this volume's thesis.

The unifying thesis of this book is that the original balance of principles underlying the NPT, which can be distilled through an application of the principles of treaty interpretation contained in Articles 31 and 32 of the Vienna Convention on the Law of Treaties, has for over a decade been distorted particularly by nuclear-weapon-possessing governments, led by the United States, in favor of a disproportionate prioritization of non-proliferation principles, and an unwarranted under-prioritization of peaceful use and disarmament principles. I will argue that this distortion of principled balance by nuclear-weapon states has resulted in a number of erroneous legal interpretations of the NPT's provisions.

These misinterpretations, in turn, have been used to form the legal basis for nuclear-weapon states' policies relevant to the NPT regime, a number of which have unlawfully prejudiced the legitimate legal interests of non-nuclear weapon states (NNWS), pursuant to the NPT's grand bargain. Specifically, these policies include:

1. Requiring NNWS to exclusively source nuclear material from a multilateral fuel bank or multinational enrichment center as a condition of supply;
2. Requiring NNWS accession to the IAEA Additional Protocol as a condition of supply; and
3. Conditioning supply and recognition of rights to nuclear technologies on compliance with an IAEA Comprehensive Safeguards Agreement.

After examining the treaty interpretations and related policies of the nuclear-weapon states during what I will identify as the target decade of this study (1998–2008), I will finally proceed to examine developments in nuclear-weapon state policy and international law since the Obama administration came to power in the United States in early 2009, to see whether these recent developments manifest a serious change of course toward a restoration of the original balance of principle and prioritization underlying the NPT's grand bargain. Though these developments are recent and ongoing, I think that in several important ways they do constitute promising evidence of remediation of interpretive and policy excesses of the past. However, some imbalances, often derived from incorrect treaty interpretation, still linger in diplomatic rhetoric and should be rectified.

1

Nuclear Energy and International Law

I. Nuclear Energy

In order to make these arguments, we must begin with a brief explanation of the technologies which are the subject of the NPT. First, however, a disclaimer. I am keenly aware of the dangers of practising what can been called 'law office science'; a close cousin to 'law office history.' These terms describe the attempts of a lawyer to venture outside of the comfort of his/her professional disciplinary training and into the substance of the issues which the law under examination seeks to regulate. This tends to proceed almost as successfully as when a nuclear physicist seeks to understand and apply the common law rule against perpetuities. Nevertheless, in order to provide meaningful legal interpretation, a lawyer must come to an understanding of the subject matter of the law sufficient to understand its complexity and the application of the legal sources to it. It is in this spirit, and with this disclaimer, that I offer the following explanation.[1]

At its essence, the NPT regulates nuclear energy in its varied applications. The most important principle arising from an analysis of the materials and technologies associated with nuclear energy, which an interpreter of the NPT must understand, is the profoundly dual-use nature of those materials and technologies. I use the term 'dual-use' here because it is a term of art which means that the materials and technologies have both military and civilian applications. However, more accurately, the term here should be 'multi-use,' due to the various subcategories of uses of nuclear energy, particularly in the civilian sector. However, to keep with the established convention, I will use the term dual-use throughout this book. *It cannot be overemphasized that the dual-use nature of materials and technologies associated with nuclear energy underlies all of the difficulties in regulating nuclear energy through international legal sources.*

What do I mean by the dual-use nature of nuclear energy materials and technologies? To understand this, we must briefly go into the physics of the natural

---

[1] See generally Joseph Cirincione, *Bomb Scare: The History and Future of Nuclear Weapons* (2007); Jeremy Bernstein, *Nuclear Weapons: What You Need to Know* (2008).

phenomenon of nuclear fission. Two elements in the periodic table, or more accurately two specific isotopes of elements in the periodic table, Uranium-235 and Plutonium-239, are peculiarly capable of sustaining a nuclear fission fast chain reaction. Although other isotopes of uranium and plutonium, as well as some other elements, will fission when bombarded with neutrons under the right conditions, the peculiarity of U-235 and P-239 is that when they are present in sufficient quantity (a so-called 'critical mass') they will sustain the fissile reaction in a manner which produces, among other things, enormous amounts of energy. In fact, a fast fission reaction of all the 2.58 trillion trillion (that's twenty-two zeros) uranium atoms in one kilogram of U-235 yields an explosive energy equal to ten thousand tons of dynamite.[2]

That is to say, a fast fission reaction of the atoms in a kilogram of U-235 will release this amount of explosive energy *under certain conditions*, e.g. when this critical mass of U-235 forms the core of a nuclear warhead. Under other conditions, when the slow neutron supply maintaining the chain reaction is controlled by a moderator, such as water or graphite control rods, the fissioning process of U-235 can be sustained and its energy can be released and harnessed without the typically inconvenient result of an explosive blast, e.g. when U-235 is a part of the uranium oxide fuel in a light water nuclear reactor. Again, the most important thing to glean from this discussion is that it is the sustained fast fission reaction of the selfsame materials, U-235 and P-239, which produces both the explosive energy release of a nuclear warhead as well as the controlled energy release in a nuclear reactor. This is the dual-use nature of nuclear energy.

But what about the materials themselves, the critical mass of U-235 in the core of a nuclear warhead and the critical mass of U-235 in the core of an electricity-producing nuclear reactor? What are the differences between the materials which produce these different energy outputs? The essential answer is isotope proportion. The critical mass of uranium in the core of a modern nuclear warhead is generally around 85–90 per cent U-235, with U-238, the primary naturally occurring isotope of uranium, comprising the other 10–15 per cent. At 85 per cent purity of U-235, a critical mass of uranium is considered to be 'weapons grade.' At over 20 per cent purity of U-235, a critical mass of uranium is considered 'weapons usable,' as material of this purity is sufficient for producing a crude weapon, and is classified as highly enriched uranium (HEU). By comparison, the critical mass of uranium at the core of a civilian nuclear reactor is typically low-enriched uranium (LEU) (i.e. under 20 per cent U-235 purity), and tends to be between 3.5–5 per cent U-235 purity.[3] These basic categories are consistent in the context

---

[2] See Joseph Cirincione, *Bomb Scare: The History and Future of Nuclear Weapons* (2007) p. 6. The bomb that was dropped on Hiroshima in 1945 had 64 kilograms of U-235 at its core.
[3] Ian Hore-Lacy, *Nuclear Energy in the 21st Century: The World Nuclear University Primer* (2006) p. 38.

of P-239, though the purity percentages differ.[4] So again, it is the same materials that are being used to produce both a nuclear explosion on one hand, and electricity on the other. They are simply present in different concentrations.

And what of the creation or manufacture of these different materials? Is there any way to distinguish between production of fissile materials for use in nuclear weapons on one hand and electricity generation, or other civilian use, on the other? In the context of uranium, the short answer is that in order to produce HEU, even up to weapons grade, one essentially performs the exact same processes upon a quantity of U-238 as one performs to make LEU for use in civilian nuclear reactors, only one performs the process repeatedly and for a longer duration.

Processes which increase the concentration of the U-235 isotope in a mass of uranium are referred to collectively as enrichment processes. All of these processes exploit the small difference in atomic weight between U-235 and the primary naturally occurring uranium isotope, U-238. All involve the initial transformation of the uranium mass into gaseous form. Then various processes are applied to the uranium gas in order to accumulate higher concentrations of U-235. Historically these have included electromagnetic separation of the isotopes, gaseous diffusion, and gas centrifuge techniques among others. By far the most common and economically efficient means of enriching uranium, however, is the use of cascades of gas centrifuges.[5] These spin at high velocities and create centrifugal force which causes the slightly heavier U-238 gas molecules to collect around the edges of the cylinder, and the lighter U-235 gas molecules to collect in the center of the cylinder. The U-235 rich gas in the center of the cylinder is then siphoned off into the next level of the centrifuge cascade. Each time the gas runs through a centrifuge, the concentration of U-235 increases. This process is repeated thousands of times until a high enough concentration of U-235 is produced in the sample. With sufficient uranium gas to continuously feed the process, this gas centrifuge cascade method can produce uranium enriched all the way to weapons grade.

Processes for producing P-239 are quite different. Plutonium is not a naturally occurring element. It is produced inside nuclear reactors by bombarding natural uranium with neutrons, which produces a phenomenon called beta decay in which one neutron in the uranium nucleus transforms into a proton and releases an electron. This process occurs in all nuclear reactors, but some reactors, known as breeder reactors, are designed specifically to maximize this process. In order to extract the plutonium from the uranium rods, a process of chemical separation is employed, commonly referred to as reprocessing. The uranium rods are subjected to a series of chemical baths in solvents such as nitric acid. Reprocessing is an expensive, heavy industrial process and requires a separate facility from the reactor

---

[4] P-239 is usually coupled in a critical mass with P-240, its less fissile isotopic cousin. Plutonium is considered weapons grade at 90%–95% P-239 purity, and fuel grade at around 82% P-239 purity.

[5] Joseph Cirincione, *Bomb Scare: The History and Future of Nuclear Weapons* (2007) p. 8.

with specialized heavy equipment and lead shielding.[6] Reprocessing plutonium to achieve a weapons grade concentration of P-239 requires specific and fairly readily detectable measures to be employed at the reactor site.

While plutonium can be used as a fuel for nuclear reactors, most power production nuclear reactors are thermal reactors, most commonly light water reactors, which use LEU. However, plutonium has become the primary core material for modern, sophisticated nuclear weapons due to its greater energy-producing capabilities per unit of mass as compared to uranium. Again, though, producing plutonium particularly to weapons grade requires a separate and relatively easily detectable reprocessing facility, as well as specialized single use methods of production. Reprocessing facilities are also highly resource intensive to build and maintain. Thus, while plutonium itself is dual-use, its processes of creation are more easily distinguishable in their intended end uses than are the processes of uranium enrichment.

In summary, then, in the context of uranium the processes of production of fissile materials are exactly the same whether fissile material is being produced for a nuclear warhead, or for civilian power generation or other peaceful uses. The essential difference in the production process for material of weapons grade purity, as opposed to reactor fuel purity, lies only in the extent and duration of the application of those processes to the uranium. As noted above, LEU is the most common reactor fuel material. This fact, along with the essential indistinguishability of the processes for creation of weapons grade vs. reactor fuel grade uranium, make this element the subject of most concern among proliferation experts and government officials regarding its dual-use energy production capacity.

In the context of plutonium, by contrast, the processes for production of weapons grade plutonium on the one hand and reactor fuel grade plutonium on the other are more easily distinguishable. However, because of the relatively high fixed costs of producing plutonium, its less common use in civilian power generation facilities, and the relative ease in detection of production of weapons grade plutonium, this element is of lesser concern to proliferation experts and government officials than is uranium.

II. International Law

With this brief review of the principal materials and technologies which are the subject of the NPT, we will now proceed to an accounting of the pre-NPT history of efforts to regulate these technologies through the sources of international law and international institutions. We will begin with the first ever resolution of the newly formed United Nations General Assembly, which was passed at its seventeenth plenary meeting on January 24, 1946.

---

[6] Joseph Cirincione, *Bomb Scare: The History and Future of Nuclear Weapons* (2007) pp. 8–9.

In Resolution 1, entitled 'Establishment of a Commission to Deal with the Problems Raised by the Discovery of Atomic Energy,' the General Assembly created the Atomic Energy Commission (AEC), which was to be composed of a representative of each state on the Security Council and Canada. The AEC was given a mandate to 'proceed with utmost despatch and inquire into all phases of the problem' of the discovery of atomic energy, and to make specific proposals:

(a) 'for extending between all nations the exchange of basic scientific information for peaceful ends';
(b) 'for control of atomic energy to the extent necessary to ensure its use only for peaceful purposes';
(c) 'for the elimination from national armaments of atomic weapons and of all other major weapons adaptable to mass destruction'; and
(d) 'for effective safeguards by way of inspection and other means to protect complying States against the hazards of violation and evasions.'[7]

The reason for the inclusion of this action in the very first General Assembly resolution was of course the fact that the world had only months earlier found out about the development by the United States of nuclear fission weapons, and their use on the cities of Hiroshima and Nagasaki, Japan in August 1945. In this resolution, the General Assembly extended its authority to consider issues of arms control, to include consideration of issues regarding nuclear weapons and 'all other weapons adaptable to mass destruction,' thereby clarifying the application of the Charter's terms to both conventional and WMD technologies, as that distinction began to be made from this time.

The early history of the AEC, perhaps not surprisingly, was to be a controversial one.[8] The U.S. Representative to the AEC, Bernard Baruch, presented a plan to the Security Council in June 1946 which included a proposal to establish a treaty-based organization to be called the International Atomic Development Authority (IADA), the task of which was to own, operate, manage, and license all atomic energy research and production facilities on behalf of the nations of the world. It was in essence a proposal to disarm all states of atomic weapons and create an international organization to control nuclear materials and distribute them equitably for peaceful uses, including the authority to maintain an inspection regime in all countries making use of such materials. According to the Baruch plan, the United States, as the sole possessor of the secrets of the full nuclear fuel cycle, was not to be subject to the authority of the IADA until the organization's control regime had been fully established, holding the atomic knowledge in

---

[7] Para. 5.
[8] See Haralambos Athanasopulos, *Nuclear Disarmament in International Law* (2000) ch 2; B. Bechhoefer, *Postwar Negotiations for Arms Control* (1961).

'sacred trust' for all humankind, and at the same time maintaining a strategic advantage over the Soviet Union.[9]

The Soviet Union, for its part, forwarded a counter proposal which would entail the creation of two new treaty regimes; one to immediately and universally outlaw nuclear weapons, and the other to organize the controls of the AEC and guarantee procedures for sharing of nuclear information and technologies between states for peaceful purposes. This counter proposal, of course, would have neutralized the U.S. nuclear advantage, but would also have left disarmament efforts largely in the hands of national governments, with an international organization having only limited rights to conduct periodic inspections of nuclear facilities.[10]

The result of these conflicting proposals was a compromise reached in the General Assembly by the passage of Resolution 41 on December 14, 1946, which used the recommendation power of the General Assembly under Article 11(1) of the U.N. Charter for the first time. Resolution 41 is divided into nine paragraphs, in which the General Assembly makes two statements of recognition of 'general principles of cooperation in the maintenance of international peace and security' and six 'recommendations with regard to such principles' to the Security Council.

The two statements of recognition are:

1. 'the necessity of an early general regulation and reduction of armaments and armed forces';[11] and

2. 'that essential to the general regulation and reduction of armaments and armed forces, is the provision of practical and effective safeguards by way of inspection and other means to protect complying states against the hazards of violations and evasions.'[12]

Based upon these statements of general principle, the General Assembly recommends in Resolution 41, *inter alia*, that:

the Security Council expedite consideration of the reports which the Atomic Energy Commission will make to the Security Council and that it facilitate the work of the Commission, and also that the Security Council expedite consideration of a draft convention or conventions for the creation of an international system of control and inspection, these conventions to include the prohibition of atomic and all other major weapons adaptable now and in the future to mass destruction and the control of atomic energy to the extent necessary to ensure its use only for peaceful purposes.[13]

And further that,

the Security Council give prompt consideration to formulating the practical measures, according to their priority, which are essential to provide for the general regulation and reduction of armaments and armed forces and to assure that such regulation and reduction of armaments and armed forces will be generally observed by all participants and not uni-

---

[9] See Daniel Cheever, 'The U.N. and Disarmament,' 19 *International Organization* (1965) 453, 468–470.
[10] Ibid.   [11] Para. 1.   [12] Para. 5.   [13] Para. 4.

laterally by only some of the participants. The plans formulated by the Security Council shall be submitted by the Secretary-General to the Members of the United Nations for consideration at a special session of the General Assembly. The treaties or conventions approved by the General Assembly shall be submitted to the signatory States for ratification in accordance with Article 26 of the Charter.[14]

The Security Council responded to General Assembly Resolution 41 on February 14, 1947 with Security Council Resolution 18, in which it resolved:

1. 'to work out the practical measures for giving effect to General Assembly resolution [...] 41...';[15]

2. 'to consider as soon as possible the report submitted by the Atomic Energy Commission and to take suitable actions to facilitate its work';[16] and

3. 'to set up a commission consisting of representatives of the members of the Security Council with instructions to prepare and submit to the Security Council [...] the proposals (a) for the general regulation and reduction of armaments and armed forces, and (b) for practical and effective safeguards in connection with the general regulation and reduction of armaments, which the commission may be in a position to formulate in order to ensure the implementation of the above-mentioned resolution [...] of the General Assembly [...]'[17]

Thus, the bold and imaginative, if rather one-sided, Baruch plan withered on the bureaucratic vine of the United Nations. The studies and recommendations called for by the Security Council in Resolution 18 did not in the end result in plans being submitted to member states, as the commission created by the resolution was divided on fundamental issues.[18] This inability of the political organs of the U.N., and particularly the Security Council, to act on issues of arms control due to political deadlock between the superpowers was to become an often repeated outcome, and formed the primary cause of the failure of the United Nations to make any meaningful progress in developing multilateral arms control law through the succeeding decades of the Cold War.

The next substantial progress in regulating nuclear energy through international law and institutions came as the result of another American proposal, this time put forward by the U.S. President himself in a speech to the U.N. General Assembly on December 8, 1953. President Dwight Eisenhower's address, which has come to be known as the 'Atoms for Peace' plan, in many fundamental ways forms the principled underpinning both of the International Atomic Energy Agency (IAEA) created in 1958, and later of the NPT itself.[19] Because of its

---

[14] Para. 2.   [15] Para. 1.   [16] Para. 2.   [17] Para. 3.

[18] See Daniel Cheever, 'The U.N. and Disarmament', 19 *International Organization* (1965) 453, 470.

[19] Joseph Pilat, 'Introduction,' in Joseph Pilat, ed., *Atoms for Peace: A Future after Fifty Years?* (2007) pp. 3–4. ('The IAEA was created in 1958, and reflected in its statute the twin Atoms-for-Peace objectives of the prevention of proliferation and the promotion of the peaceful uses of atomic energy. The Agency was in all ways the institutional realization of the Atoms-for-Peace vision.' 'Noncompliance with safeguards since that time has also raised questions about the treaty [the NPT]

essential role in enunciating the principles which would come to frame the international legal and institutional regime for regulating nuclear energy, I will excerpt a significant portion of the speech here:

The United States would seek more than the mere reduction or elimination of atomic materials for military purposes. It is not enough to take this weapon out of the hands of the soldiers. It must be put into the hands of those who will know how to strip its military casing and adapt it to the arts of peace. The United States knows that if the fearful trend of atomic military build up can be reversed, this greatest of destructive forces can be developed into a great boon, for the benefit of all mankind.

The United States knows that peaceful power from atomic energy is no dream of the future. That capability, already proved, is here—now—today. Who can doubt, if the entire body of the world's scientists and engineers had adequate amounts of fissionable material with which to test and develop their ideas, that this capability would rapidly be transformed into universal, efficient, and economic usage. To hasten the day when fear of the atom will begin to disappear from the minds of people, and the governments of the East and West, there are certain steps that can be taken now.

I therefore make the following proposals:

The Governments principally involved, to the extent permitted by elementary prudence, to begin now and continue to make joint contributions from their stockpiles of normal uranium and fissionable materials to an international Atomic Energy Agency. We would expect that such an agency would be set up under the aegis of the United Nations [. . .] Undoubtedly initial and early contributions to this plan would be small in quantity. However, the proposal has the great virtue that it can be undertaken without the irritations and mutual suspicions incident to any attempt to set up a completely acceptable system of world-wide inspection and control.

The Atomic Energy Agency could be made responsible for the impounding, storage, and protection of the contributed fissionable and other materials. The ingenuity of our scientists will provide special safe conditions under which such a bank of fissionable material can be made essentially immune to surprise seizure. The more important responsibility of this Atomic Energy Agency would be to devise methods whereby this fissionable material would be allocated to serve the peaceful pursuits of mankind. Experts would be mobilized to apply atomic energy to the needs of agriculture, medicine, and other peaceful activities. A special purpose would be to provide abundant electrical energy in the power-starved areas of the world. Thus the contributing powers would be dedicating some of their strength to serve the needs rather than the fears of mankind.

The United States would be more than willing—it would be proud to take up with others 'principally involved: the development of plans where by such peaceful use of atomic energy would be expedited [. . .]'

I would be prepared to submit to the Congress of the United States, and with every expectation of approval, any such plan that would:

First—encourage world-wide investigation into the most effective peace time uses of fissionable material, and with the certainty that they had all the material needed for the

itself. Embodying at its heart the Atoms-for-Peace bargain—that is, access to peaceful applications of atomic energy in exchange for verified pledges to forego proscribed military uses of the atom—the fate of the NPT regime and Atoms for Peace are inexorably intertwined.')

conduct of all experiments that were appropriate; Second—begin to diminish the potential destructive power of the world's atomic stockpiles; Third—allow all peoples of all nations to see that, in this enlightened age, the great powers of the earth, both of the East and of the West, are interested in human aspirations first, rather than in building up the armaments of war; Fourth—open up a new channel for peaceful discussion, and initiate at least a new approach to the many difficult problems that must be solved in both private and public conversations, if the world is to shake off the inertia imposed by fear, and is to make positive progress toward peace.

President Eisenhower's Atoms for Peace plan is essential to understanding both the IAEA and the NPT because it enunciated, for the first time together, the three principles which would come to form the core principles of the NPT, often referred to as the NPT's three pillars.[20] These three principles are:

1. encouragement of the peaceful uses of atomic energy;
2. prevention of proliferation of nuclear weapons; and
3. disarmament of existing stockpiles of nuclear weapons.

Mohamed ElBaradei, former Director-General of the IAEA, has said of the Atoms for Peace plan:

Atoms for Peace was an explicit recognition of the dual use nature of atomic energy, and stemmed from the belief in its potential beyond that of the destructive capability of nuclear weapons as a means by which to benefit humanity. The speech invoked a solemn commitment to the ideal that nuclear science and technology should be used exclusively for peaceful purposes.[21]

Joseph Pilat has very usefully commented specifically on the three core principles in the Atoms for Peace plan:

The president sought to expedite the development of the peaceful uses of nuclear energy. By offering the benefits of peaceful nuclear technology to those states that renounced nuclear weapons, he also sought to promote non-proliferation. The proposal was an arms control measure as well, as it foresaw the United States and other nuclear-weapons states providing excess nuclear material to an international authority that would use it for peaceful rather than military purposes [...] The President reasoned that nuclear material committed to peaceful uses would not be available for weapons, and believed that because weapon materials were so difficult to produce this would result in reductions in nuclear arms. With this end in mind, he called for the uranium producers and nuclear-weapons states to contribute fissile material to an international pool. To be administered by an international authority under the aegis of the United Nations, this pool would be used in the general interest— primarily to provide electrical power to regions of the world starved for energy.[22]

---

[20] Joseph Pilat, 'Introduction,' in Joseph Pilat, ed., *Atoms for Peace: A Future after Fifty Years?* (2007) p. 1.

[21] 'Foreword,' in Joseph Pilat, ed., *Atoms for Peace: A Future after Fifty Years?* (2007) p. xiii.

[22] Joseph Pilat, 'Introduction,' in Joseph Pilat, ed., *Atoms for Peace: A Future after Fifty Years?* (2007) pp. 1, 2, 3, and 5; See also generally David Fischer, *Stopping the Spread of Nuclear Weapons: The Past and the Prospects* (1992) pp. 34–37; Richard Hewlett and Jack Holl, *Atoms for Peace and War 1953–1961: Eisenhower and the Atomic Energy Commission* (1989).

President Eisenhower's Atoms for Peace concept clearly comprehended and expressed the dual-use nature of nuclear energy materials and technologies, as well as the inherent linkages between the principles of peaceful use, non-proliferation, and disarmament. These linkages would be later codified through the NPT's *quid pro quo* structure of reciprocal obligations. However, in the years immediately following its introduction, President Eisenhower's Atoms for Peace plan did not fully materialize as the President intended it to. As David Fischer has commented:

> There were three flaws in the plan. Eisenhower believed—mistakenly—that shortage of nuclear material would be the chief constraint on the nuclear weapon race and equally mistakenly that a rapid expansion of nuclear power, fuelled by supplies from the IAEA, would absorb the material 'syphoned off' to the IAEA. Surprisingly, too, the plan did not seem to take account of the fact that the hydrogen bomb would enable an attacker vastly to multiply the damage it could inflict with much the same amount of fissile material and that the Soviets had shown that they had mastered the technology of making hydrogen bombs.[23]

The IAEA was created five years later in 1958. Again, the Atoms for Peace concept, as institutionalized in the IAEA, was for the IAEA to be a repository of fissile material gathered primarily from nuclear-weapon states. This material was then to be shared out under strict controls to those nations which renounced nuclear weapons and which desired the fuel for civilian projects such as power generation. This process was to result in disarmament objectives on the front end (i.e. for suppliers), non-proliferation objectives at the choke point (i.e. control and supervision by the IAEA), and the advancement of peaceful uses of nuclear energy particularly for development purposes on the back end (i.e. for developing country recipients). It was an elegant plan which, like so many other elegant diplomatic plans, fell victim to the politics and suspicions of its time. Thus, while the IAEA Statute is structured essentially in accordance with the Atoms for Peace concept, and while the agency could have theoretically and institutionally served as a fuel bank and conduit as Eisenhower conceived, in the end there was simply not enough support in either of the superpowers for giving over significant amounts of fissile material from their own reserves to super-national governance.[24]

Over time, the IAEA's role became a somewhat more modest one, acting as an intermediary between states for programs of nuclear energy technology exchange and development assistance, and administering safeguards by agreement with states on their nuclear facilities. The IAEA's safeguarding role became more prominent over the succeeding decades, and particularly after its formal inclusion in the NPT safeguard system through the provisions of NPT Article III.

---

[23] David Fischer, *Stopping the Spread of Nuclear Weapons: The Past and the Prospects* (1992) p. 35.
[24] Ibid.

Notwithstanding the IAEA's imperfect implementation of President Eisenhower's vision, the conceptual lineage of the IAEA as an institution clearly runs directly from the Atoms for Peace plan. The conceptual influence of the Atoms for Peace plan also importantly proceeds to and through the diplomatic movement begun in earnest in the late 1950s, through the remarkable catalyst of the government of Ireland, in favor of the establishment of a multilateral treaty regulating nuclear energy in both its civilian and military applications as a source of binding international law. The beginning of this movement in diplomatic circles can be traced to proposals made by Ireland to the United Nations General Assembly during its thirteenth session in 1958.

These proposals took two forms. The first was a draft resolution offered to the General Assembly, which sought to:

establish an ad hoc committee to study the dangers inherent in the further dissemination of nuclear weapons and recommend to the General Assembly at its fourteenth session appropriate measures for averting these dangers.[25]

The second preambular paragraph of this draft resolution recognized that:

the danger now exists that an increase in the number of States possessing nuclear weapons may occur, aggravating international tension and the difficulty of maintaining world peace, and thus rendering more difficult the attainment of a general disarmament agreement [. . .][26]

The second form of the Irish proposals was a set of proposed additions to a seventeen-power draft resolution on the suspension of nuclear weapons tests. Pursuant to these proposed amendments, the draft would provide that states:

shall not supply other states with nuclear weapons while these negotiations are taking place and during the period of any suspension of tests that may result therefrom.[27]

It further called upon 'all states which are not now producing nuclear weapons to refrain from undertaking their manufacture' during the same term.

Mr Frank Aiken, Minister for External Affairs for Ireland, argued that there were two especial reasons why the proliferation of nuclear weapons needed urgently to be checked:

The first was the slowness with which negotiations toward general disarmament were proceeding. The second was that failure to halt the spread of nuclear weapons during the long period of negotiations on general disarmament was likely to make those negotiations abortive.[28]

With regard to the proposed amendments to the seventeen-power draft resolution, Mr Aiken argued:

---

[25] GAOR, 13th Sess., Anns., a.i. 64, 70, and 72, Doc A/C.1?L.206, 17 Oct. 1958.
[26] Ibid.
[27] Ibid. at Doc. A/3974 and Add. 1 and 2, 3 and 4 Nov. 1958, para. 22.
[28] Ibid. at 970th mtg, 31 Oct. 1958, para. 49.

It was essential that the 'nuclear powers' should undertake not to transfer nuclear weapons to other states, if manufacture of those weapons by the 'non-nuclear powers' was to be avoided. Indeed, until the 'nuclear powers' formally undertook to refrain from doing so, the 'non-nuclear powers' might fear a possible transfer to an enemy or rival, and strive to offset that risk by trying to manufacture their own nuclear weapons.[29]

As Mohamed Shaker has explained:

The danger was conceived by Mr. Aiken as increasing not only in proportion to the number of states possessing nuclear weapons but in geometric progression. While nuclear weapons were in the hands of a few highly developed states which had much to lose and little to gain by a nuclear war, and therefore felt a sense of deep responsibility regarding their use, the smaller states would have much less to lose and a temptation to exploit the enormous temporary advantage deriving from the possession of these weapons. Also by falling into the hands of revolutionary groups and organizations—and as history has shown, local wars and revolutions almost always involved great-power rivalry—the use of nuclear weapons by a small state or a revolutionary group could easily set off a world-wide nuclear war.[30]

While a good deal of support existed as to the substance of the Irish proposals, there was concern that the establishment of a new committee to review the issue of nuclear proliferation would largely duplicate the work already underway in the U.N. Disarmament Commission, which was to be enlarged in the same General Assembly session to include all U.N. members. With regard to the proposed amendments to the seventeen-power draft resolution, it was eventually decided by the Irish representative that the question of the proliferation of nuclear weapons should, in order to garner the maximum level of support, be kept separate from the question of nuclear testing. Thus, timing and other circumstances surrounding the Irish proposals in 1958 were perceived as non-ideal, and the Irish delegation withdrew them.[31]

However, efforts by the Irish delegation to the General Assembly on the issue of nuclear weapons proliferation, and particularly on the subject of an international convention on nuclear weapons proliferation, continued over the next three years. These efforts eventually resulted in the unanimous passage by the General Assembly on December 4, 1961 of a resolution on the 'prevention of wider dissemination of nuclear weapons.'[32] Because of the efforts of the Irish delegation leading up to the passage of this resolution, it has become commonly referred to in non-proliferation studies circles as the 'Irish Resolution.' The resolution:

1. Calls upon all states, and in particular upon the states at present possessing nuclear weapons, to use their best endeavours to secure the conclusion of an international agreement containing provisions under which the nuclear states

---

[29] Ibid. at para. 52.
[30] Mohamed Shaker, *The Nuclear Non-proliferation Treaty: Origin and Implementation 1959–1979*, Vol. I (1980) p. 5.
[31] See ibid. at 9–10.   [32] General Assembly Resolution 1665.

would undertake to refrain from relinquishing control of nuclear weapons and from transmitting the information necessary for their manufacture to states not possessing such weapons, and provisions under which states not possessing nuclear weapons would undertake not to manufacture or otherwise acquire control of such weapons;

2. Urges all states to cooperate to those ends.

The Irish Resolution of 1961 was remarkable in laying out for the first time in a broad multilateral statement some of the basic principles of a treaty regulating nuclear weapons proliferation; principles which would eventually underpin the provisions of Articles I and II of the NPT. It was further remarkable in placing upon nuclear-weapons-possessing states the primary onus of responsibility for the negotiation and conclusion of such a treaty.[33]

For their part, the superpowers voiced early support for the principles contained in the Irish Resolution. The United States had that same year put forward proposals to the General Assembly entitled 'Declaration on Disarmament: The United States Programme for General and Complete Disarmament in a peaceful World,' which included the provision:

States owning nuclear weapons shall not relinquish control of such weapons to any nation not owning them and shall not transmit to any such nation the information or material necessary for their manufacture. States not owning nuclear weapons shall not manufacture such weapons, attempt to obtain control of such weapons belonging to other states, or seek or receive information or materials necessary for their manufacture.[34]

Proposals forwarded to the General Assembly by the Soviet Union the same year under the heading 'Memorandum of the Government of the Union of Soviet Socialist Republics on Measures to Ease International Tension, Strengthen Confidence among States and Contribute to General and Complete Disarmament' included, under the subheading '[m]easures to prevent the further spread of nuclear weapons,' the following paragraph:

The Soviet Government considers that there is at present a possibility of concluding an agreement by which the nuclear powers would undertake not to give nuclear weapons to other countries, and those states which do not possess nuclear weapons would undertake not to make them or obtain them from the nuclear powers.[35]

Even with the general support of the superpowers, it was not until 1965 that the General Assembly next agreed upon a significant resolution progressing the agenda of achieving a treaty on nuclear weapons proliferation. In Resolution 2028 the General Assembly, acting under its powers pursuant to Article 11(1) of

---

[33] Mohamed Shaker, *The Nuclear Non-proliferation Treaty: Origin and Implementation 1959–1979*, Vol. I, (1980) p. 25.
[34] GAOR, 16th Sess., Anns. (Vol. I), a.i. 19, Doc. A/4891, 25 Sept. 1961 (Stage I, para. C, sub-para (e)).   [35] Ibid. at para. 22.

the U.N. Charter, agreed upon five 'main principles' which were to underpin a treaty on the proliferation of nuclear weapons. The negotiation of the treaty was entrusted by the General Assembly in Resolution 2028 to the auspices of the Conference of the Eighteen-Nation Committee on Disarmament (ENDC), a Geneva-based multilateral negotiation forum established in 1961 with close institutional ties to the United Nations. The five principles agreed in Resolution 2028 were:

(a) The treaty should be void of any loopholes which might permit nuclear or non-nuclear Powers to proliferate, directly or indirectly, nuclear weapons in any form;

(b) The treaty should embody an acceptable balance of mutual responsibilities and obligations of the nuclear and non-nuclear Powers;

(c) The treaty should be a step towards the achievement of general and complete disarmament and, more particularly, nuclear disarmament;

(d) There should be acceptable and workable provisions to ensure the effectiveness of the treaty; and

(e) Nothing in the treaty should adversely affect the right of any group of States to conclude regional treaties in order to ensure the total absence of nuclear weapons in their respective territories.

The principles in Resolution 2028 were the product of the Irish proposals of 1958, as well as the Irish Resolution of 1961 and four subsequent years of discussions of nuclear non-proliferation particularly in the ENDC and in the U.N. Disarmament Commission. During these discussions, both the United States and the Soviet Union presented draft treaties to U.N. organs, giving further support to the continuing momentum for the establishment of a multilateral convention.[36]

The five principles of Resolution 2028 became important guiding considerations in the negotiations which followed between 1965 and 1968 on a treaty text for the NPT, and their meaning and correct interpretation were the subject of much debate. The ENDC became the focal point for negotiations, and forum for convergence of resolutions passed by the General Assembly and the Disarmament Commission.

Members of the ENDC took wide soundings from other nations not formally members of the group, and included those inputs in the formulation of treaty drafts. Issues such as the sharing of control between nuclear powers and non-nuclear powers—an ability desired by the U.S. and its European allies but disapproved of by the Soviet Union—and the safeguards and inspection regime to be included in Article III of the NPT, were the subject of protracted

---

[36] The U.S. draft treaty was presented to the ENDC on August 17, 1965, and the Soviet draft treaty was presented to the General Assembly on September 24, 1965.

negotiation between the superpowers and among the wider membership of the ENDC.

However, to this point in the diplomatic history of the NPT, the members of the ENDC, and particularly the two superpowers, had been concerned almost exclusively with the issue of nuclear weapons non-proliferation. Indeed, neither of the other two pillars which had been part of the Atoms for Peace plan and which would eventually come to underpin the NPT—peaceful use of nuclear energy and nuclear disarmament—were mentioned in the articles of any of the U.S.–Soviet drafts prior to the identical treaty drafts of August 24, 1967. Incidentally, this early exclusive focus on non-proliferation in the agreed super-power drafts explains the title of the NPT as it was preserved in the final version of the text. Somewhat inexplicably, the title was never updated to reflect the broader object and purpose of the treaty, as it took shape in the later stages of negotiation. In his seminal work on the diplomatic history of the NPT, Mohamed Shaker has commented with regard to the late advent of focus on peaceful uses of nuclear energy:

Fears were expressed by [NNWS] that the NPT, by instituting [...] control on their peaceful nuclear activities in order to prevent the proliferation of nuclear weapons, would hamper their full access to the knowledge and technology of the peaceful atom most needed for their future progress and prosperity; [...] and that the Treaty would place them at the mercy of the nuclear-weapon States which would continue to enjoy their privileged position as the major suppliers of nuclear fuel and necessary equipment. Freedom to exploit the atom for peaceful purposes to the benefit of the non-nuclear weapon states was considered by the [NNWS] as the most tangible counterparts to their renunciation to acquire nuclear weapons [...] It is against this background that the importance and significance of Article IV and the corresponding preambular paragraphs can be understood and appreciated. In contrast with Articles I, II and III which have all remained unaltered since they were first presented in identical treaty drafts by the original co-authors, (i.e., the United States and the Soviet Union), Article IV was not only introduced for the first time by the latter upon the request and initiative of non-nuclear-weapon States but also underwent considerable changes before its final formulation to satisfy non-nuclear-weapon States' demands.[37]

The late attention to peaceful use issues in the diplomatic history of the NPT can thus be explained as being motivated by the fears of NNWS that the restrictive provisions regarding nuclear weapons proliferation, which were the near exclusive subject of the drafts to that point in the process, might be interpreted to prohibit even some peaceful nuclear activities. Many NNWS wanted it to be made clear in the final draft of the treaty that there was to be a balance of priority between the two principles of non-proliferation and peaceful use. They therefore demanded, ultimately successfully, the guarantees of Article IV both as a

---

[37] Mohamed Shaker, *The Nuclear Non-proliferation Treaty: Origin and Implementation 1959–1979*, Vol. I, (1980) pp. 274–275.

recognition of right, and as a reciprocal obligation primarily incumbent upon NWS to aid them in their development of peaceful uses of nuclear energy.

Similar to the negotiating history of Article IV, the submission of identical treaty drafts by the U.S. and U.S.S.R. on August 24, 1967 contained only pre-ambular references to disarmament, and no mention of disarmament in any treaty article. However, from September to November of 1967, a movement grew among important NNWS desiring that the obligations they were to undertake in Articles I and II be equitably met by the nuclear-weapon states through a treaty obligation to disarm.[38] Among the states placing such proposals on record were Mexico, India, Brazil, Sweden, Romania, Switzerland, Canada, the United Arab Republic, and Germany. The result of these efforts was the inclusion of Article VI for the first time in the identical treaty drafts of January 18, 1968. Again, Mohamed Shaker has shed some light on the reasons for its inclusion in the final version of the treaty:

The nature of the measures envisaged in [Article VI] left no doubt that the nuclear-weapon States were directly implicated by the obligation. Both the United States and the Soviet Union admitted, in fact, their primary responsibility. Their responsibility was looked upon by the non-nuclear-weapon States not only in the context of achieving a more secure world but as a quid pro quo for the latter's renunciation of nuclear weapons. It is true that the majority of non-nuclear-weapon States were unable in any case to pro-duce nuclear weapons by their own means, but their renunciation of nuclear weapons was felt to be meaningless if it was not met by a definite commitment on the part of the nuclear-weapon States in the field of disarmament and arms control. It was even a question of principle more than a question of security. There was no illusion that security would have been guaranteed merely by the adoption of certain arms control and disarmament measures by the nuclear-weapon States. The following statement by Brazil's representative at the ENDC illustrates this point: 'We are not questioning whether or not the nuclear Powers should stay nuclear until a final solution can be brought on the question of nuclear disarmament; but it seems to us imperative that the obligations imposed on the non-nuclear nations should be met on the other side by significant commitments related to the subject matter of the treaty.'[39]

Thus, in brief, the inclusion of Article VI was the other chief principled conces-sion sought by NNWS, in order to ensure that the discriminatory situation of rights and obligations between the categories of NPT parties, codified in Articles I and II with regard to nuclear weapons, would not be a permanent one.[40] Article

---

[38] Mohamed Shaker, *The Nuclear Non-proliferation Treaty: Origin and Implementation 1959–1979*, Vol. II, (1980) p. 564.

[39] Ibid. at pp. 564–565.

[40] See Joseph Cirincione, *Bomb Scare*, (2007) pp. 30–31; Christopher Chyba, 'Second-Tier Suppliers and Their Threat to the Nuclear Non-proliferation Regime,' in Joseph Pilat, ed., *Atoms for Peace: A Future after Fifty Years?* (2007) pp. 120–122; Mohamed Elbaradei, 'Towards a Safer World,' *The Economist*, October 16, 2003 ('In the climate of the mid-to-late-1960's in which the NPT nego-tiations took place, this bargain was the best that could be achieved. But the asymmetry it endorsed was never intended to be permanent').

VI additionally and importantly recognizes the inherent link between the imperative of stopping the further proliferation of nuclear weapons, and the imperative of disarmament of existing nuclear weapons stockpiles.[41] It is in the text of Article VI that we find the most concrete evidence that the NPT was from its inception conceived of not as the final word on the subject of nuclear weapons, or of nuclear energy generally. Article VI explicitly conceives of a treaty, to be concluded subsequent to the conclusion of the NPT, which is to obligate its parties to general and complete disarmament. This is clearly in contrast to the substance of the NPT, which does not prohibit possession of nuclear weapons by NWS. This evidence from the text of the NPT itself, along with a number of General Assembly resolutions, clearly establishes that the NPT was understood at its founding to be a temporary and intermediate step on the road toward full nuclear disarmament, and not the final word on the subject.[42] However, NNWS parties to the NPT particularly considered disarmament to be a key principle to be codified in the NPT. They saw it as an important reciprocal concession to be made by NWS in exchange for the non-proliferation obligations that the NNWS would be undertaking in the treaty. And on a larger normative level, disarmament was seen among many of the NPT's parties as an important principle and goal for the international community to strive towards, and it was felt that the NPT was an important intermediate step toward that end.

In both of these later movements in the diplomatic history of the NPT—the movement for inclusion of principles of peaceful use of nuclear energy, and the movement for inclusion of disarmament principles—we can see both a recognition of the dual-use nature of nuclear energy technologies, as well as the inherent linkages between the three principles which would come to be known as the three pillars of the NPT: peaceful use, non-proliferation, and disarmament. We can see also that through the diplomatic give and take preceding the signing of the NPT, particularly between the NWS and NNWS camps, it became clear that the treaty would need to maintain a careful balance between these three principles, so that no one principle could ever disproportionately impose itself upon the others. The structure of the NPT, with its framework of *quid pro quo* differential and reciprocal obligations between the two categories of states parties, was to be the method for codifying that balance into law.

On March 11, 1968, the United States and the Soviet Union submitted to the ENDC a joint draft treaty. This text was made the subject of several revisions over

---

[41] Mohamed Shaker, *The Nuclear Non-proliferation Treaty: Origin and Implementation 1959–1979*, Vol. II, (1980) p. 564. On the link between disarmament and non-proliferation, see generally Joseph Cirincione, *Bomb Scare*, (2007) pp. 32–33; Mohamed ElBaradei, 'Towards a Safer World,' *The Economist*, October 16, 2003; Mohamed Shaker, 'Toward Universal Non-proliferation and Disarmament,' in Joseph Pilat, ed., *Atoms for Peace: A Future after Fifty Years?* (2007) pp. 65–66; Christopher Chyba, 'Second-Tier Suppliers and Their Threat to the Nuclear Non-proliferation Regime,' in Joseph Pilat, ed., *Atoms for Peace: A Future after Fifty Years?* (2007) p. 123.

[42] See UNGA Resolutions 2028(c) and 2373 (Preambular Paragraphs).

the course of the succeeding two months, but was finalized in a draft of May 31 and submitted to the General Assembly. The draft was adopted as Resolution 2373 by the General Assembly on June 12, 1968 by a vote of 95 to 4 with 21 abstentions, included among which were France and three members of the ENDC. The NPT was opened for signature on July 1, 1968 at Washington, London, and Moscow.[43] It was signed that first day by the three depository governments and by more than fifty other states. The treaty entered into force on March 5, 1970, when, according to Article IX, the three depository governments and forty other states had deposited their instruments of ratification.[44]

The diplomatic history of the NPT, *when taken as a whole*, therefore, establishes clearly that the NPT is not fundamentally about regulating nuclear weapons proliferation, as it is often summarily described to be. It is, in fact, fundamentally about regulating nuclear energy in its full dual-use nature and range of applications. Again, taken as a whole, this diplomatic history makes clear that the NPT is underpinned by three inherently linked, and presumptively equal, principled pillars—peaceful use of nuclear energy, non-proliferation of nuclear weapons, and disarmament of nuclear weapons stockpiles—and not only one. *The NPT would never have come into being if the principles of peaceful use and disarmament had not been included along with the principle of non-proliferation.*[45] This balanced multi-principled underpinning is clearly reflected in the structure and text of the NPT as we will see below, and its conceptual lineage can be clearly traced back at least through to President Eisenhower's Atoms for Peace proposal. This conclusion regarding the principled underpinning of the NPT is absolutely crucial to understand when approaching the legal interpretation of the NPT. It is a fact which is frequently misunderstood by legal commentators on the NPT, which misunderstanding has led to incorrect legal interpretations of the provisions of the NPT.

---

[43] Treaty on the Non-proliferation of Nuclear Weapons, opened for signature July 1, 1968, 21 U.S.T. 483, T.I.A.S. No. 6839, 729 U.N.T.S. 161.

[44] On the NPT generally see Mason Willrich, *Non-proliferation Treaty: Framework for Nuclear Arms Control* (1969); Mohamed Shaker, *The Nuclear Non-proliferation Treaty: Origin and Implementation 1959–1979* (1980); M. Fry, N. Keatingue, and J. Rotblat, eds, *Nuclear Non-proliferation and the Non-proliferation Treaty* (1990); Ian Bellamy, Coit Blacker, and Joseph Gallacher, *The Nuclear Non-proliferation Treaty* (1985); Charles Moxley, *Nuclear Weapons and International Law in the Post Cold War World* (2000); Haralambos Athanasopulos, *Nuclear Disarmament in International Law* (2000); Lloyd Jensen, *Return from the Nuclear Brink: National Interest and the Nuclear Non-proliferation Treaty* (1974); John Rhinelander and Adam Scheinman, eds, *At the Nuclear Crossroads: Choices about Nuclear Weapons and Extension of the Non-proliferation Treaty* (1995); Susanna Schrafsetter, *Avoiding Armageddon: Europe, The United States and the Struggle for Nuclear Non-proliferation, 1945–1970* (2004); David Thomson, *A Guide to the Nuclear Arms Control Treaties* (2001); Jayantha Dhanapala, *Multilateral Diplomacy and the NPT: An Insider's Account* (2005); Jozef Goldblat, ed., *Nuclear Disarmament: Obstacles to Banishing the Bomb* (2000).

[45] See Lewis Dunn, 'The NPT: Assessing the Past, Building the Future,' 16(2) *Non-proliferation Review* (July 2009) 158–160.

2

Approach to Interpretation

I originally intended to entitle this volume *A Holistic Interpretation of the Nuclear Non-proliferation Treaty*. However, my editor and other colleagues eventually convinced me that modern associations of the concept of 'holism' with New Age healing and philosophy would likely make this title confusing to readers, who might expect a free scented candle with each purchase of the volume. I have therefore resigned myself to the current title. However, I continue to think that the word 'holistic,' in its dictionary and more traditional meaning, can be very usefully employed to characterize the method of interpretation I will use in examining the provisions of the NPT and in drawing the conclusions supporting this volume's thesis.

The concept of holism has been applied in many different disciplinary contexts, e.g. to medicine, nutrition, ecology, economics, anthropology, sociology. In all contexts, however, holism stresses the importance of the whole of a system and the interdependence of its parts. It argues that to understand any part of a system, the system as a whole must be understood, as well as the role of the examined part within that system. It argues that a full understanding of a system, or any part of that system, cannot be gained through a separate analysis of its parts outside of their context within the system.[1]

I have chosen to employ this concept of holism to describe the method of legal interpretation that I will use in this volume, because I think it parsimoniously and usefully expresses the correct interpretive method established in international law for the interpretation of treaties, as codified in the 1969 Vienna Convention on the Law of Treaties (VCLT). And I am not alone in this understanding. In its 2005 Report in the *EC-Customs Classification of Chicken Cuts* case, the World Trade Organization's Appellate Body observed: 'Interpretation pursuant to the customary rules codified in Article 31 of the Vienna Convention is ultimately a holistic exercise that should not be mechanically subdivided into rigid components.'[2]

---

[1] See, e.g., D.C. Phillips, *Holistic Thought in Social Science* (1976).
[2] WT/DS269/AB/R (adopted September 27, 2005), para. 176.

The rules of treaty interpretation contained in VCLT Articles 31 and 32 are binding as a matter of treaty law upon all parties to the VCLT, and they have additionally been consistently recognized by the International Court of Justice (ICJ) and other international tribunals as reflective of rules of customary international law.[3] VCLT Articles 31 and 32 are therefore binding upon all states, and apply to the interpretation of all treaties, including (due to their customary law quality) those concluded before the coming into force of the VCLT in 1980.[4] The text of VCLT Articles 31 and 32 is as follows:

Article 31
General rule of interpretation

1. A treaty shall be interpreted in good faith in accordance with the ordinary meaning to be given to the terms of the treaty in their context and in the light of its object and purpose.
2. The context for the purpose of the interpretation of a treaty shall comprise, in addition to the text, including its preamble and annexes:
    (*a*) any agreement relating to the treaty which was made between all the parties in connection with the conclusion of the treaty;
    (*b*) any instrument which was made by one or more parties in connection with the conclusion of the treaty and accepted by the other parties as an instrument related to the treaty.
3. There shall be taken into account, together with the context:
    (*a*) any subsequent agreement between the parties regarding the interpretation of the treaty or the application of its provisions;
    (*b*) any subsequent practice in the application of the treaty which establishes the agreement of the parties regarding its interpretation;
    (*c*) any relevant rules of international law applicable in the relations between the parties.
4. A special meaning shall be given to a term if it is established that the parties so intended.

Article 32
Supplementary means of interpretation

Recourse may be had to supplementary means of interpretation, including the preparatory work of the treaty and the circumstances of its conclusion, in order to confirm the meaning resulting from the application of article 31, or to determine the meaning when the interpretation according to article 31:

(*a*) leaves the meaning ambiguous or obscure; or
(*b*) leads to a result which is manifestly absurd or unreasonable.

---

[3] See, e.g., the *India/Malaysia* case, ICJ Reports, 2002, para. 37; the *Libya/Chad* case, ICJ Reports, 1994, paras 6, 21–22. See also Ian Brownlie, *Principles of Public International Law* (6th edn, 2003) pp. 602–607; Malcolm Shaw, *International Law* (5th edn, 2003) p. 839; Richard Gardiner, *Treaty Interpretation* (2008) pp. 12–19.
[4] See Richard Gardiner, *Treaty Interpretation* (2008) pp. 12–19.

A brief review and summary of these provisions on treaty interpretation reveals the spirit of holism which underpins them. In essence, a treaty provision is to be interpreted according to the plain meaning of its terms, as those terms are informed by their situation within the context of the whole of the treaty itself and all of its other constituent provisions, with due regard being given in their interpretation to the object and purpose of the treaty within which they are situated. The primary roles in treaty interpretation which VCLT Article 31 assigns to contextual analysis, and to the object and purpose of the treaty as a whole, are clear evidence of the holistic nature of the approach to treaty interpretation mandated by the VCLT.

Exactly how an Article 31 analysis is to proceed is a matter of much debate among lawyers and judges. However, some important principles relating to this process can be distilled. One is that the four terms mentioned by Article 31(1) in connection with the process of interpretation—namely good faith, ordinary meaning, context, and object and purpose—do not represent separate, sequential interpretive steps. In important ways, these terms and their roles in the process of treaty interpretation are interrelated. Indeed, the relationship between these terms and their use in the process of treaty interpretation represents yet another sense, separate from and additional to the one identified above, in which the rules of treaty interpretation in the VCLT are holistic in nature. In fact the term 'holistic' has been employed by a number of commentators in describing this relationship. As a World Trade Organization dispute resolution panel noted in its 1999 panel report in a case between the European Communities and the United States:

Text, context and object-and-purpose correspond to well established textual, systemic and teleological methodologies of treaty interpretation, all of which typically come into play when interpreting complex provisions in multilateral treaties. For pragmatic reasons the normal usage, and we will follow this usage, is to start the interpretation from the ordinary meaning of the 'raw' text of the relevant treaty provisions and then seek to construe it in its context and in the light of the treaty's object and purpose. However, the elements referred to in Article 31—text, context and object-and-purpose as well as good faith—are to be viewed as one holistic rule of interpretation rather than a sequence of separate tests to be applied in a hierarchical order. Context and object-and-purpose may often appear simply to confirm an interpretation seemingly derived from the 'raw' text. In reality it is always some context, even if unstated, that determines which meaning is to be taken as 'ordinary' and frequently it is impossible to give meaning, even 'ordinary meaning', without looking also at object-and-purpose.[5]

Similarly in the context of the WTO Dispute Settlement Understanding, Michael Lennard has more recently noted that:

[t]he Appellate Body has embraced the essentially textual approach, and it has also recognized the 'holistic' nature of that interpretive task—acknowledging that even the question

---

[5] Panel Report, *United States—Sections 301–310 of the Trade Act of 1974* (*US—Section 301*), WT/DS152/R, para. 7.22.

of what is the 'ordinary meaning' of a term needs to be informed by the context in which that term is used, rather than there being a strictly sequential process of first finding your dictionary meaning and then sequentially examining the context and object and purpose [. . .] these elements do not represent a number of tests that must be ticked or crossed robotically in a particular sequence—they represent, rather, a disciplined and holistic approach to determining the relevance and weight of materials in interpreting a treaty provision, in whatever order the materials are actually considered.[6]

The International Law Commission, the original drafters of VCLT Article 31, note in their commentary on that article that:

[t]he Commission, by heading the article 'General Rule of Interpretation' in the singular and by underlining the connexion between paragraphs 1 and 2 and again between paragraph 3 and the two previous paragraphs, intended to indicate that the application of the means of interpretation in the article would be a single combined operation. All the various elements, as they were present in any given case, would be thrown into the crucible and their interaction would give the legally relevant interpretation. Thus [Article 31] is entitled 'General *Rule* of Interpretation' in the singular, not 'General *Rules*' in the plural, because the Commission desired to emphasize that the process of interpretation is a unity and that the provisions of the article form a single, closely integrated rule.[7]

The title of Article 31 further makes clear that the article contains the general and primary rule of treaty interpretation. This is, importantly, in contrast to the title of Article 32, which just as clearly indicates that the considerations in that article are merely supplementary to the general rule in Article 31. Thus, as between Articles 31 and 32, there is a clear hierarchy and sequence established in the VCLT. Again, precisely how this sequence is to be worked out in practice is the source of some considerable disagreement. On the correct use specifically of the preparatory work of a treaty (the *travaux préparatoires*) in the process of interpretation, the comments of Sir Humphrey Waldock, who was Special Rapporteur for the Convention, are particularly useful:

There is, however, a difference between examining and basing a finding upon *travaux préparatoires*, and the Court itself has more than once referred to them as confirming

---

[6] Michael Lennard, 'Navigating by the Stars: Interpreting the WTO Agreements,' *Journal of International Economic Law*, 5(17) (2002) 22–23. See also Frederico Ortino, 'Treaty Interpretation and the WTO Appellate Body Report in US-Gambling: A Critique,' *Journal of International Economic Law*, 9(1) (March 2006).

[7] Yearbook of the ILC, 1966, Vol. II, pp. 219–220. See also *Aguas del Tunari v. Bolivia* (ICSID ARB/02/03), Award of 21 October 2005, para. 91:

Interpretation under Article 31 of the Vienna Convention is a process of progressive encirclement where the interpreter starts under the general rule with (1) the ordinary meaning of the terms of the treaty, (2) in their context and (3) in light of the treaty's object and purpose, and by cycling through this three step inquiry iteratively closes in upon the proper interpretation. In approaching this task, it is critical to observe two things about the general rule [. . .] First, the Vienna Convention does not privilege any one of these three aspects of the interpretation method. The meaning of a word or phrase is not solely a matter of dictionaries and linguistics [. . .]

an interpretation otherwise arrived at from a study of the text. Moreover, it is the constant practice of States and tribunals to examine any relevant *travaux préparatoires* for such light as they may throw upon the treaty. It would therefore be unrealistic to suggest, even by implication, that there is any actual bar upon mere reference to *travaux préparatoires* whenever the meaning of the terms is clear [. . .] Today, it is recognized that some caution is needed in the use of *travaux préparatoires* as a means of interpretation. They are not [. . .] an authentic means of interpretation. They are simply evidence to be weighed against any other relevant evidence of the intentions of the parties, and their cogency depends on the extent to which they furnish proof of the *common* understanding of the parties as to the meaning attached to the terms of the treaty. Statements of individual parties during the negotiations are therefore of small value in the absence of evidence that they were assented to by the other parties.[8]

Travaux materials can therefore be a part of interpretive analysis at any point in the process, but the interpreter is only to have recourse to the *travaux* in an operational sense, as source material upon which to base an interpretive finding, when confirming meaning already established through the Article 31 process, or when determining meaning after the Article 31 process has left the meaning obscure or ambiguous or has led to an absurd or unreasonable result. However, in these latter contexts in which *travaux* material is used to confirm or determine meaning, the interpreter should take care not to rely disproportionately upon single statements of persons involved in the negotiating process, as Waldock cautions. Only *travaux* material which establishes the common understanding of the negotiating parties is to be afforded probative value in interpretation.

This last caution frequently goes unobserved by legal interpreters of the NPT. It has been a very commonly employed tool in the NPT interpreter's belt to take individual statements of state officials active in the NPT negotiating process—typically officials from NWS parties to that process—and hold such statements up as having exceptional insight and probative value in interpretation of provisions of the NPT. Indeed, some commentators commit the dual sin of not only operationally relying upon such cherry-picked statements of individual officials from the *travaux*, but actually basing their analysis primarily upon this supplementary material instead of upon the process mandated by the general rule in VCLT Article 31.[9]

---

[8] *Third Report on the Law of Treaties*, Yearbook of the ILC, 1964, Vol. II, p. 58, paras 20–21.
[9] See 'A Recipe for Success at the 2010 Review Conference,' Dr Christopher A. Ford, United States Special Representative for Nuclear Non-proliferation, Opening Remarks to the 2008 NPT Preparatory Committee, Palais des Nations, Geneva, Switzerland, April 28, 2008, p. 1; Robert Zarate, 'The NPT, IAEA Safeguards and Peaceful Nuclear Energy: An "Inalienable Right," but Precisely to What?' in Henry Sokolski, ed., *Falling Behind: International Scrutiny of the Peaceful Atom* (2008).

I. Context and Object and Purpose in Interpretation of the NPT

A. Context

So much for a general discussion of the interpretive method to be applied in this book, and which will underpin the book's thesis. I will now move on to a more targeted discussion of the role of context, and object and purpose, in the particular exercise of interpretation of the provisions of the NPT. The idea in VCLT Article 31 of interpreting treaty provisions in their context means of course viewing each provision for the purpose of interpretation not as an isolated rule or recognition of right, but as a part of the larger normative whole of the treaty. It means viewing each provision as having a particular place and role among all the other provisions of the treaty, and as having a meaning which is informed by the meanings of those other provisions, as well as by the structure of the treaty itself. In interpreting the NPT, this idea of context in VCLT Article 31 requires an interpretive analysis of each provision which is informed by both the internal normative structure and meaning of the other provisions of the treaty, as well as the external or macro structure of the treaty's framing by its parties.[10]

By the internal normative structure of the NPT, I mean the essential separation of the principles of the NPT into three principled pillars, as previously discussed. These again are non-proliferation of nuclear weapons, peaceful use of nuclear energy technologies, and nuclear weapons disarmament. Looking to the provisions of the NPT, Articles I, II, and III essentially comprise the non-proliferation pillar; Articles IV and V essentially comprise the peaceful use pillar; and Article VI essentially comprises the disarmament pillar. Articles VIII through XI are essentially procedural in nature.

Thus, when interpreting a provision of the NPT located within one of these subject groupings, it is important for the interpreter to bear in mind that the provision in question is located among other provisions in its subject grouping, and even more importantly that its subject grouping is only one of the three normative subject groupings within the treaty. This understanding of the context of a provision both within and among the three principled pillars of the treaty can have significant implications for interpretation, as will be demonstrated below.

By the external or macro structure of the treaty's framing by its parties, I mean the character of the NPT as a contract treaty essentially codifying a *quid pro quo* bargain between two categories of states parties, resulting in differential and reciprocal obligations as between the two categories of parties. From the original Irish proposals in 1958, an international agreement purposed in stopping nuclear weapons proliferation had been conceptualized as one consisting of two distinct

---

[10] See Richard Gardiner, *Treaty Interpretation* (2008) pp. 177–185.

sets of obligations; one set for states already in possession of nuclear weapons, and a different set for states not in possession of nuclear weapons. States possessing nuclear weapons were to take upon themselves the obligation not to proliferate nuclear weapons or related technologies to states that did not possess nuclear weapons. For their part, states not possessing nuclear weapons were to take upon themselves an obligation neither to acquire such weapons from nuclear-weapon states, nor to manufacture such weapons indigenously.

As discussed previously, in exchange for their commitment to forego the possession of nuclear weapons, non-nuclear weapon states eventually demanded two concessions from the nuclear-weapons-possessing states. First, they demanded that the treaty provide not only a recognition of their right to use nuclear technologies for purposes of civilian power generation, but also a further reciprocal obligation on the part of nuclear-weapon states and other supplier states to provide positive assistance to non-nuclear weapon states in the development of their civilian nuclear programs.[11] Second, they further demanded that nuclear-weapon states undertake an obligation to move toward nuclear disarmament in good faith, as a part of concurrent efforts toward general and complete disarmament.[12]

This *quid pro quo* relationship of differential and reciprocal obligations between nuclear-weapon states and non-nuclear weapon states which the NPT came to codify, has become known as the 'grand bargain' of the NPT, and is the fulfillment of the guiding principle of balanced mutuality enunciated in U.N. General Assembly Resolution 2028(b).[13] The fact that the NPT is the codification of a *quid pro quo* relationship between two classes of states parties, each class having differing rights and obligations accorded them under the treaty, serves to differentiate the NPT from most other large multilateral treaties, e.g. the 1948 Genocide Convention and the 1982 Law of the Sea Convention. These other broadly subscribed multilateral treaties are referred to in legal terminology as *traité-loi*, or lawmaking treaties, and have as their chief characteristic under this classification a set of rules which are applied universally across the full spectrum of states parties. Generally speaking, lawmaking treaties do not set up a *quid pro quo* relationship between states parties or groups thereof, and there is no consideration given between states in exchange for the undertaking of obligations.[14] Thus, lawmaking treaties are comparable to a degree with legislation under domestic law, binding each member equally to their rules without consideration.[15]

[11] See Joseph Cirincione, *Bomb Scare*, (2007) pp. 30–31.
[12] See, e.g., General Assembly Resolutions 1378, 1660, 1664, 1665, 1722.
[13] See Christopher Chyba, 'Second-Tier Suppliers and Their Threat to the Nuclear Non-proliferation Regime,' in Joseph Pilat, ed., *Atoms for Peace: A Future after Fifty Years?* (2007) pp. 120–122.
[14] See generally, however, Hugo Caminos and Michael Molitor, 'Progressive Development of International Law and the Package Deal,' 79 *American Journal of International Law* (1985) 871.
[15] See Peter Malanczuk, *Akehurst's Modern Introduction to International Law* (7th edn, 1997) pp. 37–38; Hugh Thirlway, 'The Sources of International Law,' in Malcolm Evans, ed., *International*

The NPT, because of the fundamental *quid pro quo* nature of the obligations contained in it, and the separation of states parties into two groups with distinct sets of rights and obligations, should rather be classified as a *traité-contrat*, or contract treaty; a treaty format more commonly used in private international law to define business transactions.[16] It should be clear that this classification as a contract treaty, and not a lawmaking treaty, does not in any way affect the binding nature of the commitments entered into by the states parties to the NPT under international law.[17] Nor does it result in different rules of interpretation being applied to the treaty. However, this difference in classification of the NPT can have an impact upon the actual interpretation and application of the NPT's terms. While the same VCLT rules on interpretation, contained in Articles 31 and 32, apply to treaties under both the contract and lawmaking classifications, as Rudolph Bernhardt has explained, those rules may properly be applied to produce differing results depending upon a treaty's classification.[18]

Among the implications of the contract treaty nature of the NPT, as an element of the context of its terms, are the unique results of a material breach of a contract treaty by a category of states parties. When considering a multilateral lawmaking treaty, a material breach by one party or a group of parties may or may not serve to so significantly affect the interests of the other parties to the treaty that they will be able to suspend the operation of the treaty as between themselves and the state(s) in breach, or terminate it outright. Article 60 of the VCLT addresses the consequences of treaty breach, and provides that the non-breaching parties to the treaty in this situation must unanimously agree to suspend or terminate the treaty. The only ways for an individual party, or non-unanimous group of parties, to lawfully suspend their observance of the treaty in this situation are for the aggrieved state(s) to argue that they are 'specially affected' by the breach, or that the breach 'radically changes the position of every party with respect to the further performance of its obligations under the treaty.' In the case of a multilateral lawmaking treaty, these latter arguments for suspending observance of the treaty, absent unanimous agreement among the treaty parties, will be difficult to make.

However, in the case of a contract treaty, because of the *quid pro quo* reciprocal structure of the treaty's commitments, a material breach by one or a group of

---

Law (2nd edn, 2006) pp. 119–120; Rudolph Bernhardt, *Treaties*, in Encyclopedia of Public International Law, Vol. IV, pp. 928–929; Ian Brownlie, *Principles of Public International Law* (6th edn, 2003) p. 12 ('Law-making treaties create *general* norms for the future conduct of the parties in terms of legal propositions, and the obligations are basically the same for all parties.')

[16] See ibid.

[17] Hugh Thirlway, 'The Sources of International Law,' in Malcolm Evans, ed., *International Law* (2nd edn, 2006) pp. 119–120.

[18] Rudolph Bernhardt, *Treaties*, in Encyclopedia of Public International Law, Vol. IV (2000) pp. 928–929; *Interpretation in International Law*, in Encyclopedia of Public International Law, Vol. II (1995) pp. 1421–1422.

parties will almost certainly strike at the heart of the treaty's object and purpose, and much more easily be argued to 'specially affect' the non-breaching parties, and to 'radically change [] the position of every party with respect to the further performance of its obligations under the treaty.' Thus, a material breach by one party, and *a fortiori* an entire category of states parties to a contract treaty, will provide strong arguments for the aggrieved category of parties to the treaty, individually or collectively, to suspend the operation of the treaty as between themselves and the breaching state(s), pursuant to VCLT Article 60.[19]

B. Object and purpose

When seeking to divine the object and purpose of a treaty for purposes of interpretation pursuant to VCLT Article 31, a common starting point for the interpreter is the treaty's preamble, which is typically written to convey the considerations underlying the parties' motivation for concluding the treaty.[20] Examining the preamble of the NPT provides significant evidence of the object and purpose of the treaty, and will be my starting point in this analysis. Before beginning that analysis, however, it is important to note one further interpretive principle regarding the divination of a treaty's object and purpose. Which is that, notwithstanding that this element of the VCLT's Article 31 analysis is expressed in the singular, a treaty's object and purpose can be found to be comprised of multiple principles.[21] As the WTO Appellate Body has explained:

[. . .] most treaties have no single, undiluted object and purpose but rather a variety of different, and possibly conflicting, objects and purposes. This is certainly true of the *WTO Agreement*. Thus, while the first clause of the *WTO Agreement* calls for the expansion of trade in goods and services, this same clause also recognizes that international trade and economic relations under the *WTO Agreement* should allow for 'optimal use of the world's resources in accordance with the objective of sustainable development,' and should seek 'to protect and preserve the environment.' The Panel in effect took a one-sided view of the object and purpose of the *WTO Agreement* when it fashioned a new test not found in the text of the agreement.[22]

The NPT's preamble is comprised of twelve paragraphs of varying length. Divided up thematically, these paragraphs can be grouped into four categories, with one category representing each of the three principled substantive pillars of the NPT, and a fourth category addressing safeguards, which are essentially procedural in nature. With regard to the three substantive pillars of the NPT, under the peaceful use of nuclear energy category can be included the following two preambular paragraphs:

[19] Yael Ronen comes to essentially the same legal conclusion regarding VCLT Article 60 in her book *The Iran Nuclear Issue* (2010).
[20] Richard Gardiner, *Treaty Interpretation* (2008) pp. 192–197.
[21] Ibid. at p. 195.
[22] *US Import Prohibition of Certain Shrimp and Shrimp Products*, WT/DS58/AB/R, para. 17 (1998).

Affirming the principle that the benefits of peaceful applications of nuclear technology, including any technological by-products which may be derived by nuclear-weapon States from the development of nuclear explosive devices, should be available for peaceful purposes to all Parties of the Treaty, whether nuclear-weapon or non-nuclear weapon States,

Convinced that, in furtherance of this principle, all Parties to the Treaty are entitled to participate in the fullest possible exchange of scientific information for, and to contribute alone or in cooperation with other States to, the further development of the applications of atomic energy for peaceful purposes [...]

Under the non-proliferation of nuclear weapons category can be included the following three preambular paragraphs:

Considering the devastation that would be visited upon all mankind by a nuclear war and the consequent need to make every effort to avert the danger of such a war and to take measures to safeguard the security of peoples,

Believing that the proliferation of nuclear weapons would seriously enhance the danger of nuclear war,

In conformity with resolutions of the United Nations General Assembly calling for the conclusion of an agreement on the prevention of wider dissemination of nuclear weapons [...]

Finally, under the disarmament of nuclear weapons category can be included the following five preambular paragraphs:

Declaring their intention to achieve at the earliest possible date the cessation of the nuclear arms race and to undertake effective measures in the direction of nuclear disarmament,

Urging the cooperation of all States in the attainment of this objective,

Desiring to further the easing of international tension and the strengthening of trust between States in order to facilitate the cessation of the manufacture of nuclear weapons, the liquidation of all their existing stockpiles, and the elimination from national arsenals of nuclear weapons and the means of their delivery pursuant to a Treaty on general and complete disarmament under strict and effective international control,

Recalling that, in accordance with the Charter of the United Nations, States must refrain in their international relations from the threat or use of force against the territorial integrity or political independence of any State, or in any other manner inconsistent with the Purposes of the United Nations, and that the establishment and maintenance of international peace and security are to be promoted with the least diversion for armaments of the world's human and economic resources,

Recalling the determination expressed by the Parties to the 1963 Treaty banning nuclear weapon tests in the atmosphere, in outer space and under water in its Preamble to seek to achieve the discontinuance of all test explosions of nuclear weapons for all time and to continue negotiations to this end [...]

This thematic grouping of the NPT's preambular paragraphs into categories corresponding to the NPT's three substantive pillars provides significant insights into the object and purpose of the NPT. The NPT's preamble demonstrates that it is not a treaty exclusively or even primarily focused on nuclear weapons proliferation. Rather, it is a treaty primarily addressed to regulating nuclear energy in its full dual-use nature and range of applications. The parties to the NPT signaled clearly through the paragraphs of the preamble that the treaty's object and purpose is to be found in *all three of its principled pillars*, representing the full dual-use nature of nuclear energy, and not in any one principle above the others.

From a simple quantitative perspective, as demonstrated above there are two preambular paragraphs addressing the peaceful use of nuclear energy, three paragraphs addressing weapons proliferation, and five paragraphs addressing disarmament. It would certainly be impossible to draw from this evidence the conclusion that the non-proliferation pillar is the exclusive or even the primary object and purpose of the NPT, as has been maintained by a number of officials of nuclear-weapon states.[23] Again, from a purely quantitative perspective, the disarmament of the nuclear weapons pillar is represented by two more preambular paragraphs than is the non-proliferation pillar, consisting of almost three times as many words as the preambular paragraphs associated with non-proliferation. I do not mean to argue that such quantitative methods of examining the paragraphs of a treaty's preamble are dispositive of the treaty's object and purpose. However, I do think that a thematic division of preambular paragraphs, and observations based thereon, can help to identify the object and purpose of a treaty, and is particularly useful in cases where that object in purpose is comprised of multiple principles, as in the case of the NPT.

While it is the most common starting point, the preamble is not the only important source material for divining a treaty's object and purpose. In this exercise, the interpreter should also look to the substance and structure of the treaty as a whole to determine its object and purpose.[24] As noted previously, when conducting an interpretive analysis under VCLT Article 31, inquiries into the plain meaning, context, and object and purpose of a treaty should not be, and indeed cannot be, conducted as isolated or sequential inquiries. This principle is evidenced at this stage of the object and purpose analysis. There would appear to be little difference between an analysis of the substance and structure of a treaty for purposes of determining the context of a subject provision on the one hand, and an analysis of the substance and structure of a treaty for purposes of divining the treaty's object and purpose to aid in interpretation of the same provision. Thus, it is reasonable to import into this stage of object and purpose analysis those conclusions drawn from the contextual analysis of the substance and structure of the NPT conducted above. This includes conclusions concerning the three-pillared internal substantive structure of the NPT, as well as conclusions concerning the *quid pro quo* bargain-based, contract treaty nature of the NPT.

---

[23] See, e.g., 'A Recipe for Success at the 2010 Review Conference,' Dr Christopher A. Ford, United States Special Representative for Nuclear Non-proliferation, Opening Remarks to the 2008 NPT Preparatory Committee, Palais des Nations, Geneva, Switzerland, April 28, 2008, p. 1.

[24] Richard Gardiner, *Treaty Interpretation* (2008) pp. 196–197.

All of these conclusions drawn from an analysis of the object and purpose of the NPT come together to establish a number of fundamental principles which, along with their context, should inform legal interpretations of the plain meaning of provisions of the NPT. The first such principle is, as stated above, that the object and purpose of the NPT is to be found in all three of its principled pillars (i.e. peaceful use, non-proliferation, and disarmament) representing the full dual-use nature of nuclear energy, and not exclusively or primarily in any one of these pillars.

The second principle flows from this first principle, and it is that all three of the principled pillars comprising the object and purpose of the NPT should be considered to be presumptively equal in legal weight, i.e. that none of the pillars should be presumed to be of higher prioritization in interpretation of the NPT's provisions than any other. This second principle is supported not only by the presence in the treaty's preamble of numerous paragraphs addressing each of the three pillars, but it is also supported by the presence of multiple articles of the treaty addressing each one of the pillars. It is further supported by the fact of the *quid pro quo* nature of the structure of the NPT, and its character as a contract treaty. This is because it would be unreasonable, absent evidence of the specific intent of the parties, to prioritize substantive principles demanded by one or the other side in a reciprocal bargain-based agreement. Absent such evidence of the parties' intent, it is only reasonable to assume that the balance among the principled pillars of a contract treaty is an equal one, with no one principle to be presumptively prioritized over any other in interpretation of the provisions of the treaty.

There is an important caveat here. This second principle of the object and purpose analysis of the NPT, i.e. that all three of the principled pillars comprising the object and purpose of the NPT should be considered to be presumptively equal in legal weight, should be applied as a presumption in interpretation of the NPT's provisions. There are, however, instances in the NPT's provisions where there is evidence in the text of the specific intent of the parties as to the relationship between treaty articles or principles, sometimes representing the relationship between principled pillars. The clearest examples of this are to be found in Article III(3) and Article IV(1). When such evidence of the specific intent of the parties is to be found in the text, this evidence will constitute an exception to this presumption, and the terms of the particular provision will govern the relationship between the articles or principles, inclusive of the relationship between principled pillars.

C. VCLT Article 32 analysis

It will be recalled that VCLT Article 32 provides that, as a supplement to the primary method of treaty interpretation provided for in VCLT Article 31, the *travaux préparatoires*, or preparatory work of a treaty may be referenced 'in order to confirm the meaning resulting from the application of Article 31.' Such recourse to the *travaux* should be undertaken subsequent to and only as a confirmational supplement to the primary analysis conducted pursuant to the terms of Article 31.

In the case of the NPT, as concluded in Chapter 1 above, the diplomatic history of the NPT and the preparatory work of the treaty, when taken as a whole, serve to clearly confirm the conclusion drawn from context and object and purpose analysis that the NPT is not fundamentally addressed to the regulation of nuclear weapons proliferation, as it is often described to be. This diplomatic history and preparatory work establish, rather, that the NPT is, in fact, fundamentally addressed to regulating nuclear energy in its full dual-use nature and range of applications. Furthermore, when taken as a whole, the diplomatic history and preparatory work of the NPT clearly confirm the conclusion that the NPT is underpinned by three inherently linked, and presumptively equal, principled pillars—peaceful use of nuclear energy, non-proliferation of nuclear weapons, and disarmament of nuclear weapons stockpiles—and not only one. Again, the preparatory work of the treaty makes abundantly clear that the NPT would never have come into being if the principles of peaceful use and disarmament had not been included along with the principle of non-proliferation. This balanced, multi-principled underpinning has a conceptual lineage which can be clearly traced back at least through to President Eisenhower's Atoms for Peace proposal.

In summary, then, the review and analysis of the diplomatic history and preparatory work of the NPT in Chapter 1 serves, pursuant to VCLT Article 32, to interpretively confirm a number of the essential conclusions drawn from interpretation of the NPT pursuant to Article 31.

II. Conclusions

So what conclusions can be drawn from this chapter's review of the rules of interpretation contained in VCLT Articles 31 and 32, and the application of those rules, in particular the concepts of context and object and purpose, to the NPT? When performed in the holistic fashion recommended by international courts and tribunals, an analysis of the VCLT Article 31 elements of context and object and purpose, in the case of the NPT, establishes a number of important guiding principles which should be used in interpretation of the provisions of the NPT. These are:

1. The NPT is substantively and structurally comprised of three primary principled pillars—i.e. civilian use of nuclear energy, non-proliferation of nuclear weapons, and disarmament of nuclear weapons.
2. These three pillars correspond to the *quid pro quo* negotiating demands of the two sets of states parties represented in the macro level contract treaty structure of the NPT.

3. The three principled pillars of the NPT represent the dual-use character of nuclear energy applications. The NPT is fundamentally addressed to regulating nuclear energy in its full dual-use nature and range of applications, and is not exclusively or even primarily addressed to regulating only nuclear weapons.

4. These three principled pillars *together* comprise the object and purpose of the NPT. They are inherently linked and interdependent upon each other in their meaning, and must be viewed in a balanced manner. When conducting that balancing, the three pillars should be understood as presumptively juridically equal, i.e. none of the pillars should be presumed to be of higher prioritization in legal interpretation of the NPT's provisions than any other.

3

NWS Nuclear Policy and Interpretation
of the NPT

This, then, brings us to the problems of legal interpretation of the NPT, and the policies which have been justified pursuant thereto, which this book seeks to address. I am arguing here that in policy and practice, particularly by NWS governments and led by the United States, the non-proliferation pillar of the NPT has for over a decade been disproportionately and incorrectly prioritized at the expense of the peaceful use and disarmament pillars of the treaty. This unbalanced position toward the NPT has been transformed into specific policy proposals and actions which have been implemented in circumscription of the legitimate legal interests of non-nuclear weapon states particularly. This disproportionate prioritization in policy, and the specific proposals for amending the nuclear non-proliferation regime which have flowed from it, have been justified by government officials in nuclear-weapon states by ultimately erroneous interpretations of NPT law. I will proceed in the following chapters to make out each element of this thesis.

I will begin in this chapter by examining NWS nuclear policy and interpretations of the NPT during the target decade. I will offer as primary evidence a review of the statements made by states parties to the various formal meetings held under the banner of the NPT—i.e. the NPT Review Conferences (or 'RevCons') which occur once every five years, and the NPT Preparatory Committee meetings (or 'PrepComs'), which typically occur for three consecutive years preceding a Review Conference. These statements provide solid source material for analysis and evaluation of trends in states' policies toward the NPT, and legal interpretations of the NPT, as they are single subject documents (i.e. on the subject of the NPT) and are given on a recurring basis by the same governments.

I. Epochs of Policy toward Nuclear Weapons

Even as superpower tensions remained high in the early 1960s, both the U.S. and Soviet governments determined that a coordinated process of limitation of nuclear weapons and ultimately reversal of the nuclear arms race would be beneficial to their national interests. Arms control became, in essence, an alternative means of preserving the balance of power between the superpowers, which would be less risky and less costly than unbridled stockpiling of nuclear weapons.[1] The result was a decades-long process of diplomatic work, the fruits of which were a number of milestone bilateral treaties which progressively set limits upon nuclear weapons and delivery technologies, and ultimately obligated the superpowers to make deep cuts in their nuclear arsenals.

A word briefly on definition of terms. Cold War efforts by the superpowers particularly to forbid among themselves the possession of certain nuclear weapons delivery technology (e.g. through the Anti-Ballistic Missile Treaty (ABM)), and to limit and eventually reduce nuclear weapons stockpiles (e.g. through the SALT I, SALT II, and INF treaties) should properly be understood as efforts of arms control, and not nuclear weapons disarmament. These two terms—arms control and disarmament—are often used interchangeably in discourse concerning nuclear weapons, but they are in fact quite different concepts. Arms control efforts are efforts which seek and which are designed by policy to effect a limitation or reduction of their subject weapons technologies, but which do not intend nor are designed by policy to achieve complete elimination of those weapons. Arms control efforts are typically designed to decrease the cost and risk associated with stockpiling of weapons, but they maintain a conception of the continued presence of those weapons in military arsenals. They are not part of a policy program the object of which is the elimination of their subject weapons from national arsenals.

Disarmament efforts, on the other hand, are part of such a policy program whose stated object is the complete elimination of their subject weapons from national arsenals, even if that program is to be implemented through multiple, progressive steps. Thus, while arms control efforts and disarmament efforts may look similar, in that the short-term aim of both is to limit and reduce their subject weapons technologies, they are in fact quite different in that disarmament efforts are clearly framed within a policy program the object of which is complete elimination from national arsenals. This is why the Cold War treaties mentioned above between the U.S. and the U.S.S.R. are perfect examples of arms control efforts, and not disarmament efforts. These treaties were not a part of a stated program of elimination of nuclear weapons from the arsenals of the superpowers. The policy of both the U.S. and the U.S.S.R. during the Cold War clearly continuously conceived of a retention of nuclear weapons in their national arsenals.[2]

To be clear, this distinction in terms as between arms control and disarmament is not intended to diminish in any way the very positive results achieved through the conclusion and implementation of arms control treaties such as the Cold War instruments cited above. And indeed, in the post-Cold War era, great strides have

---

[1] See Jozef Goldblat, *Arms Control: The New Guide to Negotiations and Agreements* (2002) p. 71.
[2] See Joseph Cirincione, *Bomb Scare: The History and Future of Nuclear Weapons* (2007) ch 3.

been made to cut the number of nuclear weapons in the national arsenals of the U.S. and Russia pursuant to additional arms control treaties including the 1991 START I, 1993 START II, and 2002 SORT treaties. As this volume is being written, hopes are high for the ratification of the 2010 Prague Treaty as a successor to the START I treaty.

This distinction in terms is useful, however, in the identification of true disarmament efforts, as called for by Article VI of the NPT—or to be more precise, the identification of the general absence of such disarmament efforts. As will be discussed below, evidence of arms control efforts is often tendered by nuclear-weapon states, and in particular the United States, in order to attempt to show compliance with the disarmament requirements of Article VI. This erroneous approach to the obligations of Article VI will be shown below to comprise a part of the obfuscatory efforts of NWS, and particularly the United States, towards the disarmament obligations of the NPT.

In the early post-Cold War period, the focus of international attention and policy with regard to nuclear issues continued to be on arms control efforts. This can be seen clearly in the landmark START I and START II treaties concluded respectively in 1991 and 1993. However, in terms of their statements to NPT meetings, the NWS clearly seemed to conceive of the NPT as being underpinned by the three pillars of disarmament, non-proliferation, and peaceful use. Their statements reflected the understanding, which as discussed above had been transmitted to them through the long course of diplomatic history related to the NPT, that these three principled pillars were in balance in the NPT and shared an equal prioritization in the treaty. The statements by the NWS parties to the 1995 NPT Review Conference, for example, are quite balanced in their thorough and at times meticulous review of their respective national policies related to each of the three pillars. In the 1995 statements issued by the NWS, there is an absence of emphasis on overlap between the pillars resulting in a need for prioritizing any one over another. Each pillar is taken essentially on its own merits and importance in reviewing state actions relative to it.

This approach to the NPT essentially continued in the NWS party statements to the 1997 PrepCom meetings. The statement by U.S. representative Lawrence Scheinman explicitly emphasizes a balanced approach to the three pillars. As he states in his characteristically learned fashion:

The NPT is more than the sum of its parts. Its three main goals—preventing the spread of nuclear weapons; promoting nuclear disarmament; and promoting cooperation in the peaceful uses of nuclear energy under an effective safeguards system—are mutually reinforcing and cannot be considered in isolation. This perspective defines what we believe should be a second priority, namely that there be a balanced and thorough treatment of all aspects of the treaty—both in our deliberations during the PrepCom meetings and at the 2000 NPT Review Conference itself. To this end, Mr. Chairman, my delegation has come fully prepared to deliberate on all substantive issues related to the operation of the treaty [. . .] Treating the process as a referendum on the efforts of any less than all parties, or giving unequal emphasis to any of the treaty's goals, would be neither productive nor constructive and certainly would not serve our shared interests in creating a meaningful and effective process [. . .] The United States is no less committed to peaceful nuclear cooperation than to non-proliferation and nuclear disarmament goals of the treaty.[3]

The statement by China to the 1997 PrepCom echoes these sentiments:

The three major objectives of the treaty, namely, nuclear disarmament, nuclear non-proliferation and peaceful uses of nuclear energy, are equally important and mutually complementary, and none of them should be neglected. The review process should be comprehensive and balanced, giving equal attention to the three objectives, and should take into consideration those principles and objectives set forth in the 20 operative paragraphs of the 'principles and objectives' document.[4]

The 1998 NPT PrepCom meetings, however, seem to represent something of a turning point in the balance of attention and priority given at least by the United States to the three principled pillars of the NPT. While the statement jointly submitted by the NWS parties, as well as the individual statements of the other NWS individually, seem to maintain the traditional balance of attention and priority among the pillars, there is some evidence in the statement by U.S. Ambassador Norman Wulf to the 1998 PrepCom of a nascent shift in emphasis and prioritization toward the non-proliferation pillar and away from the peaceful use and disarmament pillars. In this statement for the first time we begin to see a prominent emphasis on non-proliferation themes such as 'universal adherence to the NPT,' 'promoting full compliance with the NPT,' and 'strengthening the NPT safeguards system'—phrases which will come to be stock themes for later U.S. representatives to NPT meetings. Furthermore, there is less in Ambassador Wulf's statement on the subject of peaceful use of nuclear energy than in previous U.S. statements.[5]

The explanation for this emerging shift, at this particular time in the late 1990s and in the early years of the new decade, is almost certainly to be found in the political and security climate surrounding NPT meetings during these years. Though the 1998 PrepCom took place only weeks before the Indian and Pakistani nuclear tests in May of 1998, concern regarding these tests was clearly on the minds of U.S. and other officials over the next several years. U.S. Secretary of State Madeleine Albright delivered the U.S. general statement to the 2000 NPT Review Conference, in which she stated that the Indian and Pakistani tests 'were a serious challenge to the global

---

[3] U.S. Statement to the First Preparatory Committee Meeting for the 2000 NPT Review Conference, April 8, 1997.

[4] Statement by H.E. Mr Sha Zukang, Ambassador for Disarmament Affairs and Head of Delegation of the People's Republic of China at the First Session of the Preparatory Committee for the 2000 Review Conference of the Parties in the Treaty on the Non-Proliferation of Nuclear Weapons, April 8, 1997.

[5] Statement by Ambassador Norman A. Wulf, Representative of the United States of America, to the Second Session of the Preparatory Committee Meeting for the 2000 NPT Review Conference of the Parties to the Treaty on the Non-proliferation of Nuclear Weapons. April 27, 1998.

non-proliferation regime.'[6] At the same time, tensions were high over Iraq's non-cooperation with the U.N./IAEA monitoring and verification program prescribed by U.N. Security Council Resolution 687, leading to the withdrawal of the international inspectors from Iraq in December of 1998. From 1998–2002 suspicions began to grow regarding the possibility of a reconstituted Iraqi nuclear weapons program. Furthermore, the frustrating state of the 1994 Agreed Framework process with North Korea, its intermittent missile tests and evidence of missile proliferation activity, and its ultimate 2003 withdrawal from the NPT, added to the environment of concern regarding nuclear non-proliferation during this time.

In Ambassador Norman Wulf's words:

I would not say that there was a conscious effort to make a shift in policy but there clearly was a different reality that we were experiencing in 1998 and thereafter. The Cold War was over, nuclear material was being taken out of weapons inventories, adherence was almost universal and two countries had been found to have violated their NPT obligations. We had a permanent NP—now we needed to ensure that it provided the security benefits to its adherents by ensuring that countries complied with its provisions.[7]

These non-proliferation concerns can be clearly felt in Ambassador Wulf's next statement to the NPT PrepCom meetings in 2002. In this statement, Ambassador Wulf leads off with thirteen paragraphs detailing nuclear non-proliferation concerns, and explicitly citing 'violations of the NPT' by Iraq and North Korea. The balance of the statement is comprised of only three paragraphs on disarmament, and three paragraphs on peaceful use—demonstrating a quantitatively unbalanced treatment of the pillars. But perhaps even more importantly, there is also an important substantive change in rhetoric with regard to peaceful use in this statement, as well as an explanation for this change. In the statement's third paragraph on peaceful use, Ambassador Wulf observes:

The NPT has led to peaceful nuclear cooperation among nations, with benefits extending across the globe. But just like the other benefits of the Treaty, they will not be preserved without strong support for strict compliance with the NPT's non-proliferation undertakings.[8]

This statement is remarkable for its, at the time uniquely, explicit linkage between the non-proliferation and peaceful use pillars of the NPT and its assertion that the rights of NNWS and the obligations of supplier states under Article IV of the treaty were conditional upon the 'strict compliance' of NNWS with their obligations particularly pursuant to Article II. The explanation for this change in rhetoric is expressed earlier in the statement:

We also must be vigilant for other NPT parties whose membership in the Treaty belies their real intentions. Iraq cloaked itself in the respectability of the NPT while deliberately flouting its obligations under the Treaty.[9]

[6] U.S. Statement to NPT Review Conference, United Nations, New York, April 24, 2000.

[7] Email correspondence with the author, August 2, 2009. On file with author.

[8] Statement by Ambassador Norman A. Wulf, Representative of the United States of America, to the First Session of the Preparatory Committee Meeting for the 2005 NPT Review Conference of the Parties to the Treaty on the Non-proliferation of Nuclear Weapons, April 8, 2002.

[9] Ibid.

The international community's experience with Iraq, and the revelations in the early 1990s of how close Iraq had come to developing a nuclear weapon while an NPT NNWS party had brought home, in striking fashion, the potential for abuse by NNWS of the nuclear energy technologies made available to them by supplier states under the NPT grand bargain. This realization led to ultimately successful efforts to tighten Nuclear Suppliers Group supply criteria for NNWS. It also led to a recharacterization in the minds and statements of NWS officials, and those of the U.S. particularly, of the contours of the rights and obligations contained in NPT Article IV. Whereas in past statements regarding the Article IV right of NNWS to nuclear cooperation the treaty language characterizing this as an 'inalienable right' was commonly cited, rhetoric began to change from this point onward to recognizing generally the rights and obligations under Article IV, but emphasizing at the same time that these rights and obligations were not absolute. In Ambassador Wulf's 2002 statement, and much more so in subsequent statements by Bush-era U.S. representatives, this emphasis upon the limitations placed upon the Article IV rights and obligations by the non-proliferation obligations in Articles I and II of the treaty becomes clear.

With the terrorist attacks of September 11, 2001 and the Bush administration's resulting 'global war on terror,' there is a very palpable increase in the degree of the shift of emphasis toward nuclear non-proliferation, and away from nuclear disarmament and nuclear peaceful use, reflected in U.S. statements to NPT meetings. Other signs of a fundamental shift in U.S. policy toward an emphasis on non-proliferation concerns and away from disarmament and peaceful use concerns are evident in the first years of the Bush administration. One clear example is the decision by the Bush administration to abandon the Comprehensive Test Ban Treaty which had been signed by President Clinton but never approved by the U.S. Senate. Another is the U.S. decision to unilaterally withdraw from the 1972 Anti-Ballistic Missile Treaty in 2001, and to construct a provocative missile shield in Eastern Europe.

It is during the Bush era that the disproportionate prioritization of the non-proliferation pillar of the NPT, and the marginalization of the disarmament and peaceful use pillars, comes to full bloom in U.S. policy. U.S. representatives Andrew Semmel, John Bolton, Stephen Rademaker, and Christopher Ford demonstrate this unbalancing in their statements to NPT meetings in 2003, 2004, 2005, 2007, and 2008. In addition to this marked change in substantive policy toward the NPT, it is also worth noting that the tone of the U.S. statements during this period changes to one that is much more combative, accusatory, aggressive, and defensive than in years past.

My argument concerning the disproportionate prioritization of the non-proliferation pillar of the NPT at the expense of the disarmament and peaceful use pillars, particularly in U.S. policy but also in the policy of other NWS parties, will thus be dated from 1998 through to the end of the Bush administration in the U.S. in 2008. I will refer to this time period as the target decade or target era of this study.

As noted, this trend in policy can be seen in the statements of U.S. representatives in the late 1990s and the early years of the new millennium; however, it reaches new levels of radicalism during the Bush administration in the U.S., as seen in the statements of U.S. representatives Semmel, Bolton, Rademaker, and Ford. Their statements not only show a profoundly disproportionate prioritization of non-proliferation over disarmament and peaceful use, but unlike Ambassador Wulf's statements in the late 1990s they additionally state explicitly legal interpretations of the NPT in support of these unbalanced policies. These legal interpretations, and their implementation through policy and state action, will be discussed at length below. While the U.S. certainly led the pack of NWS in this disproportionate prioritization of non-proliferation, and legal interpretations pursuant to it, there were during the Bush years several other NWS parties to the NPT who followed suit to differing degrees in their statements, as will be shown below. Thus, I argue that this is a trend which, though led by the U.S., is also seen in the statements of other NWS, and is an important dynamic in international relations related to the NPT.

I will proceed in this chapter by dividing up my argument and supporting evidence into three sections, corresponding to the three principled pillars of the NPT. I will begin with an examination of NWS statements of policy toward the NPT, and legal interpretation of the NPT in support of those policies, during the target era, on issues of nuclear non-proliferation. I will then move on to statements of policy and legal interpretation during this era on issues of nuclear peaceful use. Finally, I will examine statements of policy and legal interpretation during this era on issues of nuclear disarmament.

Having completed this examination of both policy and legal statements, I will then proceed in the next chapter to argue, again in sections corresponding to the three pillars, that a number of these legal interpretations of provisions of the NPT are incorrect, by reference to fundamental principles of the law of treaty interpretation. Having demonstrated the erroneous nature of these legal interpretations, I will conclude by arguing that a number of NWS actions and proposals, some of which involve the instrumentality of the Nuclear Suppliers Group, and which are based upon these incorrect legal interpretations, are therefore themselves unlawfully prejudicial toward or circumscriptive of the legitimate legal interests of NNWS under the NPT's grand bargain.

II. Non-Proliferation

The proliferation of nuclear weapons has long been a top national and international security concern. During the decades of the Cold War, this concern about nuclear proliferation was largely, though not exclusively, confined to concern regarding vertical, or intra-state, proliferation within the superpowers. In the post-Cold War period, however, these concerns have expanded to include the dangers of horizontal proliferation of nuclear weapons, to both states and non-state actors who are new nuclear weapons possessors.[10]

Since the end of the Cold War, high-profile cases of actual or suspected horizontal proliferation of nuclear weapons and related technology abound, including the cases of Iraq, India, Pakistan, North Korea, Libya, Iran, and Syria. The perceived threat posed, particularly by horizontal nuclear weapons proliferation, is continually on the lips of government officials, and is the focus of a broad range of both non-proliferation, and more forceful and proactive counterproliferation efforts. In the international organizational/normative arena, non-proliferation issues are frequently the subject of United Nations General Assembly and Security Council resolutions, and of course the work of the International Atomic Energy Agency, and the informal Nuclear Suppliers Group.[11]

In the context of NPT NWS, and particularly U.S., statements to NPT meetings during the target decade of 1998–2008, these statements frequently follow a standard structural template. Non-proliferation issues are generally addressed first. The discussion of non-proliferation issues, including Article I and II obligations, Article III safeguards obligations, and specific cases of proliferation concern, typically constitutes the bulk of the statement. Frequent emphasis is placed upon the need to achieve both 'universal adherence' to and 'full compliance' with the non-proliferation obligations in Articles I–III of the NPT. This full compliance with NPT non-proliferation obligations is frequently stressed as constituting a sequential prerequisite for the observance by the NWS and other supplier states of their obligations under both the peaceful use and disarmament pillars, as well as for the enjoyment by NNWS of their rights under Article IV.

While this template is followed throughout the target decade, the degree to which discussion of non-proliferation issues dominates the statements increases dramatically from 2003 onwards. The beginning of this increasing trend clearly coincides with the U.S.-led global war on terror, following the attacks of September 11, 2001. On February 11, 2004 U.S. President Bush delivered a landmark speech on the topic of WMD proliferation and its relevance to the war on terror. In this speech, Bush discussed at length the threat posed by the proliferation of weapons of mass destruction, and announced seven proposals 'to strengthen the world's efforts to stop the spread of deadly weapons.' The fourth and fifth of these proposals dealt specifically with the proliferation threat posed by what Bush characterized as a 'loophole' in the NPT. As Bush explains:

The Nuclear Non-Proliferation Treaty was designed more than 30 years ago to prevent the spread of nuclear weapons beyond those states which already possessed them. Under this treaty, nuclear states agreed to help non-nuclear states develop peaceful atomic energy if

---

[10] See generally Daniel H. Joyner, *International Law and the Proliferation of Weapons of Mass Destruction* (2009) Introduction.

[11] See generally ibid. ch 1.

they renounced the pursuit of nuclear weapons. But the treaty has a loophole which has been exploited by nations such as North Korea and Iran. These regimes are allowed to produce nuclear material that can be used to build bombs under the cover of civilian nuclear programs.[12]

This characterization of the NPT Article IV right to peaceful nuclear cooperation as a 'loophole' of the treaty was new and singular. I will return to this characterization of the NPT right to peaceful use below and discuss it and its implications more thoroughly. For the moment, however, it is important to note that the proposals which Bush made to close this 'loophole' in the NPT, including NNWS acceptance of foreign source nuclear fuel supply and accession to the IAEA Additional Protocol as conditions of nuclear cooperation, clearly prioritized non-proliferation concerns over peaceful use concerns. This placement of the peaceful use pillar of the NPT in secondary status to the non-proliferation pillar, is a theme which runs through U.S., and to a lesser extent other NWS, statements to NPT meetings from 2003 through 2008.

What is most remarkable about NWS statements during the 2003–2008 era, at least from an international legal perspective, however, is the explicit and implicit legal interpretations of the NPT which are offered in these statements in order to justify this disproportionate prioritization of non-proliferation over both peaceful use and disarmament principles. These interpretations employ a variety of terminology, but at their essence they share a similar theme, which is that the non-proliferation pillar of the NPT is the principal, primary, central, or core principled pillar of the treaty, and that the other two pillars are of secondary or lesser status and weight. For example, the United Kingdom's statement to the 2005 Review Conference clearly views the non-proliferation pillar as the *primus inter pares*, as illustrated by the following passage:

Mr. President, let me say at the outset: we recognize the need for balanced implementation of the Treaty and we support progress in all its areas, as our record demonstrates. However, we believe that progress in non-proliferation is important in its own right.[13]

Similarly, in its statement to the 2008 PrepCom, France observed:

The first requirement is to confirm the relevance and credibility of the Treaty by providing a suitable response to the serious violations of it by States that have circumvented the norm of non-proliferation it puts in place. It is not acceptable for a small number of States, supported by clandestine networks, to breach their obligations while at the same

---

[12] Remarks by U.S. President George W. Bush on Weapons of Mass Destruction Proliferation. Fort Lesley J. McNair—National Defense University, Washington D.C., February 11, 2004.
[13] Statement by Ambassador John Freeman, Head of UK Delegation, to the Seventh Review Conference of the Treaty on the Non-Proliferation of Nuclear Weapons, New York, May 5, 2005.

time claiming the benefit of their rights, thus undermining the very foundations of the Treaty. I add that the commitment on which the NPT is founded, which is to prevent proliferation, cannot under any circumstances be made conditional upon progress towards the other goals of the Treaty.[14]

In this statement by France, there is a clear expression of the primacy of the non-proliferation pillar of the NPT, and of its absolute nature even in cases of tension with the 'other goals' of the treaty, which are through this language reduced to decidedly subsidiary concepts.

The statements most explicitly and forcefully expressing this legal interpretation regarding the relationship between the principled pillars of the NPT are those of the U.S. delegations from 2003–2008. In his statement to the 2003 PrepCom, U.S. representative Andrew Semmel observed, 'The central purpose of the NPT is to prevent the spread of nuclear weapons.'[15] U.S. representative Stephen Rademaker expands on this idea in his statement to the 2005 PrepCom:

Today, the Treaty is facing the most serious challenge in its history due to instances of noncompliance. Although the vast majority of member states have lived up to their NPT non-proliferation obligations that constitute the Treaty's most important contribution to international peace and security, some have not [. . .] This Review Conference provides an opportunity for us to demonstrate our resolve in reaffirming our collective determination that noncompliance with the Treaty's core non-proliferation norms is a clear threat to international peace and security.[16]

The clearest iterations of this unbalanced legal interpretation favoring the non-proliferation pillar come from U.S. representative Christopher Ford in his statements to the 2007 and 2008 PrepComs. As he explains in his 2008 statement:

The NPT, and the broader non-proliferation regime of which it forms a vital part, powerfully serves the security interests of all its States Party by helping combat the further spread of nuclear weapons [. . .] By accomplishing its core non-proliferation purpose, the NPT also powerfully serves the interest of the other goals to which States Party committed themselves in the Treaty's text, including promotion of the peaceful uses of nuclear technology, and progress toward nuclear disarmament [. . .] The world today is vastly safer and more secure than the one in which the NPT was opened for signature, and part of the reason for this has been the success of States Party in ensuring compliance with the

---

[14] Statement by H.E. Ambassador Jean-François Dobelle, Permanent Representative of France to the Conference on Disarmament, Head of the French Delegation, to the Second Session of the Preparatory Committee for the 2010 NPT Review Conference, April 28, 2008.

[15] Statement by Dr Andrew K. Semmel, Alternative Representative of the United States of America, to the Second Session of the Preparatory Committee for the 2005 NPT Review Conference. Peaceful Nuclear Cooperation: NPT Article IV, Geneva, Switzerland, May 7, 2003.

[16] Statement by Stephen G. Rademaker, United States Assistant Secretary of State for Arms Control, to the 2005 Conference of the Treaty on the Non-proliferation of Nuclear Weapons, New York, May 2, 2005.

non-proliferation obligations that during the NPT's negotiation were referred to as 'the core of the Treaty.'[17]

In his repetition that the non-proliferation pillar of the NPT represents its 'core' principles, and that the peaceful use and disarmament pillars merely represent the 'other goals' of the treaty, Ford could hardly have been clearer in his opinion that the treaty provisions containing these 'other goals' are subsidiary in nature to the NPT's 'core' non-proliferation provisions.

This common NWS statement template, which places in clear priority the non-proliferation principles of the NPT, is in stark contrast to the statements of many NNWS parties to the NPT, and particularly developing countries, at NPT meetings during the target era. NNWS, and particularly developing states, tend to stress in their statements the need for balance among the three NPT pillars. A classic statement of this position comes from Malaysia in its address to the 2005 RevCon, as representative of the over 100 states members of the Non-Aligned Movement (NAM):

The NPT is at a crossroads, with its future uncertain. The historic compromise reached 37 years ago between nuclear-weapon States and non-nuclear-weapon States over disarmament, proliferation and peaceful uses of nuclear technology remains unfulfilled. Today as we meet, the stress is on proliferation, rather than disarmament in good faith. The lack of balance in the implementation of the NPT threatens to unravel the NPT regime, a critical component of the global disarmament framework [. . .] I wish to call upon all States Parties, nuclear-weapon States and non-nuclear-weapon States, to recognize the importance of the full and non-selective implementation of the Treaty in nuclear disarmament, non-proliferation and the peaceful uses of nuclear technology—the three pillars of the Treaty.[18]

Similarly, in its statement to the 2008 NPT PrepCom, Brazil's representative noted:

Over the past years, the international community has witnessed disturbing developments in the disarmament and non-proliferation agenda. While an increasing emphasis has been given to non-proliferation, nuclear disarmament has received scant attention. Meager progress in the latter has been—much to the international community's dismay—the result of unilateral decision by Nuclear Weapons States instead of coming from multilaterally negotiated, irreversible and verifiable agreements [. . .] Brazil also acknowledges that one of the challenges facing the NPT is related to proliferation attempts, both overt and concealed, within or outside the Treaty's framework, carried out by both state and non-state actors. While concerns with the new developments in the international security

---

[17] See 'A Recipe for Success at the 2010 Review Conference,' Dr Christopher A. Ford, United States Special Representative for Nuclear Non-proliferation, Opening Remarks to the 2008 NPT Preparatory Committee, Palais des Nations, Geneva, Switzerland, April 28, 2008.
[18] Statement by the Hon. Syed Hamid Albar, Minister of Foreign Affairs of Malaysia, on Behalf of the Group of Non-Aligned States Parties to the Treaty on the Non-proliferation of Nuclear Weapons, at the General Debate of the 2005 Review Conference of the Parties to the Treaty on the Non-proliferation of Nuclear Weapons, New York, May 2, 2005.

agenda in this regard are legitimate, action to curb proliferation must be taken in tandem with nuclear disarmament and the use of nuclear technology for exclusively peaceful ends. We reiterate our understanding that disarmament and non-proliferation processes are closely interrelated and mutually reinforcing. A balanced implementation of the NPT with equal focus on these pillars is essential if the present challenges to the mutual undertakings on which the Treaty is based are to be surmounted.[19]

Representing the states of the Non-Aligned Movement in his statement to the 2009 PrepCom, the representative from Cuba declared:

NAM calls upon all States Parties, both the nuclear weapon and the non nuclear weapon States, to recognize the importance of the full and non-selective implementation of the three pillars [. . .] The NPT is a cornerstone of the nuclear non-proliferation and disarmament regime; it protects the world from the colossal damage of a potential nuclear war that would devastate us all. We must relentlessly pursue our aim of universalization of the regime and its total commitment and adherence by all States, while providing equal weight to the three pillars of disarmament, non-proliferation, and the pursuit of lawful nuclear energy sources.[20]

In their statements to NPT meetings, developing NNWS parties tend to speak of the three principled pillars relatively evenhandedly, and to stress the need to return balance to prioritization of the three pillars in states' nuclear policies, and not to prioritize any one of the pillars over the others. In his statement to the 2005 Review Conference, the representative from Nigeria said:

It is [...] regrettable to note that increasing efforts by some States in the past few years to pursue the objectives of non-proliferation in the use of civilian nuclear reactors may hinder the peaceful application of nuclear technology as provided for in the Treaty. In this connection, we urge State Parties to adopt appropriate measures, at this Review Conference, to preserve the inalienable right of all the Parties to the Treaty to develop research, production and use of nuclear energy for peaceful purposes without discrimination as contained in the Treaty [...] The Treaty on Non-Proliferation of Nuclear Weapons rests on three pillars of nuclear non-proliferation, nuclear disarmament and peaceful uses of nuclear energy. All States Parties share a common desire to realize the goals we have set for ourselves in relation to each of the three pillars but in doing so, there is need for caution and transparency to ensure that none of the three objectives is achieved at the expense of the other.[21]

---

[19] Statement by the Head of the Delegation of Brazil, Ambassador Luiz Felipe de Macedo Soares, to the Second Session of the Preparatory Committee to the 8th Review Conference of the Treaty on the Non-proliferation of Nuclear Weapons, April 28, 2008.

[20] Statement by Ambassador Abelardo Moreno, Permanent Representative of Cuba to the United Nations, on Behalf of the Group of Non-Aligned States Parties to the Treaty on the Non-proliferation of Nuclear Weapons, at the General Debate of the Third Session of the Preparatory Committee for the 2010 Review Conference of the States Parties to the Treaty on the Non-proliferation of Nuclear Weapons, New York, May 4, 2009.

[21] Statement by Mr Chuka Udedibia, Minister Permanent Mission of Nigeria to the UN, on Behalf of the Nigerian Delegation. Delivered at the 2005 Review Conference of States Parties to the Treaty on Non-proliferation of Nuclear Weapons, May 3, 2005.

Similarly, the Indonesian representative, again representing the 100+ states of the Non-Aligned Movement, made the following statement to the 2008 PrepCom:

The NAM States Parties regard the three pillars of NPT; nuclear disarmament, non-proliferation, and the peaceful uses of nuclear technology, as vital to an invigorated Treaty that benefits all mankind. We stress that this review cycle should focus equally on the three pillars of the NPT. The lack of balance in the implementation of the NPT threatens to unravel the NPT regime [. . .] NAM calls upon all States Parties, NWS and NNWS, to recognize the importance of the full and non-selective implementation of the Treaty in nuclear disarmament, non-proliferation, and the peaceful uses of nuclear technology, which I repeat are the three pillars of the Treaty.[22]

These differences of approach to the question of the relative priority to be given to the three principled pillars of the NPT are at their essence differences in the legal interpretation of the NPT as a conventional source of international law, as some of the NWS statements from 2003–2008 were at pains to make clear.

III. Peaceful Use

As compared to references in NWS statements to nuclear non-proliferation issues during the target era, there can be found far fewer references by the same representatives to NNWS rights of peaceful civilian nuclear use, or to the obligation of all states, particularly including NWS and other supplier countries, to assist in these uses, per Article IV of the NPT. Furthermore, on the occasions in which reference is made to issues of nuclear peaceful use, NWS official statements during this period are generally not positive endorsements of the utility and value of existing peaceful nuclear energy programs, nor of the desirability of the spread of such programs in the developing world particularly—principles which were at the heart of President Eisenhower's Atoms for Peace proposal, and which provide the underpinning for the peaceful use pillar of the NPT. Indeed on the contrary, they customarily emphasize the dangers inherent in NNWS pursuit of civilian uses of nuclear energy, and in particular their pursuit of indigenous capabilities for production of fissile materials.

These statements by NWS representatives frequently invoke this danger as the justification for a very narrow and limited view of the rights recognized and obligations created in NPT Article IV. Under this limited view, the rights and obligations of Article IV are clearly and tightly circumscribed by the non-proliferation obligations of Articles II and III. These statements make clear the view that the

[22] Statement by H.E. Gusti Agung Wesaka Puja, Ambassador of the Republic of Indonesia, on Behalf of the Group of Non-Aligned States Parties to the Treaty on the Non-proliferation of Nuclear Weapons, at the General Debate of the Second Session of the Preparatory Committee for the 2010 Review Conference of the States Parties to the Treaty on the Non-proliferation of Nuclear Weapons, April 28, 2008.

Article IV rights and obligations are secondary in priority to the non-proliferation obligations of Articles II and III, and are only operative on condition of prior, full, and demonstrated compliance with these normatively superior non-proliferation obligations.

Again, as noted above, one of the clearest statements of the rationale underpinning this marginalization of the peaceful use principles of Article IV is to be found in U.S. President Bush's February 11, 2004 speech in which he characterizes the rights and obligations related to peaceful use in Article IV as a 'loophole' in the treaty—one that has been and will continue to be exploited by certain NNWS to cover their true aims of nuclear proliferation.[23] This negative characterization of the principles of peaceful use codified in Article IV would become a theme running through statements of U.S. representatives to NPT meetings from 2004–2008, and can also be seen reflected in the statements of other NWS during this period as well. It further served as the theoretical underpinning for a number of proposals advanced by NWS during this era, aimed at limiting the access of NNWS to what are considered 'sensitive' civilian nuclear fuel cycle technologies.

Bush's negative characterization of Article IV principles was immediately parroted by U.S. representative John Bolton in his statement to the 2004 PrepCom:

There is a crisis of NPT noncompliance, and the challenge before us is to devise ways to ensure full compliance with the Treaty's non-proliferation objectives. Without such compliance by all members, confidence in the security benefits derived from the NPT will erode. To address this serious problem, President Bush recently announced a series of proposals that are aimed at strengthening compliance with the obligations we all undertook when we signed the Treaty. These proposals will address a fundamental problem that has allowed nations like Iran and North Korea to exploit the benefits of NPT membership to develop their nuclear weapons programs. The President is determined to stop rogue states from gaining nuclear weapons under cover of supposed peaceful nuclear technology. As President Bush said on February 11, 'Proliferators must not be allowed to cynically manipulate the NPT to acquire the material and infrastructure necessary for manufacturing illegal weapons.'[24]

U.S. representative Stephen Rademaker had a similar message regarding the relationship between the non-proliferation and peaceful use pillars of the NPT in his statement to the 2005 PrepCom:

The NPT is fundamentally a treaty for mutual security. It is clear that the security of all member states depends on unstinting adherence to the Treaty's non-proliferation norms by all other parties [. . .] Today, the Treaty is facing the most serious challenge in its history

---

[23] Remarks by U.S. President George W. Bush on Weapons of Mass Destruction Proliferation. Fort Lesley J. McNair—National Defense University, Washington D.C., February 11, 2004.

[24] Statement by United States Under Secretary of State for Arms Control and International Security John R. Bolton, to the Third Session of the Preparatory Committee for the 2005 Review Conference of the Treaty on the Non-proliferation of Nuclear Weapons. 'The NPT: A Crisis of Non-Compliance,' New York, April 27, 2004.

due to instances of noncompliance. Although the vast majority of member states have lived up to their NPT non-proliferation obligations that constitute the Treaty's most important contribution to international peace and security, some have not [. . .] U.S. support for the NPT extends far beyond our determined efforts to reinforce the Treaty's core non-proliferation norms. The benefits of peaceful nuclear cooperation comprise an important element of the NPT. Through substantial funding and technical cooperation, the United States fully supports peaceful nuclear development in many states, bilaterally and through the IAEA. But the language of Article IV is explicit and unambiguous: states asserting their right to receive the benefits of peaceful nuclear development must be in compliance with their non-proliferation obligations under Articles I and II of the NPT. No state in violation of Articles I or II should receive the benefits of Article IV. All nuclear assistance to such a state, bilaterally or through the IAEA, should cease.[25]

In his statement to the 2008 PrepCom on behalf of the United States, Christopher Ford similarly pointed out the dangers inherent in the spread of civilian nuclear programs:

First, there is wide international understanding that the proliferation of the capability to produce fissile material usable in nuclear weapons poses grave dangers to the non-proliferation regime. The difficulty in obtaining fissile material is the principal obstacle to developing nuclear weapons, and the unchecked or unsafeguarded acquisition of material-production capabilities by countries with potential nuclear weapons ambitions is antithetical to the cause of non-proliferation.[26]

However, the United States was not alone during the target era in noting the threat posed by the spread of civilian nuclear programs, and in stressing the limited and circumscribed nature of the Article IV rights and obligations. In his statement to the 2005 RevCon, French representative François Rivasseau emphasized the conditional nature of the Article IV right:

My country will ensure that the right to 'nuclear energy for peaceful purposes' recognized in Article IV of the NPT be preserved and fully exercised for countries that unambiguously comply with their international obligations [. . .] I wish to recall in this respect the conditions required to have the right to nuclear power within the meaning of Article IV of the Treaty, namely: compliance with the obligations to ensure non-proliferation and implement IAEA safeguards on the one hand; and the pursuit of 'peaceful purposes' on the other in accordance with the principle of good faith. It is evident that a State failing to comply with its obligations to ensure non-proliferation and implement IAEA safeguards and the peaceful purposes of whose nuclear activities could not be recognized, would not be entitled to enjoy the stipulations of Article IV.[27]

---

[25] Statement by Stephen G. Rademaker, United States Assistant Secretary of State for Arms Control, to the 2005 Conference of the Treaty on the Non-proliferation of Nuclear Weapons, New York, May 2, 2005.

[26] See 'A Recipe for Success at the 2010 Review Conference,' Dr Christopher A. Ford, United States Special Representative for Nuclear Non-proliferation, Opening Remarks to the 2008 NPT Preparatory Committee, Palais des Nations, Geneva, Switzerland, April 28, 2008.

[27] Statement to the 2005 Review Conference of the Parties to the Treaty on the Non-proliferation of Nuclear Weapons, May 5, 2005.

In the same vein, in his statement to the 2008 PrepCom, French representative Jean-François Dobelle remarked:

My country fully supports the inalienable right recognized for parties to the Treaty to develop nuclear energy for peaceful purposes, but it recalls that according to the provisions of Article IV, that right is not unconditional. Indeed, under the terms of the Treaty, such entitlement is subject to the following conditions:

- Firstly, conformity with the non-proliferation obligations laid down in Articles I and II of the Treaty, and acceptance of the IAEA safeguards as defined in Article III;
- Secondly, the pursuit, in accordance with the principle of good faith, of 'peaceful purposes'.

Indeed, the right to peaceful use must not be diverted to allow the use of nuclear materials, equipment and technology for purposes contrary to the intentions of the Treaty. No State failing to meet its obligations with regard to non-proliferation and the application of IAEA safeguards, or whose nuclear activities are not directed toward identifiable peaceful ends, can claim the benefit of the stipulations contained in Article IV [...] we must promote mutual understanding of the conditions to be met for the exercise of the right to make peaceful use of atomic energy, a right that must be enjoyed by as many States as possible insofar as they abide by their non-proliferation obligations and pursue in good faith activities directed at peaceful goals.[28]

Also in 2008, in his statement to the PrepCom on behalf of Russia, Anatoly Antonov made the following observation particularly with regard to the maintenance and spread of indigenous enrichment capabilities by developing states:

We can see today that countries are increasingly interested in developing nuclear energy as a reliable resource ensuring their energy security. This is a natural process. It gives ample opportunities for international cooperation. First of all, those should be taken to supply countries developing their own atomic energy with nuclear fuel in a reliable and assured manner. One way is that every country can establish its own facilities to enrich uranium, produce fuel and further reprocess it. Yet, it is a very complicated process not only in terms of funds, but also in terms of intellectual, scientific, physical and technical resources. Is moving along this path justified when the world market is capable of meeting both current and future needs in this area? It is unlikely so.[29]

And in their joint statement to the 2008 PrepCom, following their recitation of recognition of the Article IV right to peaceful use, the five NWS made sure to emphasize the limited and conditional nature of that right, and to discourage the maintenance and spread of indigenous fuel cycle programs in NNWS:

---

[28] Statement by H.E. Ambassador Jean-François Dobelle, Permanent Representative of France to the Conference on Disarmament, Head of the French Delegation, to the Second Session of the Preparatory Committee for the 2010 NPT Review Conference, April 28, 2008.

[29] Statement by H.E. Ambassador Anatoly Antonov, Head of the Delegation of the Russian Federation at the Second Session of the Preparatory Committee for the 2010 Review Conference of the Parties to the Treaty on the Non-Proliferation of Nuclear Weapons, April 28, 2008.

We note that a growing number of States Party is showing interest in developing nuclear programmes aimed at addressing their long-term energy requirements and other peaceful purposes. We are ready to co-operate with States Party in the development of nuclear energy for peaceful uses and we emphasise the requirement for compliance with non-proliferation obligations and for development of research, use and production of nuclear energy to be solely for peaceful purposes. We believe such international co-operation should contribute to the full implementation of the NPT and enhance the authority and effectiveness of the global non-proliferation regime.

We welcome the work of the International Atomic Energy Agency on multilateral approaches to the nuclear fuel cycle and encourage efforts towards a multilateral mechanism to assure access for all countries to nuclear fuel services as a viable alternative to the indigenous development of enrichment and reprocessing.[30]

A. NWS peaceful use policies

This negative and limited view of the peaceful use pillar of the NPT is reflected in a number of proposals and high-level efforts by NWS during the target decade aimed at circumscribing and conditioning the right of NNWS to nuclear fuel cycle technologies, and at changing the conditions under which supplies of nuclear technologies are made to NNWS by NWS and other supplier states. These proposals and efforts include:

1. Requiring NNWS to exclusively source nuclear material from a multilateral fuel bank as a condition of supply;
2. Requiring NNWS accession to the IAEA Additional Protocol as a condition of supply; and
3. Conditioning supply and recognition of rights to nuclear technologies on compliance with an IAEA Comprehensive Safeguards Agreement.

I will proceed to consider each of these in turn.

1. *The NSG*

In order to discuss and evaluate these proposals and efforts, however, a preliminary discussion of the Nuclear Suppliers Group (NSG) is necessary. I will only include herein a summary description and discussion of the NSG. For a more detailed discussion of the NSG's history and functioning, please see, *inter alia*, my previously published work.[31]

---

[30] Statement on behalf of China, France, the Russian Federation, the United Kingdom of Great Britain and Northern Ireland, and the United States of America, to the 2008 Non-Proliferation Treaty Preparatory Committee, delivered by Ambassador John Duncan, UK Ambassador for Multilateral Arms Control and Disarmament, May 9, 2008.

[31] See generally Daniel H. Joyner, 'The Nuclear Suppliers Group: History and Functioning,' 11(2) *International Trade Law & Regulation* (2005) 33–42; ibid. 'The Nuclear Suppliers Group: Present Challenges and Future Prospects,' 11(3) *International Trade Law & Regulation* (2005) 84–96.

Article III.2 of the NPT provides the international legal basis for all nuclear export controls. It specifies that all parties to the treaty will not transfer nuclear (fissionable) materials, as well as 'any equipment or material especially designed or prepared for the processing, use or production of special fissionable material' to non-nuclear weapon states for peaceful purposes unless such material is subject to the IAEA safeguards specified in Article III.1.[32]

This provision, providing only the most vague of standards both on the subject of criteria for applying national export controls, and on the question of exactly what materials should be the subject of national export controls, created an urgent need for clarification of the NPT's meaning in this regard. This was particularly the case as the regulation of trade in nuclear-related technologies between states formed the most practical continuing concern for states in possession of such technologies, and the issue area in which the implementation of NPT rules was to be most impactful upon the national laws and policies of the NWS and other supplier states of nuclear-related technologies.

Due to this need, in March 1971, shortly after the NPT's entry into force, a group of nuclear supplier states gathered for the purpose of clarifying the technical implications of NPT export controls, as well as to establish a continuing forum for interpretation of Article III.2's broad export control provisions. This meeting was the nucleus of a group which came to be known as the Zangger Committee, after its first Chairman, Professor Claude Zangger.

The Zangger Committee continued to meet periodically and eventually established both a set of Understandings adopted by all Committee members, and a trigger list composed of items the export of which should 'trigger' the requirement of safeguards. The Zangger Committee's Understandings were published in September 1974 as IAEA document INFCIRC/209, and are divided into two separate memoranda addressing export controls on a category of items described in Article III.2. Memorandum A covers source and special fissionable material, and Memorandum B covers equipment and material specifically designed or prepared for the processing, use, or production of special fissionable material. The memoranda provide that nuclear suppliers should, in the context of a transfer of subject items to a non-nuclear weapon state not party to the NPT,

(a) obtain assurances from the recipient state that the exported materials will not be used in a nuclear explosion;
(b) subject such items, and materials on the trigger list produced through their use, to IAEA safeguards; and
(c) ensure that items on the trigger list are not re-exported to a third party recipient state unless that recipient state meets the criteria laid out in (a) and (b).

---

[32] See ibid.

The trigger list, which clarifies and provides detail regarding the equipment listed in the memoranda, is updated regularly in accordance with technological innovations. The Zangger Committee's trigger list and memoranda together comprised the first major agreement among supplier states regarding nuclear export controls.

The explosion of a nuclear device by India in May 1974, in addition to increased activity among other NNWS to create a full nuclear fuel cycle, led to heightened concern among supplier states regarding nuclear proliferation. In 1975 a new group of supplier states met in London with the purpose of supplementing the Zangger Committee's work in the field of nuclear export controls. Over successive meetings, this group became known unofficially as the 'London Club,' and officially as the Nuclear Suppliers Group (NSG). The NSG's chief distinction from the Zangger Committee was initially to be found in the character of its membership. The Zangger Committee had from its inception been comprised exclusively of NPT member states. The NSG by contrast was consciously envisioned to include non-parties to the NPT and, importantly, France, a major supplier state not yet a party to the NPT and therefore also not a member of the Zangger Committee. The establishment of the NSG thus expanded the number of important voices and interests in deliberations regarding nuclear export control standards.[33]

In 1976 NSG member states produced a document entitled 'Guidelines on Nuclear Transfers,' which was accepted by all fifteen members in 1977 and published in February 1978 as IAEA document INFCIRC/254. The NSG guidelines incorporated the Zangger Committee trigger list and largely mirrored the Zangger Committee's Understandings, with the notable addition of going beyond the context of the NPT to cover nuclear transfers to any non-nuclear weapon state. The NSG guidelines further tightened export control standards in a number of areas including in the transfer of nuclear facilities and technology supporting them.

Following the adoption of the guidelines in 1977, the NSG did not meet again officially for thirteen years, although during this time the NSG Guidelines were implemented by member states through national measures and twelve more states from both the West and the East formally accepted the Guidelines. However, the NSG entered a period of renewed activity beginning with the end of the Cold War—a revival which was largely spurred by the experience of the 1990–91 Gulf War and the revelations of Iraq's mature, and clandestine, WMD development programs.

These revelations brought home to supplier states in compelling fashion the necessity of greater attention to harmonization and tightening of multilateral nuclear export controls in general. This was particularly perceived as it became clear that items and technologies used exclusively in the processes of weapons

---

[33] See Tadeusz Strulak, 'The Nuclear Suppliers Group,' 1(1) *The Non-proliferation Review* (Fall 1993).

manufacture were not the only or even the most important problem for export control systems to deal with. As the war progressed, and particularly in its aftermath, it became clear that one of the greatest facilitators of the formidable Iraqi nuclear weapons program was the importation, through various methods ranging from open purchase to covert indirect acquisition, of items from Western companies which were not exclusively used in the production of fissile materials and other elements of a nuclear weapons program, but which were rather dual-use in nature, again items which had legitimate civilian uses but which could also be adapted for use in weapons programs.[34]

The trigger lists and foundational principles both of the Zangger Committee and the NSG had up to that point been concentrated on fissile materials and those items and technologies 'especially designed' for their production, as specified in Article III.2 of the NPT. Now, however, it was realized that a sizeable 'dual-use gap' existed as between the normative foundations of the multilateral nuclear export control regimes and the realities of the modern security environment. The recognition of this dual-use gap, and a commonly perceived imperative to narrow it, contributed significantly to the revival of the NSG.[35]

At the NSG plenary meeting in the Hague in March 1991, the members agreed to bring the NSG control list up to date by broadening it to include the items which had been added to the Zangger Committee's control list since the last NSG meeting in 1977. However, the most noteworthy achievement of the Hague meeting was the decision to create a supplementary regime within the NSG framework to control exports of nuclear-related dual-use materials and technology. This arrangement was formally adopted by the twenty-seven NSG members at the 1992 plenary meeting in Warsaw, and both the resulting guidelines and trigger list were published by the IAEA in July 2002 as INFCIRC/254/REV 1.Part 2.

The NSG arrangement for dual-use nuclear export controls, now referred to as NSG Part 2, consists of a set of guidelines for transfers of nuclear dual-use items and a list of approximately sixty-five items including equipment and technology. The 'Basic Principle' of the guidelines states that suppliers should not authorize transfers of equipment, materials, software, or related technology identified on the list if (1) they are to be used by a non-nuclear-weapon state in a nuclear explosive activity or an unsafeguarded nuclear fuel cycle; (2) there is in general an unacceptable risk of diversion to such an activity; or (3) the transfers are contrary to the objective of averting the proliferation of nuclear weapons.

When considering the role of the NSG as a normative regime, and its influence upon the actions of its participants, it is important to bear a number of

---

[34] James Holmes and Gary Bertsch, 'Tighten Export Controls,' *Defense News*, May 5, 2003. David Albright and Mark Hibbs, 'Iraq and the Bomb, Were They Even Close?' *The Bulletin of Atomic Scientists* (April 1992) 16–28; David A. Kay, 'Denial and Deception of WMD Proliferators,' 18(1) *The Washington Quarterly* (November 1994) 90.

[35] See Carlton E. Thorne, ed., *A Guide to Nuclear Export Controls* (5th edn, 2002).

points in mind. The first is that the guidelines and the trigger lists of the NSG are not formally binding legal documents. 'Membership' in the NSG (or 'participation' as is the favored phrase of the Group) is accomplished through a joint, informal declaration of adherence to the guidelines. Second, the NSG is not, strictly speaking, a multilateral normative regime, if by multilateral one means an institution or regime in which any state may be included according to its own will. Rather, the NSG, like all the other international export control regimes (e.g. the Australia Group, the Missile Technology Control Regime, and the Wassenaar Arrangement) is technically speaking a plurilateral regime, in which membership is only extended to states on the basis of the consensual vote of the existing group of participants, currently numbering forty-five. It is this plurilateral aspect of the institutional character of the NSG, along with its track record which many developing countries perceive as being unduly restrictive toward states legitimately attempting to develop civilian power generation facilities, which has led many NNWS to criticize the NSG as constituting a supplier state 'cartel.'[36]

Notwithstanding their legal informality and these criticisms by developing states, the NSG guidelines and trigger list do have a significant influence upon the policies of its participating states, and the implementation of NSG standards in the national law of participants is expected by their fellows in the Group, among other reasons in order to prevent the collective action problem of undercutting.[37]

This, then, is the context for understanding the proposals, first made by U.S. President Bush in his February 2004 speech, for amending the NSG Guidelines on Nuclear Transfers in order to more stringently limit trade in both single use and dual-use nuclear technologies to NNWS developing states. Immediately after characterizing the Article IV NPT right to nuclear energy development as a 'loophole' in the treaty, Bush continued as follows:

So today, as a fourth step, I propose a way to close the loophole. The world must create a safe, orderly system to field civilian nuclear plants without adding to the danger of weapons proliferation. The world's leading nuclear exporters should ensure that states have reliable access at reasonable cost to fuel for civilian reactors, so long as those states renounce

---

[36] See, e.g., NAM Summit Declaration, Cartagena, Colombia, 18–20 Oct. 1995. Available at <http://www.nam.gov.za/xisummit/index.html>. In this Declaration, NAM members 'noted with concern the growing restraint placed on access to material, equipment and technology for peaceful uses of nuclear energy by the developed countries through imposition of ad-hoc export control regimes.'

[37] Paragraph 4(b) of the 1992 dual-use regime Memorandum of Understanding states that member governments 'should not authorize a transfer of equipment, materials, software, or related technology identified in the Annex which is essentially identical to a transfer which was not authorized by another Subscribing Government where this decision was notified pursuant to subparagraph (a), without consulting the Subscribing Government which provided the notice.' The observance of this rule on undercutting transfers is vital to the maintenance of an effective procedure for information sharing in the area of denial notifications. This principle and the other implementing principles of the MOU for 'leveling the playing field' among members became available for acceptance by all NSG members in 1997.

enrichment and reprocessing. Enrichment and reprocessing are not necessary for nations seeking to harness nuclear energy for peaceful purposes.

The 40 nations of the Nuclear Suppliers Group should refuse to sell enrichment and reprocessing equipment and technologies to any state that does not already possess full-scale, functioning enrichment and reprocessing plants. This step will prevent new states from developing the means to produce fissile material for nuclear bombs. Proliferators must not be allowed to cynically manipulate the NPT to acquire the material and infra-structure necessary for manufacturing illegal weapons.

For international norms to be effective, they must be enforced. It is the charge of the International Atomic Energy Agency to uncover banned nuclear activity around the world and report those violations to the U.N. Security Council. We must ensure that the IAEA has all the tools it needs to fulfill its essential mandate. America and other nations support what is called the Additional Protocol, which requires states to declare a broad range of nuclear activities and facilities, and allow the IAEA to inspect those facilities.

As a fifth step, I propose that by next year, only states that have signed the Additional Protocol be allowed to import equipment for their civilian nuclear programs. Nations that are serious about fighting proliferation will approve and implement the Additional Protocol.[38]

I will proceed to examine these two proposals, before moving on to consider efforts to limit NNWS' Article IV rights by reference to Article III and compliance with IAEA safeguards agreements.

2. *Fuel bank membership as a condition of supply*

The first of Bush's proposals was in essence a proposal for a change to the NSG guidelines in order to cut off supplies of nuclear fuel and technology from supplier states to all NNWS that maintain domestic enrichment and reprocessing capabilities. He further proposed that no state that does not already have enrichment and reprocessing facilities should be provided materials and technologies for developing such facilities by NSG participants. Instead, Bush proposed that, for states that do renounce their rights to maintain domestic enrichment and reprocessing capabilities, '[t]he world's leading nuclear exporters should ensure that [they] have reliable access at reasonable cost to fuel for civilian reactors.'[39] In later comments by U.S. as well as other NWS officials, it became clear that this proposal translated into an initiative to change NSG guidelines in order to make membership in an international fuel bank facility a condition of supply of nuclear fuel and other technologies.

Bush's proposal clearly drew inspiration from analysis and proposals made by IAEA Director-General Mohamed ElBaradei in 2003 in an op-ed published in the *Economist* magazine. In the op-ed, ElBaradei explained:

Uranium enrichment is sophisticated and expensive, but it is not proscribed under the NPT. Most designs for civilian nuclear-power reactors require fuel that has been 'low-enriched', and many research reactors operate with 'high-enriched' uranium. It is not uncommon, therefore, for non-nuclear-weapon states with developed nuclear infrastruc-

---

[38] Remarks by U.S. President George W. Bush on Weapons of Mass Destruction Proliferation. Fort Lesley J. McNair—National Defense University, Washington D.C., February 11, 2004.
[39] Ibid.

tures to seek enrichment capabilities and to possess sizeable amounts of uranium that could, if desired, be enriched to weapons-grade [. . .] Under the current regime, therefore, there is nothing illicit in a non-nuclear-weapon state having enrichment or reprocessing technology, or possessing weapon-grade nuclear material. And certain types of bomb-making expertise, unfortunately, are readily available in the open literature. Should a state with a fully developed fuel-cycle capability decide, for whatever reason, to break away from its non-proliferation commitments, most experts believe it could produce a nuclear weapon within a matter of months [. . .] the margin of security under the current non-proliferation regime is becoming too slim for comfort. We need a new approach.

My proposal has three parts: First, it is time to limit the processing of weapon-usable material (separated plutonium and high-enriched uranium) in civilian nuclear pro-grammes, as well as the production of new material through reprocessing and enrichment, by agreeing to restrict these operations exclusively to facilities under multinational con-trol. These limitations would need to be accompanied by proper rules of transparency and, above all, by an assurance that legitimate would-be users could get their supplies.[40]

The basic idea of the international fuel bank facilities envisioned by both ElBaradei and Bush is not new. Indeed, it hearkens back to the proposal by U.S. representative Bernard Baruch in 1946 to establish an International Atomic Development Authority, as well as to the original conception of the International Atomic Energy Agency expressed by President Eisenhower in his Atoms for Peace proposal in 1953. The idea of a repository of fissile material procured from sup-plier states, under some form of collective international control, and to be used for the purpose of supplying developing countries with nuclear fuel for civilian energy production, underpins all of these proposals. NWS officials in the Bush era simply revived this old idea in their proposals. However, what they added to the fuel bank concept is the proposal that such internationally controlled fuel banks, combined with a limited number of multinational enrichment centers, be the *exclusive* source of supply of nuclear fuel for developing NNWS parties to the NPT; an exclusivity encompassing the requirement of renunciation of NNWS rights to maintain indigenous enrichment and reprocessing capabilities. These proposals further include the idea that the NSG guidelines should be amended to require such exclusive sourcing of nuclear fuel as a condition of supply of other nuclear-related technologies, including dual-use technologies.

Since Bush's 2004 address, proposals for exclusive sourcing of NNWS nuclear fuel from international fuel banks, and multinational enrichment centers, as well as the idea of fuel bank membership as an NSG condition of supply, have been adopted and advocated by a number of other NWS govern-ments. Russia, in particular, has expressed its endorsement of such proposals

---

[40] 'Towards a Safer World,' *The Economist*, October 16, 2003. See the development of these ideas in a report published by an IAEA expert group at INFCIRC/640, dated February 2005; Tariq Rauf and Zoryana Vovchok, 'Fuel For Thought,' *IAEA Bulletin* 49(2) (March 2008) 59–63 ('The vision of a new framework is that all new enrichment and reprocessing should be exclusively under multi-national control and eventually all such sensitive nuclear fuel cycle technologies are operated multi-laterally with an assurance of supply mechanism.')

on a number of occasions. For example, in his statement to the 2008 PrepCom, Russian Representative Anatoly Antonov noted:

Today countries are increasingly interested in developing nuclear energy as a reliable resource ensuring their energy security [. . .] One can often hear that a country cannot completely depend on the situation in the market or on the political will of some States. These are legitimate concerns. We think they can be allayed on the basis of multilateral approaches to the nuclear fuel cycle, intended to provide an economically reasonable and feasible alternative to establishing all its elements at a national level [. . .] The former Russian President, Vladimir Putin, suggested we work together to develop global nuclear energy infrastructure and to set up multinational centers to provide nuclear fuel cycle services. Our first step was to establish the International Uranium Enrichment Center on the basis of the enrichment plant in Angarsk. Kazakhstan takes part in it, with Armenia finalizing its accession procedures. Those participating in the Center will have a guaranteed access to enrichment services to meet their nuclear fuel needs without developing their own production facilities.[41]

In furtherance of these initiatives regarding international fuel banks, a number of specific proposals have been developed for fuel bank and other fuel cycle facilities. At least twelve such proposals have been produced—some by individual states, such as Russia's Global Nuclear Infrastructure Initiative to be headquartered at Angarsk, and the United States' Global Nuclear Energy Partnership; some by coalitions of states, such as the Six Country Concept (Reliable Access to Nuclear Fuel) presented by France, Germany, Russia, the Netherlands, the U.K., and the U.S.; and at least one by a non-governmental organization—the Nuclear Threat Initiative Proposal to be administered by the IAEA.[42] These proposals at least originally all shared in the essentials of the fuel bank concept described above. However, some have gone further and would additionally potentially provide independent enrichment and fuel return and reprocessing services. Almost all have conceived, or yet conceive of their services, along with those of multinational enrichment centers as being the exclusive source of nuclear fuel for recipients.[43]

Reception of such proposals by developing NNWS—the potential recipients of such international fuel sourcing services—has been largely negative.[44] Many

---

[41] Statement by H.E. Ambassador Anatoly Antonov, Head of the Delegation of the Russian Federation at the Second Session of the Preparatory Committee for the 2010 Review Conference of the Parties to the Treaty on the Non-Proliferation of Nuclear Weapons, April 28, 2008.

[42] See generally Tariq Rauf and Zoryana Vovchok, 'Twelve Proposals on the Table,' 49(2) *IAEA Bulletin* (March 2008); Fiona Simpson, 'Reforming the Nuclear Fuel Cycle: Time is Running Out,' 38(7) *Arms Control Today* (September 2008); 'EU Pledges Funds for IAEA Fuel Bank,' 39(1) *Arms Control Today* (February 2009).

[43] The only proposal which has not required exclusivity is the German Multilateral Enrichment Sanctuary Project (MESP).

[44] See Statement by the Delegation of the Republic of Indonesia on behalf of the Group of Non-Aligned States Parties to the Treaty on the Non-Proliferation of Nuclear Weapons, at the Second Session of the Preparatory Committee for the 2010 Review Conference of the States Parties to the Treaty on the Non-Proliferation of Nuclear Weapons. April 28–May 9, 2008. On Cluster 3 Issues.

have expressed concerns that exclusive sourcing of nuclear fuel from fuel banks and other foreign-controlled sources would unacceptably circumscribe their rights under Article IV of the NPT. Indeed, at the IAEA Board of Governors' meeting on June 18, 2009, the Board blocked a proposal by IAEA Director-General Mohamed ElBaradei to move forward on the Agency's plans to establish and administer a fuel bank, in potential partnership with a number of both private and public investors. As reported by Reuters:

While developing states agreed to let talks go on, they warned others on the IAEA's 35-nation governing board against 'attempts meant to discourage the pursuit of any peaceful nuclear technology on grounds of its alleged "sensitivity"' [. . .] '[Developing nation] delegations kept saying they felt this plan would hamper their inalienable and sovereign right under the Non-Proliferation Treaty to develop their own nuclear fuel cycle,' said a Vienna diplomat in the closed-door gathering.[45]

As Patricia Lewis has written:

The various proposals for multinational approaches to the nuclear fuel cycle and assurance of supply are having a difficult time gaining traction in the developing world. There are persistent fears that the nuclear supplier countries are plotting price-fixing cartels and that they have a long term aim of infringing on Article 4 rights.[46]

Even as rhetoric regarding the exclusive-sourcing aspect of multilateral fuel banks seems to have been dropped by at least the U.S. government since Barack Obama assumed the U.S. presidency in 2009, as will be more fully discussed below, many NNWS are still dubious of the fuel banks because of their conceptual provenance,

---

('The [NAM] Group rejects, in principle, any attempts aimed at discouraging certain peaceful nuclear activities on the ground of their alleged "sensitivity." Concerns related to nuclear non-proliferation shall not in any way restrict the inalienable right of all states to develop all aspects of nuclear science and technology for peaceful purposes.'); Statement by H.E. Ambassador Maged Abdel Fatah Abdel Aziz, Permanent Representative of the Arab Republic of Egypt, before the Third Session of the Preparatory Committee to the 2010 NPT Review Conference, May 4, 2009. ('Egypt notes with growing concern attempts by some to reinterpret Article IV of the Treaty in a manner that aims to restrict the ability of non-nuclear weapon states to benefit from their rights by creating artificial categories of "sensitive" and "non-sensitive" nuclear technologies or "responsible" and "irresponsible" states. Egypt also views with concern efforts by the Nuclear Suppliers Group and other discriminatory arrangements to impose additional restrictions on some but not on others, in a manner that is clearly politicized and does not contribute to the implementation of the NPT's objectives, in particular its universality, as well as interference in the internal affairs of states by attempting to influence the determination of their nuclear energy requirements or to restrict their choice to achieve self-sufficiency in the area of fuel supply.') See also Leonard Weiss, 'Reliable Energy Supply and Non-proliferation,' 16(2) *Non-proliferation Review* (July 2009) 269, 274 ('Outright denial of transfers of fuel cycle technology to non-nuclear weapon states have also become the norm for nuclear suppliers, leading to complaints that one of the grand bargains upon which the NPT was founded has been reneged on,' p. 280).

[45] Sylvia Westall, 'Obama-backed Nuclear Fuel Bank Plan Stalls at IAEA,' Reuters, June 18, 2009. Available at <http://www.reuters.com/article/worldNews/idUSTRE55H58L20090618>.

[46] 'Prospects for the NPT and the 2010 Review Conference,' 40(2) *Arms Control Today* (March 2010) 19.

and the fear that they are a first step toward circumscription of NNWS rights of indigenous control over the nuclear fuel cycle.

3. *IAEA Additional Protocol membership as a condition of supply*

The second of Bush's proposals was for a change to the NSG guidelines to require NNWS accession to the IAEA Additional Protocol as a condition of supply of nuclear fuel and technologies. As in the case of the proposal for international fuel sourcing of nuclear fuel as a condition of supply, Bush's proposal regarding the IAEA Additional Protocol has since been advocated by a number of other NWS as well. In his statement to the 2005 RevCon, U.K. representative John Freeman said:

> Mr President, these examples should cause us to examine the tools we have at our disposal to counter the challenges they pose. Here I must first mention the IAEA whose work the UK supports in all areas. We believe its work underpins the NPT and stands in the front line against those who would evade or deny their international obligations. We therefore call on all Non-Nuclear Weapon States that have not yet done so to agree, bring into force and comply with, Comprehensive Safeguards Agreements and Additional Protocols to those agreements. We would like to see the combinations of a Comprehensive Safeguards Agreement and Additional Protocol accepted as a future condition of supply for sensitive nuclear materials.[47]

Similarly, in his statement to the 2008 PrepCom, Russian representative Anatoly Antonov said:

> Improving the efficiency of IAEA's verification activities is an important aspect of strengthening the nuclear non-proliferation regime. We believe that the Additional Protocol to the Safeguards Agreement is an efficient instrument to provide more opportunities to the Agency in this area. Its application allows to timely prevent and eliminate emerging non-proliferation concerns. In the future, the Additional Protocol should become a universally accepted standard to verify the compliance of States with their NPT non-proliferation obligations and an essential new standard in the field of nuclear supply arrangements.[48]

In order to understand this proposal and its implications, a brief review of the role and work of the IAEA, including the Additional Protocol, is needed. Pursuant to NPT Article III.4, all NNWS parties to the NPT must conclude a safeguards agreement with the IAEA 'for the exclusive purpose of verification of the fulfillment of its obligations assumed under this Treaty with a view to preventing diversion of nuclear energy from peaceful uses to nuclear weapons or other nuclear explosive devices.'[49] In 1972, two years after the coming into force of the NPT,

---

[47] Statement by Ambassador John Freeman, Head of UK Delegation, to the Seventh Review Conference of the Treaty on the Non-Proliferation of Nuclear Weapons, New York, May 5, 2005.

[48] Statement by H.E. Ambassador Anatoly Antonov, Head of the Delegation of the Russian Federation at the Second Session of the Preparatory Committee for the 2010 Review Conference of the Parties to the Treaty on the Non-Proliferation of Nuclear Weapons, April 28, 2008.

[49] Quote from NPT Article III.1.

the new comprehensive IAEA safeguards system was brought online and defined in document INFCIRC/153, entitled 'The Structure and Content of Agreements Between the Agency and States Required in Connection With the Treaty on the Non-proliferation of Nuclear Weapons.' INFCIRC/153 sets out the principles which should be included in a safeguards agreement between the IAEA and each NNWS. The basic system established by INFCIRC/153 is one in which states have an obligation to keep detailed records 'on all source or special fissionable material in all peaceful nuclear activities,' and to provide the IAEA with design information on facilities in which such materials are kept, as well as access to such facilities for IAEA inspectors.[50]

The IAEA's role is essentially one of verification of the details on the location and handling of nuclear materials provided to the Agency through national reporting. In order to fulfill this role, the IAEA is to engage in routine inspections of declared facilities, including sampling of the environment within and outside of such facilities. However, the INFCIRC/153 system was constructed to impose the minimum burden necessary upon NNWS, and to be applied in a manner designed 'to avoid hampering' technological development, 'to avoid undue interference' in civilian nuclear energy, and 'to reduce to a minimum the possible inconvenience and disturbance to the State.' Thus, as one result, IAEA inspectors are not granted rights of access to all parts of safeguarded facilities, but only to agreed 'strategic points' within facilities.[51]

INFCIRC/153 does provide, in Article 77, for the IAEA to be granted authority in safeguards agreements to conduct 'special inspections' in addition to these routine inspections, through which the Agency might 'obtain access in agreement with the State to information or locations in addition to the access specified in paragraph 76 above for *ad hoc* and routine inspections.' However, the idea of special inspections was met with considerable opposition from NNWS, and the system which evolved in practice over the next two decades created an environment in which IAEA inspectors did not feel able to make such requests, and in fact did not make them. Thus, the IAEA's role remained one of verification of national reports through routine inspections of declared facilities.

Despite its shortcomings in practice, due to the comprehensive character of the INFCIRC/153 system which is to cover all sites involved in nuclear fuel cycle activity within a state, this safeguards system came to be referred to as the 'Full Scope Safeguards System' (FSSG).[52]

In the aftermath of the 1991 Iraq war, IAEA inspectors returning to Iraq discovered that the Hussein regime had pursued a nuclear weapons program to an advanced stage, involving activities in facilities located all over the country. This program, according to IAEA Deputy Director of Inspections David Kay, had

---

[50] See ibid.   [51] See ibid.

[52] See Fritz Schmidt, 'NPT Export Controls and the Zangger Committee,' 7(3) *Non-proliferation Review*, CNS, (Fall–Winter 2000).

progressed to being within 12 to 18 months of acquiring sufficient fissile material to construct a nuclear explosive device.[53]

This revelation of a large-scale clandestine nuclear weapons program in a state which had signed an INFCIRC/153 agreement with the IAEA, and which was under active Agency safeguards, was troubling. Even more disturbing was the fact that one of the undeclared nuclear installations, the Tuwaitha Nuclear Research Center, was virtually next door to a declared, safeguarded research reactor. Iraq's ability to conceal such an advanced program literally under the noses of IAEA inspectors shook international confidence in the INFCIRC/153 safeguards system.[54]

Again, that system relies almost entirely upon the declarations of facilities and materials made by states, and the IAEA's role under that system is to review those declarations and accounts to verify that the numbers add up, and that all fissile material is accounted for. However, under the INFCIRC/153 system the IAEA had almost no facility for determining the completeness of such reports, or of detecting undeclared nuclear activities.

Speaking at the 46th Session of the General Assembly in 1991, IAEA Director General Hans Blix called for the construction of an IAEA safeguards system with 'more teeth.' Soon afterward, a committee of IAEA member states began negotiation on a protocol to strengthen and supplement the INFCIRC/153 system. This process led to the adoption by the IAEA Board of Governors in 1997 of the Model Additional Protocol (INFCIRC/540).

The Additional Protocol has been characterized as 'an effort to transform IAEA inspectors from accountants to detectives.'[55] It attempts to do this by supplementing the INFCIRC/153 safeguards system in two primary areas. First, the Additional Protocol requires states to produce a more expanded declaration regarding nuclear fuel cycle activity being carried out within its territory than that required by the INFCIRC/153 system. This expanded declaration is to include details on nuclear materials and the facilities involved in producing, processing, and utilizing them, as required under INFCIRC/153, but in addition must also include information on all nuclear fuel cycle-related research and development activities that do not themselves involve nuclear materials, but which may be used in the production of nuclear materials, including activities being carried out in privately owned facilities. This expansion of information required from the states significantly widens the Agency's understanding of the full range of nuclear-related activities being carried on within a state. This more complete

[53] U.S. Senate, Committee on Foreign Relations, *Nuclear Proliferation: Learning from the Iraq Experience*, Hearing before the Committee on Foreign Relations, 102 Cong., 1st Sess., October 17, 1991, p. 20.

[54] Theodore Hirsch, 'The IAEA Additional Protocol: What it is and Why it Matters,' *The Nonproliferation Review* (Fall–Winter 2004).

[55] See ibid. at 143.

understanding allows the IAEA to better assess the purpose and direction of nuclear programs within NNWS.[56]

Second, the Additional Protocol provides for the IAEA to have 'complementary access' to that which it enjoys under the INFCIRC/153 system. INFCIRC/540 gives the IAEA the right of access 'on a selective basis in order to assure the absence of undeclared nuclear material' to 'any place' on the site of a declared facility, and not only to agreed strategic points, as under the INFCIRC/153 system. It further provides for IAEA access to all sites on which information has been provided by the state regarding research and development activities on nuclear fuel cycle-related technologies, in order 'to resolve a question relating to the correctness and completeness of the information provided.'[57]

Additionally, INFCIRC/540 provides for IAEA access to 'any location specified by the Agency' in order to carry out 'location-specific environmental monitoring.' This provision enables IAEA inspectors to nominate undeclared locations at which they would like to take soil, water, and air samples in order to detect the presence of fissile materials, and thus potentially produce evidence of undeclared nuclear activities.

The notice requirements for the carrying out of inspections under the Additional Protocol are significantly shortened from their length under the INFCIRC/153 system, and are typically set at 24 hours, down from the normal one-week notice period under INFCIRC/153. The Additional Protocol further requires the state to grant multi-entry visas to inspectors. Under the INFCIRC/153 system, this was not a requirement, and the necessity in many states of inspectors obtaining entry visas, often a month-long process, served to give the state even earlier warning of impending inspections.

These supplements to the information-gathering ability of the IAEA, as well as its ability to conduct inspections in a more efficient and effective manner, are significant improvements to the Agency's ability to verify not only the correctness, but also the completeness of state declarations. They allow for increased confidence in the determinations of the IAEA that no undeclared nuclear-related activity is being carried out in a safeguarded territory.

The INFCIRC/540 Additional Protocol is voluntary for NPT member states, in that conclusion of an INFCIRC/540 agreement is not considered a part of the fundamental NNWS safeguards obligation contained in Article III.4 of the NPT. NPT NNWS may, if they choose, maintain only the standard INFCIRC/153 agreement with the IAEA. However, since its adoption in 1997, INFCIRC/540 agreements have been signed and have come into force in eighty-six IAEA member states.

Thus, in summary, the proposals by the several NWS states noted above would change the guidelines of the NSG to make accession to an Additional

---

[56] See ibid. at 143–144.   [57] See ibid.

Protocol agreement with the IAEA—a voluntarily undertaken obligation granting the IAEA enhanced rights of information gathering and inspection—a condition of supply of nuclear fuel and other technologies for developing NNWS.

4. *Conditioning supply and recognition of Article IV rights on compliance with an IAEA Comprehensive Safeguards Agreement*

On the above-mentioned list of proposals and efforts by NWS during the target era aimed at circumscribing and conditioning the rights of NNWS and the obligation of supplier states under Article IV, the third entry is efforts by NWS to condition nuclear supply and recognition of rights to nuclear technologies upon compliance with an IAEA Comprehensive Safeguards Agreement. While these efforts and their underpinning justifications were not mentioned specifically in President Bush's February 2004 speech, other NWS officials have frequently alluded to them.

In order to understand these efforts by NWS, one must go through their underpinning logic methodically. This logical progression includes a number of points of treaty interpretation. First in the chain of logical progression is the understanding, expressed by numerous NWS statements, that there is a normative link between Article IV of the NPT and Article III of the NPT. Specifically, this is an understanding that both the rights and the obligations contained in Article IV are conditional in their viability upon NNWS compliance, *inter alia*, with their obligations under Article III. As U.S. representative Andrew Semmel stated to the 2003 PrepCom:

[. . .] Article IV does not stand alone or in isolation. The inalienable right to develop nuclear energy is not an entitlement but rather flows from demonstrable and verifiable compliance with Articles I, II and III of the Treaty [. . .] All NPT parties in good standing need to reinforce the fundamental principle that Article IV benefits are extended only to NPT parties that are clearly in compliance with Articles I, II, and III.[58]

Similarly, U.K. representative John Duncan explained to the 2007 PrepCom that:

Article IV provides for the enjoyment of the benefits of the peaceful uses of nuclear energy. But these inalienable rights come hand in hand with obligations. Obligations to comply fully with the provisions of Articles I, II and III of the Treaty.[59]

French Representative Jean-François Dobelle stated to the 2008 PrepCom that:

---

[58] Statement by Dr Andrew K. Semmel, Alternative Representative of the United States of America, to the Second Session of the Preparatory Committee for the 2005 NPT Review Conference. Peaceful Nuclear Cooperation: NPT Article IV, Geneva, Switzerland, May 7, 2003.

[59] Statement by Ambassador John Duncan, Head of the UK Delegation to the First Preparatory Committee for the Eighth Review Conference of the Nuclear Non-Proliferation Treaty, April 30, 2007.

No state failing to meet its obligations with regard to non-proliferation and the application of IAEA safeguards, or whose nuclear activities are not directed towards identifiable peaceful ends, can claim the benefit of the stipulations contained in Article IV.[60]

In their combined statement to the 2008 PrepCom, the five NWS stated:

We affirm the inalienable right of all States Party to the NPT under Article IV to develop research, production and use of nuclear energy for peaceful purposes without discrimination and in accordance with the relevant provisions of the Treaty and the relevant principles on safeguards.[61]

The conditional normative link between Article IV and Article III is the first step, and is a particular point of treaty interpretation, which I will examine in detail in the next chapter. The second step in this logical progression is the understanding that noncompliance with an IAEA safeguards agreement by a NPT NNWS *per se* constitutes a violation of Article III of the NPT. During the target era, this second understanding was at times stated explicitly by NWS representatives. More often, however, the understanding was expressed by a rhetorical blurring of terms and concepts, which in effect equated, or conflated, safeguards agreement noncompliance with a violation of NPT Article III.

As was frequently the case, one of the most explicit statements of interpretation was given by U.S. representative Christopher Ford, in this case to the 2007 PrepCom:

Article III of the Treaty requires non-nuclear weapon States Party to reach and comply with safeguards agreements with the IAEA.[62]

A similarly explicit statement of this understanding was given in the joint statement of the NWS to the 2008 PrepCom:

We seek universal adherence to IAEA comprehensive safeguards, as provided for in Article III, and to the Additional Protocol and urge the ratification and implementation of these agreements.[63]

---

[60] Statement by H.E. Ambassador Jean-François Dobelle, Permanent Representative of France to the Conference on Disarmament, Head of the French Delegation, to the Second Session of the Preparatory Committee for the 2010 NPT Review Conference, April 28, 2008.

[61] Statement on behalf of China, France, the Russian Federation, the United Kingdom of Great Britain and Northern Ireland, and the United States of America, to the 2008 Non-Proliferation Treaty Preparatory Committee, delivered by Ambassador John Duncan, UK Ambassador for Multilateral Arms Control and Disarmament. May 9, 2008.

[62] 'A Work Plan for the 2010 Review Cycle: Coping with Challenges Facing the Nuclear Non-proliferation Treaty,' by Dr Christopher A. Ford, United States Special Representative for Nuclear Non-proliferation, Opening Remarks to the 2007 Preparatory Meeting of the Treaty on the Non-Proliferation of Nuclear Weapons, April 30, 2007.

[63] Statement on behalf of China, France, the Russian Federation, the United Kingdom of Great Britain and Northern Ireland, and the United States of America, to the 2008 Non-Proliferation Treaty Preparatory Committee, delivered by Ambassador John Duncan, UK Ambassador for Multilateral Arms Control and Disarmament, May 9, 2008.

A prime example of blurring or conflating safeguards agreement noncompliance with NPT breach can be seen in U.S. representative John Bolton's remarks to the 2004 PrepCom:

Despite Iran's massive deception and denial campaign, the IAEA has uncovered a large amount of information indicating numerous major violations of Iran's treaty obligations under its NPT Safeguards Agreement [. . .] If Iran continues in its unwillingness to comply with the NPT, the Council can then take up this issue as a threat to international peace and security.[64]

The final step of the logical progression is to complete the transitive sequence thus:

1. Noncompliance with an IAEA safeguards agreement constitutes a breach of NPT Article III,
2. A breach of NPT Article III results in the invalidity of the rights and obligations in Article IV,
3. Thus, noncompliance with an IAEA safeguards agreement results in the invalidity of the rights and obligations in Article IV.

This conditional linkage between NPT Articles III and IV, and the transitive conclusion that noncompliance with a safeguards agreement constitutes breach of the NPT, has been used most frequently by NWS officials with regard to Iran, as seen in John Bolton's statement above. It was used extensively by NWS officials during the target era to justify the non-recognition of Iran's right to peaceful nuclear technologies under NPT Article IV(1), as well as to justify a cessation of nuclear assistance to Iran by supplier states, pursuant to the obligation in Article IV(2).[65]

B. Legal interpretations

The negative and limited view of the peaceful use principles of the NPT, which was manifest in the statements of NWS representatives during the target decade, and which gave rise to the above-described proposals and measures for limiting access to peaceful nuclear technologies, has been justified by NWS officials by reference to legal interpretations of the provisions of the NPT and of the relative priority in the treaty to be assigned to its three principled pillars.

   While statements of legal interpretation by state representatives to NPT meetings are relatively rare—the focus of these statements tends to be more

---

[64] Statement by United States Under Secretary of State for Arms Control and International Security John R. Bolton, to the Third Session of the Preparatory Committee for the 2005 Review Conference of the Treaty on the Non-proliferation of Nuclear Weapons. 'The NPT: A Crisis of Non-Compliance,' New York, April 27, 2004.

[65] See, e.g., Statement of Andrew Semmel, Alternative Representative of the United States of America, to the Second Session of the Preparatory Committee for the 2005 NPT Review Conference: Peaceful Nuclear Cooperation, Article IV (2003).

policy-oriented than legal—there were a few exceptional statements during the target era which provide insight into the legal interpretations underpinning the policy positions of NWS states toward NPT Article IV. The clearest of these come from U.S. representatives John Bolton and Andrew Semmel.

In his statement on behalf of the United States to the 2004 PrepCom, Bolton said:

In order to address loopholes and the crisis of noncompliance with the NPT, President Bush announced four proposals that would strengthen the Treaty and the governance structures of the International Atomic Energy Agency [...]. The first proposal would close the loophole in the Treaty that allows states like Iran and North Korea to pursue fissile material for nuclear weapons under peaceful cover. Enrichment and reprocessing plants would be limited to those states that now possess them. Members of the Nuclear Suppliers Group would refuse to sell enrichment and reprocessing equipment and technologies to any state that does not already possess full-scale, functioning enrichment and reprocessing plants. Nuclear fuel supplier states would ensure a reliable supply of nuclear fuel at reasonable prices to all NPT parties in full compliance with the NPT that agreed to forego such facilities. In this way, nations could use peaceful nuclear power as anticipated by the Treaty, but not to produce fissile material for nuclear weapons. *The Treaty provides no right to such sensitive fuel cycle technologies.*[66]

Later in the same statement, Bolton directly addresses the relationship between NPT Articles II and IV:

The central bargain of the NPT is that if non-nuclear weapons states renounce the pursuit of nuclear weapons, they may gain assistance in developing civilian nuclear power. This bargain is clearly set forth in Article IV of the Treaty, which states that the Treaty's 'right' to develop peaceful nuclear energy is clearly conditioned upon parties complying with Articles I & II. If a state party seeks to acquire nuclear weapons and thus fails to conform with Article II, then under the Treaty that party forfeits its right to develop peaceful nuclear energy.[67]

A year earlier, U.S. representative Andrew Semmel had similarly included legal interpretive commentary in his remarks to the 2003 PrepCom, expanding Article IV conditionality to include Article III as well as Articles I and II:

Article IV of the NPT provides for the 'inalienable right' of all Parties to develop nuclear energy for peaceful purposes. This right is grounded firmly by the Treaty in the clear understanding that such development must be in conformity with the non-proliferation undertakings of Articles I and II. Thus, Article IV does not stand alone or in isolation. The inalienable right to develop nuclear energy is not an entitlement but rather flows from demonstrable and verifiable compliance with Articles I, II and III of the Treaty [...] All NPT parties in good standing need to reinforce the fundamental principle that

---

[66] Statement by United States Under Secretary of State for Arms Control and International Security John R. Bolton, to the Third Session of the Preparatory Committee for the 2005 Review Conference of the Treaty on the Non-proliferation of Nuclear Weapons. 'The NPT: A Crisis of Non-Compliance,' New York, April 27, 2004. Emphasis added.

[67] Ibid.

Article IV benefits are extended only to NPT parties that are clearly in compliance with Articles I, II, and III. Supplier states must forego assistance to states with suspect nuclear programs until the suspicions are resolved. The mere claim of peaceful intent is not sufficient. We all know that IAEA safeguards can never be an absolute guarantee, but states—especially those with ambitious nuclear programs—must back up their claims of peaceful intent and 'transparency' by fully implementing the IAEA's Strengthened Safeguards Additional Protocol.[68]

In addition to stressing the questionable nature of the inalienable right to peaceful nuclear energy codified in NPT Article IV as a true juridically cognizable right (i.e. by stating that it is not an independent entitlement), Semmel in this statement stresses, as would Bolton a year later, the conditional nature of this right. He argues that the inalienable right only 'flows from *demonstrable and verifiable compliance* with Articles I, II and III of the Treaty,' and that 'Article IV benefits are extended only to NPT parties that are *clearly in compliance* with Articles I, II and III.'[69] He adds that states with 'suspect nuclear programs' should be denied Article IV 'benefits' (again note, not 'rights') until these 'suspicions are resolved.'[70] Thus, Semmel clearly sees the inalienable right to peaceful nuclear energy in Article IV to not only be a conditional right, but his interpretation of that conditionality also sets quite a high bar for the fulfilling of the condition precedent of compliance with Articles I, II, and III. Indeed, according to Semmel, an NNWS nuclear program need only be 'suspect' for that state to be bereft of any entitlement to enjoy the benefits of developing nuclear energy capacity for peaceful purposes under Article IV. Such a state, he argues, should have its supplies of nuclear fuel and other technologies from supplier states cut off until these suspicions are resolved. He goes on to place the burden for clearing up these suspicions squarely upon the shoulders of the NNWS party under suspicion, noting that they 'must back up their claims of peaceful intent and "transparency,"' at least by implementation of the IAEA Additional Protocol.

Thus, Semmel clearly sees the burden of proof for meeting the conditionality test for enjoyment of the Article IV right to peaceful nuclear energy as being borne by the NNWS states who would claim that right. This could be expressed, juridically, as a rebuttable legal presumption against the Article IV right for NNWS, subject to each NNWS overcoming that presumption by bearing the burden of proof that their nuclear program meets the conditionality test of full and verifiable compliance with Articles I, II, and III of the treaty.

[68] Statement by Dr Andrew K. Semmel, Alternative Representative of the United States of America, to the Second Session of the Preparatory Committee for the 2005 NPT Review Conference. Peaceful Nuclear Cooperation: NPT Article IV, Geneva, Switzerland, May 7, 2003.

[69] Ibid. Emphasis added.

[70] In support of this position, see the Statement by H.E. Mr François Rivasseau to the 2005 Review Conference of the Parties to the Treaty on the Non-proliferation of Nuclear Weapons, General Debate, May 5, 2005 ('My country will ensure that the right to "nuclear energy for peaceful purposes" recognized in Article IV of the NPT be preserved and fully exercised for countries that unambiguously comply with their international obligations.')

C. Disarmament

Issues of nuclear disarmament and the obligations of Article VI of the NPT have their own rather enigmatic place in the statements of both NWS and NNWS officials during the target era. I use the word enigmatic in part because in this area particularly it seems that NWS and NNWS officials routinely talk past each other as opposed to talking to or with each other. NWS and NNWS officials during this era clearly had fundamentally different understandings of the correct interpretation of the Article VI obligation, and of the policies and actions required of states to bring themselves into compliance with this obligation. Furthermore, the word enigmatic in describing this area also seems appropriate because most of the statements by NWS officials of NPT Article VI during the target era appear intentionally obfuscatory in nature.

Statements by NWS officials to NPT meetings during the target era on the subject of Article VI share essential commonality of structure and substance. Indeed, they read as though a common template was shared by the speech writers of several of the NWS. This template first includes a statement that the state concerned is fully committed to their obligations under Article VI. Then, with more or less detail, depending on the particular state, they lay out their accomplishments in reducing the number of warheads on operational readiness within their arsenals.[71] Such reductions, they insist, are proof positive of their progressive compliance with their Article VI obligation.

The problem with this rhetorical template, essentially shared by the NWS during the target era, is that it is obfuscatory of the issue of the interpretation of Article VI. These statements are obfuscatory in that they give lip service to the obligation of Article VI, but they tend to be quite indeterminate as to what they understand that obligation to be. They are merely vague and absolute statements of support and compliance, generally without discussion of the detailed scope and meaning of the obligation, and how their conduct is in compliance with such a detailed view of the obligation. It must be noted incidentally that this is in stark contrast with the detailed and lengthy discussions in the same statements of the precise contours of NNWS obligations with regard to non-proliferation and peaceful use, and exact accountings and implications of NNWS policy shortcomings.

On the few occasions in which NWS officials spoke in more detailed terms about the content of the Article VI obligation, their comments, and particularly those of U.S. representatives, revealed an interpretation which holds that the Article VI obligation is one of very limited scope—in some cases approaching

---

[71] See, e.g., Statement on behalf of China, France, the Russian Federation, the United Kingdom of Great Britain and Northern Ireland, and the United States of America, to the 2008 Non-Proliferation Treaty Preparatory Committee, delivered by Ambassador John Duncan, UK Ambassador for Multilateral Arms Control and Disarmament, May 9, 2008.

non-existence. Furthermore, these statements explicitly marginalize the disarmament pillar of the NPT in prioritization and importance as compared to the non-proliferation pillar of the NPT. These intentionally vague statements, which hide an exceptionally limited understanding of the legal scope of the Article VI obligation, in full knowledge of the exceptional character of that interpretive understanding within the international community, obfuscate or obscure the points of interpretive difference between NWS and NNWS, and make meaningful exchange and debate impossible.

U.S. representative Andrew Semmel's statement to the 2003 PrepCom typifies the frequently conveyed U.S. desire to excuse more rigorous and meaningful discussion of NWS obligations under Article VI, by reference to more important and pressing problems of non-proliferation. His statement is also typical of U.S. statements both in identifying nuclear disarmament as a *goal* of the NPT and not as an *obligation*, as well as in stressing the conditional link between non-proliferation and disarmament—i.e. that disarmament goals will not be attainable without prior improvements in the NWS non-proliferation agenda:

Let me speak briefly to the question of balance in our deliberations. We understand and expect there will be considerable discussion on Article VI issues during our Preparatory Committee sessions. Indeed, much has already been said at this meeting. Nuclear disarmament is a goal of the Treaty and we should have constructive exchanges about it. However, the great majority of responsible NPT parties who value and abide by the Treaty need to recognize also the large issues at stake in actual and potential cases of noncompliance with Article II. There is a simple logic: more states with nuclear weapons means a more dangerous world. It also means that the overall NPT goal of the elimination of nuclear weapons would become even more difficult to achieve.[72]

U.S. representative John Bolton's statement to the 2004 PrepCom similarly marginalizes NPT Article VI. In one of only six sentences in his entire statement discussing Article VI issues—in which the word 'disarmament' is never used—Bolton clearly puts Article VI issues in their place when he says:

Enforcement is critical. We must increase the costs and reduce the benefits to violators, in ways such as the proliferation Security Initiative now being pursued actively around the world, and which President Bush has proposed strengthening further [. . .] We cannot hope the problem will go away. We cannot leave it to 'the other guy' to carry the full measure of the challenge of demanding full compliance. We cannot divert attention from the violations we face by focusing on Article VI issues that do not exist. If a party cares about the NPT, then there is a corresponding requirement to care about violations and enforcement.[73]

---

[72] Statement by Dr Andrew K. Semmel, Alternative Representative of the United States of America, to the Second Session of the Preparatory Committee for the 2005 NPT Review Conference. Peaceful Nuclear Cooperation: NPT Article IV, Geneva, Switzerland, May 7, 2003.

[73] Statement by United States Under Secretary of State for Arms Control and International Security John R. Bolton, to the Third Session of the Preparatory Committee for the 2005 Review Conference of the Treaty on the Non-proliferation of Nuclear Weapons. 'The NPT: A Crisis of Non-Compliance,' New York, April 27, 2004.

However, by far the most extreme position on Article VI interpretation during the target era was taken by U.S. representative Christopher Ford. Ford's statements to the NPT PrepComs in both 2007 and 2008 were clearly carefully rhetorically constructed to convey an understanding of the limited—at times approaching nonexistent—nature of the Article VI obligation upon the U.S. As he stated to the 2008 PrepCom:

> States Party know that the United States remains firmly and unequivocally committed to the disarmament goals of the Preamble and Article VI of the NPT, and indeed that we have become a leading contributor to international discussions of how to move forward toward those ends [. . .] Thanks to these efforts and to those of some of the other NWS, Article VI discourse is now gradually arriving at the place where disarmament debate *should* have been all along. In short, astonishing progress has already been achieved and is continuing, most of the NWS are becoming increasingly accustomed to a constructive degree of voluntary transparency about nuclear matters, and there seems to be a growing interest in realistic and practical discussions about the possibility of nuclear disarmament.[74]

Ford is careful here to identify the nature of the disarmament principle in NPT Article VI as a goal, rather than as an obligation. The United States, he says, is committed—note not obligated—to this goal. The limited and attenuated normative character of the Article VI obligation is again expressed in a speech Ford gave in 2007 at a conference in France:

> [. . .] the NPT nonetheless clearly expresses in its Preamble the intention of all States Party to facilitate both nuclear and general disarmament, and in its Article VI their commitment to pursue negotiations in good faith relating to those goals [. . .] The United States remains committed to the goals of the NPT, and is in full conformity with its Article VI obligations.[75]

Interestingly, Ford does in this statement acknowledge that there is an obligatory aspect to Article VI. However, he also reiterates the position that the disarmament principles in Article VI are merely goals of the treaty. This then begs the question: if disarmament principles do not constitute the obligatory aspect of Article VI, what does? We find Ford more candidly stating his view on the legal interpretation of Article VI, and answering the question of his understanding of the scope and meaning of the legal obligation in Article VI, in his non-official writings published while he served as United States Special Representative for Nuclear Non-proliferation.

In a 2007 article published in the *Non-proliferation Review*, Ford argues that the only legal obligation contained in NPT Article VI is an obligation on all

---

[74] 'A Recipe for Success at the 2010 Review Conference,' Dr Christopher A. Ford, United States Special Representative for Nuclear Non-proliferation, Opening Remarks to the 2008 NPT Preparatory Committee, Palais des Nations, Geneva, Switzerland, April 28, 2008.
[75] 'Disarmament, the United States and the NPT,' Address by Dr Christopher Ford, United States Special Representative for Nuclear Non-proliferation, delivered at the Conference on 'Preparing for 2010: Getting the Process Right,' Annecy, France, March 17, 2007.

states to pursue negotiations in good faith.[76] He argues that the International Court of Justice was incorrect in its 1996 Advisory Opinion conclusion that the Article VI obligation 'is an obligation to achieve a precise result—nuclear disarmament in all its aspects—by adopting a particular course of conduct, namely, the pursuit of negotiations on the matter in good faith.'[77] Furthermore, not only was the ICJ incorrect that the Article VI obligation is an obligation to achieve disarmament results through good faith negotiation, Ford argues that the Article VI obligation is not even an obligation of negotiation in good faith. Rather, it is merely an obligation to pursue negotiations in good faith. As he explains:

[. . .] the language about negotiations needing to be 'pursue[d] [. . .] in good faith' clearly leaves open the possibility that such negotiations might not take place, let alone succeed. It would hardly have been difficult for the drafters (as a matter of grammar and syntax, at least) to require the engagement in or conclusion of negotiations. But to specify instead merely the pursuit of negotiation in good faith acknowledges the reality that a party may honestly try, but fail—perhaps through no fault of its own, such as in the event of a failure of good faith by other parties—to bring about a meaningful negotiation or agreement [. . .]

It is clear [...] that the only sensible reading of Article VI in compliance analysis must dismiss the ICJ's ill-considered dictum about 'concluding' negotiations and retain as its touchstone only the element of good faith effort in pursuit of disarmament negotiations. If there is good faith effort toward negotiations, then there is compliance; if there is not, then there is noncompliance.[78]

He thus concludes:

The negotiating history makes quite clear that the plain language of Article VI is no accident and that its meaning is precise: all states party are required to pursue good faith negotiations toward the article's stated goals, but they are not legally required—and could not reasonably *be* legally required—to conclude such negotiations. Arguments that Article VI should require concrete disarmament steps of the nuclear weapon states, and efforts to enumerate specific mandatory steps, were rejected.[79]

Ford's argument is thus that the only legal obligation in NPT Article VI relating to disarmament is an extremely limited obligation to put forth 'good faith effort toward negotiations' on disarmament. This interpretive understanding is clearly expressed in his and other U.S. official statements to NPT meetings throughout the target era.

---

[76] Christopher A. Ford, 'Debating Disarmament: Interpreting Article VI of the Treaty on the Non-Proliferation of Nuclear Weapons,' 14(3) *Non-proliferation Review* (November 2007).

[77] *Advisory Opinion on the Threat or Use of Nuclear Weapons*, ICJ Reports, 1996, p. 26, para. 99. For explication of the ICJ Advisory Opinion, see Daniel H. Joyner, *International Law and the Proliferation of Weapons of Mass Destruction* (2009) ch 5.

[78] Christopher A. Ford, 'Debating Disarmament: Interpreting Article VI of the Treaty on the Non-Proliferation of Nuclear Weapons,' 14(3) *Non-proliferation Review* (November 2007) 403, 411.

[79] Ibid. at 408.

Based on this understanding of the limited scope of the Article VI obligation, the United States and the other NWS throughout the target decade offered, as the primary, and often exclusive, evidence of their progressive compliance with Article VI, their unilateral and at times bilateral arms reduction efforts.

The interpretive obfuscation by NWS during this decade was not lost on NNWS, whose statements frequently contain criticism of the NWS for their lack of meaningful progress in complying with what NNWS almost uniformly saw as a much more substantive disarmament obligation in NPT Article VI. Representing the 118 member states of the Non-Aligned Movement, Indonesia's statement to the 2008 PrepCom lamented:

It is most unfortunate that the NWS and those remaining outside the NPT continue to develop and modernize their nuclear arsenals, imperiling regional and international peace and security, in particular in the Middle East. The recent developments, in this regard, illustrate a trend of vertical proliferation and non-compliance by NWS towards their commitments under Article VI of the NPT.[80]

As Egypt explained in its statement to the 2008 PrepCom:

Egypt welcomes reductions made by the Nuclear Weapon States in their nuclear arsenals [. . .] We reiterate however that such reductions do not as yet meet the expectations of the vast majority of States Parties. This is especially the case in light of qualitative developments undertaken in nuclear arsenals, which reaffirm that Nuclear Weapon States continue to rely on nuclear deterrence as a salient feature in their strategic security policies. This situation casts serious doubts on commitments to nuclear disarmament and the implementation of Article VI and thus disrupts the delicate balance upon which the Treaty is based.[81]

Specifically with regard to the development by NWS of new generations of nuclear weapons, the statement by New Zealand to the 2008 PrepCom on behalf of the New Agenda Coalition (Brazil, Egypt, Ireland, Mexico, New Zealand, South Africa, and Sweden) noted:

The New Agenda Coalition welcomes indications from some nuclear-weapon States that further cuts in nuclear arsenals are being advanced. However, the Coalition remains seriously concerned that intentions to modernize other nuclear forces seem to persist. The Coalition reiterates that States should not develop new nuclear weapons or nuclear weapons with new military capabilities or for new missions, nor replace nor modernize their nuclear weapon systems, as any such action would contradict the spirit of the disarmament and non-proliferation obligations of the treaty.[82]

---

[80] Statement by H.E. Gusti Agung Wesaka Puja, Ambassador of the Republic of Indonesia, on Behalf of the Group of Non-Aligned States Parties to the Treaty on the Non-proliferation of Nuclear Weapons, at the General Debate of the Second Session of the Preparatory Committee for the 2010 Review Conference of the States Parties to the Treaty on the Non-proliferation of Nuclear Weapons, April 28, 2008.

[81] General Statement of Egypt to the Second Preparatory Committee of the 2010 NPT Review Conference, April 28, 2008.

[82] Statement by H.E. Don Mackay, Permanent Representative of New Zealand to the United Nations in Geneva, on Behalf of the New Agenda Coalition, to the Preparatory Committee for the

The interpretation of Article VI which is reflected in these statements is one which understands the legal obligation in Article VI to be a substantive disarmament obligation. Not just an obligation to pursue negotiations toward disarmament, but an obligation to achieve, at least in progressive fashion, the result of full nuclear disarmament. This interpretation views the obligation of good faith effort in Article VI as applying not just to negotiations on disarmament, but also to state policies and state actions in the progressive direction of actual nuclear disarmament. It should be noted that this interpretation is essentially consistent with the interpretation of Article VI given by the International Court of Justice in its 1996 Advisory Opinion, quoted in part above.[83]

2010 Review Conference of the Parties to the Treaty on the Non-proliferation of Nuclear Weapons, General Debate, April 28, 2008.

[83] *Advisory Opinion on the Threat or Use of Nuclear Weapons*, ICJ Reports, 1996.

4

Legal Analysis of NWS Interpretations of the NPT

Having reviewed NWS nuclear policies and legal interpretations of the NPT during the target decade of this study, I will proceed in this chapter to provide a legal analysis of these interpretations and the policies which have been justified by reference thereto. I will undertake this analysis by reference to the guiding principles of interpretation of the NPT, produced through the consideration in Chapter 2 above of the VCLT rules of treaty interpretation, and in particular the concepts of context and object and purpose. Those principles, again, are:

1. The NPT is substantively and structurally comprised of three primary principled pillars—i.e. civilian use of nuclear energy, non-proliferation of nuclear weapons, and disarmament of nuclear weapons.

2. These three pillars correspond to the *quid pro quo* negotiating demands of the two sets of state parties represented in the macro level contract treaty structure of the NPT.

3. The three principled pillars of the NPT represent the dual-use character of nuclear energy applications. The NPT is fundamentally addressed to regulating nuclear energy in its full dual-use nature and range of applications, and is not exclusively or even primarily addressed to regulating only nuclear weapons.

4. These three principled pillars *together* comprise the object and purpose of the NPT. They are inherently linked and interdependent upon each other in their meaning, and must be viewed in a balanced manner. When conducting that balancing, the three pillars should be understood as presumptively juridically equal, i.e. none of the pillars should be presumed to be of higher prioritization in legal interpretation of the NPT's provisions than any other.

My argument in this chapter is that many of the interpretations of the NPT by NWS during the target decade were legally incorrect by reference to these guiding principles of interpretation. *Essentially, these are cases of NWS officials failing to interpret the provisions of the NPT in their context and in the light of the treaty's object and purpose.* These misinterpretations have in turn formed the legal basis for policies and actions which have prejudiced the legitimate legal interests of NNWS pursuant to the NPT's grand bargain.

I will again divide my analysis into three sections, corresponding to the three principled pillars of the NPT.

I. Non-Proliferation

As reviewed in Chapter 3, NWS officials during the target era justified their disproportionate prioritization of the non-proliferation pillar of the NPT over the peaceful use and disarmament pillars of the NPT, *inter alia* by reference to the legal interpretation that the non-proliferation pillar of the NPT is the principal, primary, central, or core principled pillar of the treaty, and that the other two pillars are of secondary or lesser legal status and weight. This was in stark contrast to the statements of many NNWS parties to the NPT, and particularly developing countries, who tended to stress the need for balance and equal prioritization among the three pillars.

As concluded in Chapter 2, an analysis of the context of the NPT's provisions and the object and purpose of the NPT, as confirmed by the treaty's *travaux préparatoires*, reveals that the three principled pillars of the NPT should be understood to be presumptively juridically equal, i.e. that none of the pillars should be presumed to be of higher prioritization in legal interpretation of the NPT's provisions than any other. Thus, in arriving at the legal interpretation that the non-proliferation provisions of the NPT are the core provisions of the treaty while its peaceful use and disarmament provisions are subsidiary in interpretive status, NWS officials during the target decade simply took Articles I, II, and III of the NPT out of their proper context within the NPT, and disregarded the treaty's comprehensive object and purpose.

NWS officials during this decade did not frequently support their legal interpretations with analytical discussion. However, on the rare occasions that they, or sympathetic non-official commentators, did, they seemed to frequently ground their understandings upon cherry-picked statements taken from the NPT's *travaux préparatoires* in support of their legal interpretations. These selected statements tended to have been made by U.S. and Soviet representatives to the treaty negotiations.[1] A prime official example of this cherry picking specifically in the

---

[1] For non-official instances of the use of this incorrect interpretive technique in the context of various NPT provisions, see Jozef Goldblat, *The New Guide to Negotiations and Agreements* (2nd edn, 2002) p. 102 (interpreting the term 'manufacture' in NPT Article II solely by reference to one *travaux* statement from a U.S. representative); Andreas Persbo, 'The Case for a Stronger Safeguards Regime,' in *Perspectives for Progress: Options for the 2010 NPT Review Conference and Beyond* (Pugwash, May 2010) p. 60 (repeating Goldblat's analysis); Robert Zarate, 'The NPT, IAEA Safeguards and Peaceful Nuclear Energy: An "Inalienable Right," but Precisely to What?' in Henry Sokolski, ed., *Falling Behind: International Scrutiny of the Peaceful Atom* (SSI, 2008) p. 243 (primarily using statements from the *travaux* to interpret NPT Article IV).

context of arguing for the interpretive primacy of non-proliferation provisions can be found in U.S. representative Christopher Ford's statement to the 2008 PrepCom. Ford states at the beginning of his remarks that:

[t]he world today is vastly safer and more secure than the one in which the NPT was opened for signature, and part of the reason for this has been the success of States Party in ensuring compliance with the non-proliferation obligations that during the NPT's negotiation were referred to as 'the core of the Treaty.'[2]

Following the quoted text, Ford inserts a footnote citation, which identifies the quote as having come from a statement of a Canadian representative to the Eighteen-Nation Committee on Disarmament in 1968. Here, then, Ford is making a legal interpretation of the NPT in an official statement, and basing that interpretation solely on one source taken from the *travaux* of the treaty.

As explained in the review of VCLT treaty interpretation rules in Chapter 2 above, this is not the correct method for interpreting a treaty. The VCLT in Article 31 places clear interpretive primacy upon the plain meaning of the text of a treaty provision, taken in its context and in the light of the treaty's overall object and purpose. According to Article 32 of the VCLT, the interpreter is only to have recourse to the *travaux* in an operational sense—as source material upon which to base an interpretive finding—when confirming meaning already established through the Article 31 process, or when determining meaning after the Article 31 process has left the meaning obscure or ambiguous or has led to an absurd or unreasonable result. However, in these latter contexts in which *travaux* material is used to confirm or determine meaning, the interpreter should take care not to rely disproportionately upon single statements of persons involved in the negotiating process. Only *travaux* material which establishes the *common understanding of the negotiating parties* is to be afforded probative value in interpretation.[3]

Thus, in operationally relying upon a cherry-picked single statement of an individual official from the *travaux*, and basing his analysis exclusively upon this supplementary material instead of upon the process mandated by the general rule in VCLT Article 31, Ford commits a double interpretive sin. Here, while it is accurate as a generalization to say that the non-proliferation provisions of the NPT were perceived to be the 'core of the treaty' by the U.S., the U.S.S.R., and certain other developed states, as explained in Chapter 2 the *travaux préparatoires* of the NPT, *when taken in their entirety* show that NNWS generally did not share this perception, and had their own set of equally 'core' issues which they demanded be included in the treaty.

---

[2] 'A Recipe for Success at the 2010 Review Conference,' Dr Christopher A. Ford, United States Special Representative for Nuclear Non-proliferation, Opening Remarks to the 2008 NPT Preparatory Committee, Palais des Nations, Geneva, Switzerland, April 28, 2008.
[3] See Sir Humphrey Waldock, *Third Report on the Law of Treaties*, Yearbook of the ILC, 1964, Vol. II, p. 58, paras 20–21.

As has often been observed with regard to the record of preparatory negotiations and statements of lawmakers made in the sometimes years long process of drafting law, whether it be in the context of an international treaty or a piece of domestic legislation, most any interpretive position on the resulting law can be maintained by reference to some portion of this preparatory record.[4] One can therefore see the wisdom of the VCLT's drafters in placing primacy in treaty interpretation upon textual analysis, and in relegating *travaux* materials to a secondary interpretive role.

In summary, then, by reference to the guiding principles of interpretation of the NPT, produced through the consideration in Chapter 2 above of the VCLT rules of treaty interpretation, and in particular the concepts of context and object and purpose, it is legally incorrect to conclude that the non-proliferation pillar of the NPT, and the textual provisions which comprise it, are of higher importance or normative weight in interpretation than are the provisions comprising the peaceful use and disarmament pillars of the NPT. Interpretations by NWS officials during the target era, which concluded that the non-proliferation provisions of the NPT are the principal, primary, central, or core provisions of the treaty, were thus incorrect, as many NNWS representatives were at pains to point out in their statements.

II. Peaceful Use

As reviewed in Chapter 3, when NWS officials made reference during the target era to the development and use of peaceful nuclear technologies by NNWS, they customarily emphasized the dangers inherent in NNWS pursuit of civilian uses of nuclear energy, and in particular their pursuit of indigenous capabilities for production of fissile materials. These statements by NWS representatives frequently included a very narrow and limited view of the rights recognized and obligations created in NPT Article IV. Under this limited view, the rights and obligations of Article IV are clearly and tightly circumscribed by the non-proliferation obligations of Articles I, II, and III. These statements make clear the view that the Article IV rights and obligations are secondary in priority to the non-proliferation obligations of Articles I, II, and III, and are only operative on condition of prior full and demonstrated compliance with these normatively superior non-proliferation obligations.

In their legal interpretive arguments, U.S. representatives John Bolton and Andrew Semmel stressed the conditionality of the Article IV right. Bolton argued that the NPT provides no right to indigenous possession of the elements of the nuclear fuel cycle. And Semmel went so far as to hold that the Article IV

---

[4] See, e.g., Leonard Levy, *Original Intent and the Framers' Constitution* (1988).

inalienable right is not an independent entitlement at all, but rather operates more as a privilege, enigmatically flowing to NNWS from their compliance with Articles I, II, and III.[5]

This negative and limited view of the peaceful use pillar of the NPT, as justified by reference to these legal interpretations of Article IV, is reflected in a number of proposals and high level efforts by NWS during the target decade aimed at circumscribing and conditioning the right of NNWS to nuclear fuel cycle technologies, and at changing the conditions under which supplies of nuclear technologies are made to NNWS by NWS and other supplier states. These proposals and efforts include:

1. Requiring NNWS to exclusively source nuclear material from a multilateral fuel bank as a condition of supply;
2. Requiring NNWS accession to the IAEA Additional Protocol as a condition of supply; and
3. Conditioning supply and recognition of rights to nuclear technologies on compliance with an IAEA Comprehensive Safeguards Agreement.

A. Interpretation of Article IV(1)

As a matter of treaty interpretation, it is important to reiterate the following guiding interpretive principles, taken from the analysis in Chapter 2 above of the context of NPT provisions and the object and purpose of the NPT itself, at the beginning of an interpretive analysis of NPT Article IV(1). First is that the three principled pillars of the NPT represent the dual-use character of nuclear energy applications. The NPT is fundamentally addressed to regulating nuclear energy in its full dual-use nature and range of applications, and is not exclusively or even primarily addressed to regulating only nuclear weapons.

Second is that these three principled pillars *together* comprise the object and purpose of the NPT. They are inherently linked and interdependent upon each other in their meaning, and must be viewed in a balanced manner. When conducting that balancing, the three pillars should be understood as presumptively juridically equal, i.e. none of the pillars should be presumed to be of higher prioritization in legal interpretation of the NPT's provisions than any other.

As explained in Chapter 2, this second principle of the object and purpose analysis of the NPT—i.e. that all three of the principled pillars comprising the object and purpose of the NPT should be considered to be presumptively equal

---

[5] Statement by United States Under Secretary of State for Arms Control and International Security John R. Bolton, to the Third Session of the Preparatory Committee for the 2005 Review Conference of the Treaty on the Non-proliferation of Nuclear Weapons. 'The NPT: A Crisis of Non-Compliance,' New York, April 27, 2004; Statement by Dr Andrew K. Semmel, Alternative Representative of the United States of America, to the Second Session of the Preparatory Committee for the 2005 NPT Review Conference. Peaceful Nuclear Cooperation: NPT Article IV, Geneva, Switzerland, May 7, 2003.

in legal weight—should be applied as a presumption, or baseline in interpretation of the NPT's provisions. As noted, there are, however, instances in the NPT's
provisions where there is evidence in the text of the specific intent of the parties
as to the relationship between treaty articles or principles, sometimes representing the relationship between principled pillars. One of the clearest examples of
this is to be found in Article IV(1).

When such evidence of the specific intent of the parties is found in the text,
this evidence will constitute an exception to this presumption or baseline, and
the terms of the particular provision will govern the relationship between the
articles or principles, inclusive of the relationship between principled pillars.
However, flowing from the fundamental nature of the interpretive principles of
context and object and purpose of the treaty, as stipulated in VCLT Article 31, is
the understanding that this textual specificity should itself still be understood in
light of the overall context of the provision and the object and purpose of the
treaty—which in the case of the NPT provides for the juridical equality of the
principled pillars as the presumption or baseline from which the specificity is a
limited textual carve-out.

With these guiding principles in mind, it is possible to follow the rules of
interpretation in VCLT Articles 31 and 32 to produce a correct interpretation of
NPT Article IV(1), which is the paragraph of Article IV most relevant to NWS
arguments regarding the nature of the NNWS right to peaceful nuclear energy
technologies. Article IV(1) provides:

Nothing in this Treaty shall be interpreted as affecting the inalienable right of all the
Parties to the Treaty to develop research, production and use of nuclear energy for peace-
ful purposes without discrimination and in conformity with articles I and II of this
Treaty.

The first term of interpretive interest is the term characterizing the right described
in this paragraph as an 'inalienable right.' The plain meaning of the term 'inalienable right' is a right which cannot be given, taken, or in any way transferred away
from its holder. This term is very rare in international law. It is used with some
frequency in international human rights treaties.[6] However, when referencing the
right of a state, and not of individuals, there appears to be only one context apart
from its appearance in the NPT in which the right of a state is termed to be an
'inalienable right.' This is in the context of U.N. General Assembly resolutions
discussing the principle of permanent sovereignty over natural resources.[7] Closely

---

[6] See the Universal Declaration of Human Rights (Preamble), the International Covenant on
Civil and Political Rights (Preamble), and the International Covenant on Economic, Social and
Cultural Rights (Preamble).

[7] See U.N. General Assembly Resolutions 3171 (1973) and 3281 (1974). Similar terms occur in
the context of General Assembly resolutions on the principle of self-determination, however,
self-determination in international law is not strictly speaking a right of states, but more precisely
the right of a people in a particular geographical place to constitute or create a state.

semantically related, however, is the term 'inherent right.' Outside of the international human rights law context, the term 'inherent right' appears to occur in only one instance of treaty law. This of course is Article 51 of the United Nations Charter, which provides that:

[n]othing in the present Charter shall impair the inherent right of individual or collective self-defence if an armed attack occurs against a Member of the United Nations, until the Security Council has taken measures necessary to maintain international peace and security.

As with the 'inherent right' characterization of self-defense in Article 51 of the U.N. charter, the 'inalienable right' characterization of the right to peaceful nuclear materials and technologies in NPT Article IV conveys a particular legal meaning. In both treaties, these unique descriptions appear to designate the right thus characterized as a right which is not created by the present conventional instrument, but rather as a pre-existing right with an existence independent of the treaty, and only recognized by its terms.[8] Both the right to self-defense and the right to peaceful nuclear materials and technology are thus identified as rights of states which exist independently of treaty law. This begs the question of the jurisprudential character of these state rights—or of any other rights of states for that matter.

The concept of rights which a state holds by virtue of its statehood is one which has never been satisfactorily constructed or explained in international law, and a comprehensive list of such rights has never been agreed upon. In 1949 the newly established International Law Commission adopted a draft Declaration on Rights and Duties of States. This draft Declaration consisted of 14 draft Articles which enunciated, in broad terms, some of the basic rights and duties of states. The 1949 draft Declaration was never adopted by the General Assembly, and largely fell by the wayside as geopolitical shifts over the subsequent decades made agreement on a statement of states' 'fundamental' rights diminishingly likely. In 1970 a successor statement to the 1949 draft Articles was adopted by the General Assembly, entitled the Declaration on Principles of International Law concerning Friendly Relations and Cooperation among States.[9] This 1970 Declaration predominantly discussed principles of states' obligations, such as the obligation not to use or threaten force against other states, or otherwise to intervene in the affairs of other states. However, in its discussion of the principle of the sovereign equality of states, it does delineate some of the most basic rights of states, including the right 'freely to choose and develop its political, social, economic and cultural systems.' Neither the 1949 draft Declaration, nor the 1970 Declaration can be described as systematically addressing the subject of states' rights, and certainly cannot be claimed to list such rights exhaustively.

---

[8] See Daniel H. Joyner, *International Law and the Proliferation of Weapons of Mass Destruction* (2009) ch 7.

[9] General Assembly Resolution 2625.

Thus, in the context of the inherent right of self-defense in the U.N. Charter, and the inalienable right to peaceful nuclear materials and technology in the NPT, we are left with a conventional designation of these rights as rights inuring to all states by virtue of their statehood, but with little explanation as to the jurisprudential meaning and effect of this designation.

Perhaps the most important inquiry for the purpose of treaty interpretation is the relationship between an 'inalienable' or 'inherent' state right recognized in a treaty provision, and the other conventional terms in that treaty provision or in other provisions within the same treaty, including conventionally agreed obligations on states parties which can be read to set limits or circumscriptions upon that state right.

One of the few principles of international law clearly relevant to a discussion of the scope and meaning of the rights, or scope of legally unimpeachable acts, of states is the *Lotus* principle, announced by the Permanent Court of International Justice in a case of the same name in 1927.[10] This principle provides that 'restrictions upon the independence of States cannot [...] be presumed' and that international law recognizes that states possess 'a wide measure of discretion which is only limited in certain cases by prohibitive rules.'[11] In essence, the *Lotus* principle provides that states are free to engage in any activity they wish unless that activity has been prohibited in a source of international law. Another way to phrase the *Lotus* principle is as a recognition that states have the original or inherent or inalienable right to engage in any activity which is not prohibited to them by a positive source of international law.

Taking the *Lotus* principle as an interpretive guide, as provided for in VCLT Article 31(3)(c), for purposes of treaty interpretation a right of states recognized in a treaty should be presumed to include within its permissive terms the fullest possible range of state actions. The legal permissibility of a state engaging in these actions should be contravened by prohibitive obligations within the same treaty provision or other provisions in the same treaty, *only to the extent that the prohibited activities are clearly delineated by the conventional obligation.* The interpretive presumption of scope and meaning should lie with permissibility of state actions related to the recognized right, and not with conventional prohibitions of state actions related to the recognized right, also present in the treaty.

This interpretive reading is in complete harmony with a reading of the term 'inalienable right' in NPT Article IV(1) in this provision's context within the NPT. Article IV(1) operates within the NPT as a recognition of the residual rights of all states party, and particularly NNWS parties, to develop, produce, and use peaceful nuclear energy materials and technologies. This recognition is important in the context of the agreed obligation of NNWS in Article II of the NPT not to manufacture, obtain, or possess nuclear weapons. The conventional prohibitive obligation in Article II regarding nuclear weapons constitutes a

---

[10] PCIJ, Ser. A, No. 10, 1927.   [11] Ibid. at pp. 18 and 19.

positive international legal limitation on states' rights to engage in any nuclear activity they wish, pursuant to the *Lotus* principle. *However, Article IV(1) serves in this context to clarify that states retain all rights to engage in nuclear activities which are not clearly delineated by the conventional prohibitive obligation in Article II and by those terms forbidden to them.*

This interpretation of the term 'inalienable right' in NPT Article IV(1), which is informed by the context of Article IV(1) within the NPT and by the *Lotus* principle as a relevant rule of international law, itself provides important interpretive context for the final words of Article IV(1), which stipulate that the inalienable right of states parties to develop research, production, and use of nuclear energy for peaceful purposes must be exercised 'in conformity with articles I and II of this Treaty.'

Before proceeding, it is necessary to note that the final document of the 2000 NPT Review Conference contains the following statement:

The Conference reaffirms that nothing in the Treaty shall be interpreted as affecting the inalienable right of all the parties to the Treaty to develop research, production and use of nuclear energy for peaceful purposes without discrimination and in conformity with articles I, II and III of the Treaty.

NPT Review Conference final documents, which are as a rule adopted by the unanimous consent of conference participants, fit well under VCLT Article 31(3) (a) as sources of 'subsequent agreement between the parties regarding the interpretation of the treaty or the application of its provisions.'[12] Thus, statements from Review Conferences should be taken into account in interpretation of treaty provisions, along with context. Here, then, the treaty text of Article IV(1) which reads 'in conformity with articles I and II of this Treaty' should be interpreted taking into account that the NPT's parties have agreed on an interpretation of these words which includes Article III as well as Articles I and II. Thus, Article IV(1) should generally be read and interpreted to include a reference to Article III along with its existing reference to Articles I and II.

In these closing words of Article IV(1), then, we have a reference to obligations created by the treaty with which the right recognized in Article IV(1) is to be exercised 'in conformity.' The treaty obligations in Articles I, II, and III can be described as prohibitive or at least limiting in character, in that they prohibit certain acts related to nuclear energy, or at least limit states' freedom of action in this area. Thus, we have the situation described above in which a state right recognized in a treaty provision is to be limited or circumscribed by conventional obligations contained within the same treaty.

In light of the context of these final words of Article IV(1) within Article IV(1) itself, and the article's recognition of an 'inalienable right' which term has been

---

[12] See Burrus Carnahan, 'Treaty Review Conferences,' 81 *American Journal of International Law* (1987) 226, 229.

interpreted above, the plain meaning of the words 'and in conformity with' would seem to be usefully rephrased as '*as limited by.*' Again, in light of the context of Article IV(1) within the NPT, and its role as discussed above in clarifying that states retain all rights to engage in nuclear activities which are not clearly delineated by the conventional prohibitive obligations of the treaty, interpreting 'in conformity with' as 'as limited by' makes contextual sense.

Thus, Article IV(1) provides that the right of all states to develop, produce, and use peaceful nuclear energy materials and technologies is limited by Articles I, II, and III of the NPT. This reading is consistent with the *Lotus* principle relative to the rights of states discussed above, in providing that *states party to the NPT may engage in any peaceful use of nuclear energy materials and technology, as limited only by the clearly delineated terms of the prohibitive/limiting conventional obligations contained in Articles I, II, and III.*

This interpretation appears fully consistent with the object and purpose of the treaty, which again is composed of all three of the NPT's principled pillars in juridical equality. This principle of the combined and interdependent nature of the three pillars as the object and purpose of the treaty is in perfect harmony with an interpretation of Article IV(1) which provides for a broadly interpreted residual recognition of the right of all states to peaceful uses of nuclear energy material and technologies, as limited and circumscribed through the specific intent of the parties expressed in the text, by clearly delineated non-proliferation obligations in Articles I, II, and III. The object and purpose of the NPT thus characterized, can be confirmed by reference to the *travaux préparatoires* of the treaty taken as a whole, as discussed in Chapter 2.

B. Application of the interpretation

Having arrived at an interpretation of Article IV(1) by the use of the holistic interpretive method prescribed by the VCLT, I can now proceed to contrast that interpretation to the interpretations cited above by NWS officials during the target era, as they are clearly fundamentally at odds.

Semmel's extreme argument that the inalienable right in Article IV(1) is not a right at all, but a privilege that enigmatically flows from compliance with Articles I, II, and III is clearly erroneous, as this non-recognition of the legal status of the Article IV(1) right is contradicted by the plain meaning of the text.[13]

More common among NWS officials, however, and stated explicitly by John Bolton, is the interpretation of the conditionality of the inalienable right upon NNWS compliance with Articles I, II, and III.[14] Under the interpretation I have

---

[13] Statement by Dr Andrew K. Semmel, Alternative Representative of the United States of America, to the Second Session of the Preparatory Committee for the 2005 NPT Review Conference. Peaceful Nuclear Cooperation: NPT Article IV, Geneva, Switzerland, May 7, 2003.

[14] Statement by United States Under Secretary of State for Arms Control and International Security John R. Bolton, to the Third Session of the Preparatory Committee for the 2005 Review

advanced herein, this interpretive conclusion is incorrect. The link between Articles I, II, and III on the one hand, and the Article IV(1) right on the other is not one of conditionality. Rather, it is one of a limited conventional circumscription or limitation of an inalienable state right. Articles I, II, and III prohibit certain activities and mandate others with regard to nuclear weapons. These are obligations which NNWS have taken on themselves, and their compliance with these obligations must be determined through proper juridical mechanisms, both inside and outside of the NPT context. *However, NNWS compliance or noncompliance with these non-proliferation obligations has no* per se *conditional effect upon the residual right of NNWS to engage in the peaceful use of nuclear energy materials and technologies recognized in Article IV(1).* Such conditionality would be in disharmony with the understanding of states' rights pursuant to the *Lotus* principle, and to the role of Article IV(1) in the context of the NPT, as discussed above.

Related to the conditionality interpretation—in a sense a lesser included argument within this interpretation—and incorrect for the same reasons, is the argument by Semmel and others that the burden for resolving any suspicions regarding a NNWS's domestic nuclear program lies with the subject NNWS itself. As Semmel himself stated to the 2003 PrepCom:

Supplier states must forego assistance to states with suspect nuclear programs until the suspicions are resolved. The mere claim of peaceful intent is not sufficient [...] states—especially those with ambitious nuclear programs—must back up their claims of peaceful intent and 'transparency' by fully implementing the IAEA's Strengthened Safeguards Additional Protocol.[15]

As manifest in Semmel's comments, during the target era the NWS interpretation of the conditionality of the Article IV(1) right, as supplemented by this burden placement interpretation, became an important legal argument underpinning proposals for the requirement of accession to the IAEA Additional Protocol as a condition of nuclear supply, as such a measure would potentially enhance the ability of the NWS to determine the compliance of NNWS with their non-proliferation obligations, and thus clarify whether a particular NNWS was entitled to enjoy their right to peaceful use.

As an additional interpretation, Bolton specifically argued in his statement to the 2004 PrepCom that the NPT provides no right to enrichment and reprocessing (ENR) technologies.[16] In essence, this is an argument that, while Article

---

Conference of the Treaty on the Non-proliferation of Nuclear Weapons. 'The NPT: A Crisis of Non-Compliance,' New York, April 27, 2004.

[15] Statement by Dr Andrew K. Semmel, Alternative Representative of the United States of America, to the Second Session of the Preparatory Committee for the 2005 NPT Review Conference. Peaceful Nuclear Cooperation: NPT Article IV, Geneva, Switzerland, May 7, 2003.

[16] Statement by United States Under Secretary of State for Arms Control and International Security John R. Bolton, to the Third Session of the Preparatory Committee for the 2005 Review

IV(1) recognizes some rights to peaceful nuclear uses for NNWS, it does not recognize a right of NNWS to indigenous control over the nuclear fuel cycle.

This argument is an interpretive answer to the apparent existence of a 'loophole' in the NPT, which President Bush bemoaned and sought to close in his 2004 speech.[17] Other commentators have referred to this loophole problem as the 'latent proliferation' problem, meaning that under the NPT, NNWS can potentially develop a nuclear program which could be turned into a weapons program in relatively short order, all under the legal umbrella of the Article IV(1) inalienable right. Then, at a time of their choosing, they could break out of the treaty with a weapons program, the development of which has been assisted by the IAEA and other states under the guise of a civilian nuclear energy program.[18] Ariel Levite has referred to this as the strategy of 'nuclear hedging.'[19] The interpretive argument by Bolton, that the Article IV(1) right does not cover indigenous control over the nuclear fuel cycle, became a common argument underpinning the multilateral fuel cycle proposals discussed in Chapter 3.

However, this interpretation that NNWS do not have a right to indigenous control over the nuclear fuel cycle is incorrect. The best way to approach this analytically is to begin with first principles of international law, one of which is contained in the *Lotus* principle, discussed above.[20] Again, this principle holds that states may do what they like absent some prohibitive rule of international law which forbids a certain action. With that principle as a guide, correctly interpreting the inalienable right in Article IV(1) becomes possible. As concluded above, this right should be interpreted to provide that states party to the NPT may engage in any peaceful use of nuclear energy materials and technology, as limited only by the clearly delineated terms of the prohibitive/limiting conventional obligations contained in Articles I, II, and III. This then creates an interpretive presumption toward the legitimacy of peaceful uses of nuclear materials and technology in the absence of evidence that a particular such use is prohibited in Articles I, II, or III. ENR technologies are nowhere prohibited in NPT Articles I, II, or III. *Therefore, pursuant to the* Lotus *principle, NNWS have a right to ENR technologies and to other peaceful possessions and uses of fuel cycle technologies, just as they have the right to exist and to defend themselves.* None of these rights derive from treaties or other positive sources of international law. They are simply includable among the plenary rights inuring to a state by virtue of its statehood.

Conference of the Treaty on the Non-proliferation of Nuclear Weapons. 'The NPT: A Crisis of Non-Compliance,' New York, April 27, 2004.

[17] Remarks by U.S. President George W. Bush on Weapons of Mass Destruction Proliferation. Fort Lesley J. McNair—National Defense University, Washington D.C., February 11, 2004.

[18] See Christopher Chyba, 'Second-Tier Suppliers and Their Threat to the Nuclear Non-proliferation Regime,' in Joseph Pilat, ed., *Atoms for Peace: A Future after Fifty Years?* (2007) p. 121.

[19] 'Never Say Never Again: Nuclear Reversal Revisited,' 27(3) *International Security* (2002–2003) 59–88.

[20] PCIJ, Ser. A, No. 10, pp. 18 and 19.

If any further persuasion is needed, an analysis of the plain meaning of the terms of Article IV(1) and the associated paragraphs of the preamble of the NPT, also supports this conclusion. The inalienable right is described in Article IV(1) as a right 'to develop research, production and use of nuclear energy for peaceful purposes.' In the seventh paragraph of the preamble to the NPT, all states are recognized to be 'entitled [...] to contribute alone or in cooperation with other States to, the further development of the applications of atomic energy for peaceful purposes.' Thus, the plain meaning of the terms of Article IV(1), as read along with the preamble of the treaty, clearly conceives of states having independent control over the means to pursue research on and development of applications of nuclear energy for peaceful purposes. Enrichment and reprocessing technologies are absolutely integral technologies in the nuclear fuel cycle, and are therefore included within this entitlement.

C. Conditioning supply and recognition of Article IV rights on compliance with an IAEA Comprehensive Safeguards Agreement

I would like to pay particular analytical attention at this point to the treaty interpretations given by NWS during the target period in order to justify the conditioning of nuclear supply, and recognition of the Article IV(1) right to peaceful use, upon NNWS compliance with an IAEA Comprehensive Safeguards Agreement. As discussed in Chapter 3, there are several points of treaty interpretation included within the logical progression of interpretation maintained by NWS officials. I identified these steps of interpretive progression as occurring within the following transitive sequence:

1. Noncompliance with an IAEA safeguards agreement constitutes a breach of NPT Article III,
2. A breach of NPT Article III results in the invalidity of the rights and obligations in Article IV,
3. Thus, noncompliance with an IAEA safeguards agreement results in the invalidity of the rights and obligations in Article IV.

As I explained in Chapter 3, this conditional normative linkage between NPT Articles III and IV, and the transitive conclusion that noncompliance with a safeguards agreement constitutes breach of the NPT, was used by NWS officials during the target era in order to justify the non-recognition of Iran's right to peaceful nuclear technologies under NPT Article IV(1), as well as to justify a cessation of nuclear assistance to Iran by supplier states, pursuant to the obligation in Article IV(2).[21]

---

[21] See, e.g., Statement of Andrew Semmel, Alternative Representative of the United States of America, to the Second Session of the Preparatory Committee for the 2005 NPT Review Conference: Peaceful Nuclear Cooperation, Article IV (2003). For more detailed discussion of the Iran case, see Daniel H. Joyner, *International Law and the Proliferation of Weapons of Mass Destruction* (2009) p. 50.

The interpretation of a conditional linkage between Article III and Article IV, which forms an integral part of this transitive sequence, is an argument that I have already addressed above.[22] I concluded above that NNWS compliance or non-compliance with Articles I, II, and III has no *per se* conditional effect upon the residual right of NNWS to engage in the peaceful use of nuclear energy materials and technologies recognized in Article IV(1). This conclusion, taking away one of the two interpretive pillars of this transitive sequence, on its own renders the interpretive sequence incorrect.

However, I will assume *arguendo* for the moment that the NWS interpretation on conditionality between Article III and Article IV is correct. I will do so to show that, even if it was correct, the other interpretive pillar of this transitive sequence—that noncompliance with an IAEA safeguards agreement constitutes a breach of NPT Article III—is also incorrect.

Returning to the discussion in Chapter 3 of the identity, role, and authorities of the IAEA, it will be recalled that the IAEA is its own self-enclosed treaty-based international organization. Its existence predates that of the NPT by more than a decade. It has its own constitutional treaty—the IAEA Statute—and its own separate membership as an international organization. Its statute contains detailed rules and procedures regarding its functioning and authority. The IAEA's only legal connection to the NPT is the obligation in Article III.4 of the NPT for all NNWS parties to 'conclude agreements with the International Atomic Energy Agency to meet the requirements of this Article.'

Some have argued that the operative legal obligation for NNWS in Article III is contained in Article III.1. They point to the language in Article III.1 stating that each NNWS 'undertakes to accept safeguards as set forth in an agreement to be negotiated and concluded with the International Atomic Energy Agency [. . .]' and to the phrases 'Procedures for the safeguards required by this Article shall be followed with respect to source or special fissionable material [. . .]' and 'The safeguards required by this Article shall be applied on all source or special fissionable material [. . .]' They see in these terms an obligation in Article III.1 not only to enter into a safeguards agreement with the IAEA, but also an obligation *to comply with* the terms of that safeguards agreement.[23]

However, a closer reading of the whole of Article III renders this interpretation unpersuasive. Article III does contain an obligation for NNWS to enter

---

[22] In addition to official statements of this erroneous argument, it has additionally been made in non-proliferation literature by diplomatic and academic observers. See, e.g., John Carlson, 'Defining Noncompliance: NPT Safeguards Agreements,' 39(4) *Arms Control Today* (May 2009) 22; N. Jansen Calamita, 'Sanctions, Countermeasures, and the Iranian Nuclear Issue,' 42 *Vanderbilt Journal of Transnational Law* (2009) 1393, 1397.

[23] See, e.g., John Carlson, 'Defining Noncompliance: NPT Safeguards Agreements,' 39(4) *Arms Control Today*, (May 2009) 22 ('Noncompliance with an NPT safeguards agreement constitutes violation of Article III of the NPT, the obligation to accept safeguards on all nuclear material [. . .]').

into a safeguards agreement with the IAEA. That obligation is discussed in Article III.1, but is stated with even more clarity and specificity in Article III.4 which states: 'Non-nuclear-weapon States Party to the Treaty shall conclude agreements with the International Atomic Energy Agency to meet the requirements of this Article [. . .]'

Additionally, reading into Article III.1's provisions an independent obligation to comply with the terms of the safeguards agreement to be negotiated with the IAEA produces a redundancy from a normative system perspective. One of the fundamental system rules of international law is contained in the customary international law rule of *pacta sunt servanda* ('treaties are to be observed'), which holds that parties to a treaty are under an obligation to perform their treaty undertakings in good faith.[24] *Pacta sunt servanda* is an omnipresent rule of customary international law, binding all states and all treaties made.

Therefore, to interpret Article III.1 of the NPT as comprising an operative legal obligation would be to make its provisions redundant with the obligation clearly spelled out in Article III.4. Furthermore, to interpret Article III.1's terms as containing an obligation to comply with the terms of another treaty (a safeguards agreement) would render the terms of Article III.1 redundant and superfluous in light of the rule of *pacta sunt servanda*. An interpretation of a treaty which renders some of its terms redundant or superfluous internally, or redundant with regard to other system rules of international law, is to be avoided.[25]

The terms of Article III.1 are better interpreted in their context within Article III as describing, along with Article III.2 and Article III.3, the sort of safeguards agreement which NNWS are to enter into with the IAEA. Under this interpretation, Article III makes sense holistically, and redundancy is avoided. Paragraphs 1–3 of Article III lay out in detail the type of safeguards agreement which paragraph 4 requires NNWS to enter into with the IAEA. Indeed this is precisely what the terms of Article III.4 provide: 'Non-nuclear-weapon States Party to the Treaty shall conclude agreements with the International Atomic Energy Agency *to meet the requirements of this Article.'*[26]

Interpreted correctly, then, it is clear that the operative obligation in Article III.4 for NNWS to enter into a safeguards agreement with the IAEA, of a type described in Article III(1–3), is the extent of the legal relationship between the NPT on the one hand, and the IAEA and its safeguards agreements with states on the other.

If a state enters into a safeguards agreement with the IAEA, it accepts the IAEA's role in monitoring its compliance with its safeguards agreement, as detailed in Article XII of the IAEA Statute. As Article XII makes clear, the IAEA

---

[24] See VCLT Article 26; *Gabcikovo-Nagymaros Project* (Hung. v. Slov.), ICJ Reports, 1997, p. 7, para. 114.

[25] See Ulf Linderfalk, *On the Interpretation of Treaties: The Modern International Law as Expressed in the 1969 Vienna Convention on the Law of Treaties* (2007) pp. 109–110.

[26] Emphasis added.

has the authority to determine that a state party to a safeguards agreement is in noncompliance with that agreement. Noncompliance with a safeguards agreement is reported in the first instance by the IAEA's inspectors, whose job it is to verify the state's disclosures and accounting of the nuclear materials and activities occurring within its borders. If the IAEA inspectors report noncompliance with the terms of a safeguards agreement, Article XII(c) of the IAEA Statute details the IAEA's responsibilities and procedural options. The report on noncompliance is to be transmitted to the Director General, who will also transmit it to the IAEA Board of Governors. At this point, the Board 'shall call upon the recipient State or States to remedy forthwith any non-compliance which it finds to have occurred.' The Board shall also report the noncompliance to all IAEA members and to the U.N. Security Council and General Assembly.

If the state fails to take 'fully corrective action within a reasonable time,' the Board may take one or both of the following measures: (1) it may curtail or suspend all assistance being provided to the state by the IAEA and demand a return of assistance materials; (2) it may also act under Article XIX of the Statute and suspend the state from IAEA membership and privileges.

An interesting legal question concerns the juridical meaning of a determination of safeguards agreement noncompliance by the IAEA. Is the determination of noncompliance by the IAEA equivalent to or constitutive of a finding of material breach by the state party to the agreement, pursuant to the definition of material breach contained in VCLT Article 60? Or is it merely a preliminary finding of noncompliance that does not, *per se*, constitute a determination of material breach?[27] This is essentially a question of the role and authority of the IAEA. And this in turn becomes a fundamental question of the international legal personality of the IAEA as an international organization. And the question is whether the IAEA's international legal personality includes the authority to make a determination of material breach of safeguards agreements to which it is a party, which is an essentially judicial and not a political role.

Determining the international legal personality of an international organization is essentially a determination, made through a review of the organization's constituting instruments, of the intent of the states that created the organization. With what attributes of legal personality did the state creators of the organization intend to endow it? The practice of the organization subsequent to its founding, and the acceptance or rejection of this practice by their member states as well as non-member states, can also contribute to the contours of the organization's personality attributes.[28]

---

[27] See generally Martti Koskenniemi, 'Breach of Treaty or Non-Compliance? Reflections on the Enforcement of the Montreal Protocol,' Yearbook of International Environmental Law, Vol. 3 (1992) p. 123; Bruno Simma and Dirk Pulkowski, 'Of Planets and the Universe: Self-Contained Regimes in International Law,' 17 *European Journal of International Law* (2006) 483, 488–489.

[28] See Ian Brownlie, *Principles of Public International Law* (7th edn, 2008) p. 675; *Reparation* case, ICJ Reports, 1949, p. 174.

In the case of the IAEA, a review of its constituting instrument, the IAEA Statute, yields compelling evidence that the IAEA was not intended by its creators to exercise a judicial role. Rather, it was to perform a technical role of verifying the disclosures and accounting of nuclear materials and activities occurring within the boundaries of states that entered into safeguards agreements with the organization. A finding of noncompliance with an IAEA safeguards agreement can be based upon quite technical disclosure or accounting lapses.[29] Indeed, pursuant to paragraph 19 of INFCIRC/153 (the agency's standard comprehensive safeguards agreement), the IAEA Board of Governors may refer states to the U.N. Security Council for enforcement action upon the simple finding that Agency inspectors are 'not able to verify that there has been no diversion of nuclear material required to be safeguarded under the Agreement to nuclear weapons or other nuclear explosive devices.' And the IAEA's inspectors are highly capable and qualified in their training to make such technical determinations. These determinations are important in that they can be probative in alerting the IAEA Board of Governors and the U.N. Security Council to diversions of declared fissile materials and technologies to military uses.

However, the standards for determining technical noncompliance detailed in the IAEA Statue do not satisfactorily correlate to the standard for determining material breach, contained in VCLT Article 60, nor do they purport to. Material breach is defined in the VCLT as '(*a*) a repudiation of the treaty not sanctioned by the present Convention; or (*b*) the violation of a provision essential to the accomplishment of the object or purpose of the treaty.'

Quite the opposite, the IAEA Statute in Article XVII is explicit in its direction to the organization on steps to be taken in the event of 'any question or dispute concerning the interpretation or application of this Statute which is not settled by negotiation [...]' The organization is directed to refer all such legal questions to a proper judicial forum—the International Court of Justice. Article XVII further mandates the IAEA governing bodies to request an advisory opinion from the ICJ 'on any legal question arising within the scope of the Agency's activities.' These provisions, manifesting the intent of the creators of the IAEA, are incongruous with an interpretation that the IAEA itself possesses a judicial role and authority, including the authority to determine a material breach of IAEA safeguards agreements.

Furthermore, one must remember that IAEA safeguards agreements are bilateral treaties between the IAEA, in its exercise of legal personality explicitly granted to it by the IAEA Statute, and a state. The proposition that the IAEA itself can determine in authoritative fashion that the other party to a bilateral

---

[29] See Pierre Goldschmidt, 'Exposing Nuclear Non-Compliance,' 51(1) *Survival* (February 2009) 143; John Carlson, 'Defining Noncompliance: NPT Safeguards Agreements,' 39(4) *Arms Control Today* (May 2009) 22.

treaty, to which it itself is the other member, is in breach of its obligations under that treaty, has no precedent or analogue in international law.

The better interpretation of the IAEA's international legal personality, and its mandate with regard to determining compliance with safeguards agreements, is that an IAEA determination that a state is in noncompliance with its safeguards agreement constitutes a preliminary technical determination of noncompliance short of an allegation or finding of material breach. As Article XII of the IAEA Statute stipulates, such a finding triggers reporting requirements for the IAEA, but it also marks the beginning of a diplomatic process through which the IAEA is to work with the state to bring its actions—which again may consist of no more than reporting or accounting errors or omissions—into full compliance with the obligations of its safeguards agreement. It is only if the noncompliant state fails to take corrective action within a reasonable time that the IAEA may proceed to suspend its assistance from the organization, or ultimately to suspend its IAEA membership and privileges, pursuant to the process detailed in Article XIX.

Rather than interpreting the first finding of noncompliance as a treaty breach, it would be more correct to interpret only such a suspension pursuant to Article XIX as constituting an allegation (not a finding) by the IAEA that the other party to a bilateral treaty to which it is also a party, is in material breach of its obligations under that treaty. Such an interpretation would be consonant, and in fact in perfect harmony, with the presumptive rules on termination or suspension of a treaty as a consequence of breach, contained in VCLT Article 60. Article 60 provides that only a 'material breach of a bilateral treaty by one of the parties entitles the other to invoke the breach as a ground for terminating the treaty or suspending its operation in whole or in part.' The first finding, or subsequent findings of safeguards agreement noncompliance by the IAEA short of a finding triggering the procedures for suspension in Article XIX, should not therefore be interpreted as constituting an allegation of a material breach of the safeguards agreement. Only a determination of noncompliance which results in the IAEA's suspension of the membership of the noncompliant state under Article XIX, mirroring the remedy provided for in VCLT Article 60(1), should be interpreted as such an allegation of a material breach.

Under this interpretation, a determination by the IAEA that a state is in noncompliance with its safeguards agreement is not *per se* equivalent to or constitutive of a determination of material breach of the safeguards agreement. The IAEA simply does not have the legal personality under its statute to exercise such a judicial function. A determination of safeguards agreement noncompliance by the IAEA is better interpreted as comprising a preliminary technical finding of treaty noncompliance, short of material breach, which results in explicitly detailed rights and responsibilities of the IAEA under Article XII of its Statute.

Returning, therefore, to NPT Article III, I have demonstrated through this analysis that an IAEA determination of safeguards noncompliance does not per se *constitute a determination of a material breach of the safeguards agreement. However, even if it did, this would not result in or constitute a breach of NPT Article III. This is because, as I have explained, the operative obligation in Article III is contained in Article III.4 and consists only in an obligation for NNWS to enter into a safeguards agreement with the IAEA, of a type described in Article III(1–3).*

I have thus demonstrated that the second interpretive pillar of the transitive sequence identified above—that noncompliance with an IAEA safeguards agreement constitutes a breach of NPT Article III—is incorrect, as is the first interpretive pillar of the transitive sequence—the interpretation of a conditional linkage between Article III and Article IV. The rhetorical blurring and conflation by NWS officials during the target era of the concepts of noncompliance with an IAEA safeguards agreement, and violation of Article III of the NPT, and the resulting claim that NNWS in noncompliance with their safeguards agreement were not entitled to their Article IV(1) right to nuclear peaceful use, was all therefore simply incorrect treaty interpretation.

This conclusion does beg the following questions: How then can a breach of NPT Article III be established? What entity is authorized to make this determination? What are the legal implications or consequences of such a determination? Under the interpretation of Article III maintained herein, a breach of NPT Article III can be established if an NNWS party either fails to conclude a safeguards agreement with the IAEA, or is determined by a competent judicial authority to have materially breached a safeguards agreement, pursuant to the definition of material breach in VCLT Article 60. The other logical means of breach would be termination of or withdrawal from a safeguards agreement with the IAEA. However, the standard INFCIRC/153 safeguards agreement does not provide for termination/withdrawal in its terms. Therefore any renunciation of a safeguards agreement by an NNWS party would fall under the definition of material breach contained in VCLT Article 60.

As for who has the authority to determine a breach of Article III, the NPT is no different in this context than any other treaty. There is no specialized judicial body within the NPT normative system, inclusive of the IAEA, that has authority to determine a breach of NPT Article III. Therefore only an international judicial body with appropriate jurisdiction can perform this essentially judicial role. The NPT does not contain a provision explicitly submitting parties to the jurisdiction of the International Court of Justice for legal questions arising under the treaty, as many treaties do. Therefore, jurisdiction for the ICJ to hear a dispute arising under the NPT must be obtained through other means, detailed in the ICJ's Statute.[30]

In the event that a properly seized international judicial body were to determine that an NNWS party to the NPT had in fact breached NPT Article III, there would of course be legal implications for the breaching party as well as for the

---

[30] For more on ICJ jurisdiction in the context of non-proliferation treaties, see Daniel H. Joyner, *International Law and the Proliferation of Weapons of Mass Destruction* (2009) ch 5.

other parties to this multilateral treaty. The rights of the other parties of the NPT in the event of a material breach (if indeed a breach of NPT Article III were determined by the court to constitute a material breach of the NPT) by one party are laid out in detail in VCLT Article 60. As for the breaching party itself, it would be liable under any judgment for damages imposed by the court. However, in terms of the NPT itself and the continuing applicability of the rest of its provisions to the breaching NNWS, there would be no *per se* legal implication flowing from the breach of Article III. There would be no inherent conditionality with Article IV, as concluded herein. As a *de facto* matter, however, a state found to be in breach of Article III—if that breach were determined by the court to be a material breach of the treaty—would no doubt find many if not all of the other NPT parties exercising their rights under VCLT Article 60 to suspend the operation of the treaty as between themselves and the breaching state. This would have the practical effect of nullifying the terms of the NPT with respect to the breaching state.

D. Proposals and efforts to circumscribe the Article IV(1) inalienable right

I have so far demonstrated that the legal interpretive arguments which were employed by NWS during the target era to justify the proposals and efforts discussed in Chapter 3 for circumscribing the inalienable right recognized in Article IV(1)—the requirement of fuel bank membership, IAEA Additional Protocol adoption, and IAEA safeguards agreement compliance as conditions of supply— were fundamentally erroneous. As I stated in the introduction to this chapter, these interpretive errors are at their shared core the result of NWS officials disproportionately prioritizing the non-proliferation pillar of the NPT and incorrectly marginalizing the peaceful use pillar of the NPT, and in so doing failing to interpret the provisions of the NPT in their proper context and in the light of the treaty's correctly understood object and purpose.

In fact, in light of the correct interpretation given herein, these proposals and efforts were actions in unlawful circumscription of the right of NNWS to peaceful nuclear activities in Article IV(1) as properly understood. Each of these proposals and efforts, inasmuch as action was taken in pursuance of them, were manifestations of non-recognition of the full and proper scope of this inalienable right, and effected a prevention of trade which should have been allowed between private entities in NWS, and NNWS developing states, in exercise of their right to peaceful use of nuclear materials and technologies. These actions were therefore illegally prejudicial of the legitimate legal interests of NNWS under the grand bargain of the NPT.

These actions were arguably also in breach of the Article IV(2) obligation upon supplier states, who are therein obligated to 'cooperate in contributing alone or together with other States or international organizations to the further development of the applications of nuclear energy for peaceful purposes, especially in the territories of non-nuclear-weapon States Party to the Treaty.' I will not provide herein a full legal analysis of Article IV(2), though I have done so elsewhere.[31] It will suffice here to say that through their actions which they justified on the basis of the erroneous legal interpretations herein examined, NWS and other supplier states unjustifiably denied nuclear supply to NNWS, and were thus likely in breach of their obligation of nuclear cooperation in NPT Article IV(2) during the target era.

With regard to the proposals and efforts of NWS to make fuel bank membership, IAEA Additional Protocol adoption, and safeguards agreement compliance conditions of supply, these proposals are best seen as attempts by NWS to essentially rewrite the terms of NPT Article IV in a much more restrictive way for NNWS parties than originally written. In essence it is an attempt by a relatively small group of developed, nuclear-weapon-possessing states to restructure the grand bargain of the NPT by pressuring developing NNWS to make further concessions in the area of peaceful use than those to which they originally agreed. Procedurally, this is of course invalid, as the NPT contains provisions on modification in Article VIII which have not been followed in this context.

More substantively, the problem with such efforts to rewrite the terms of the NPT for one set of parties (NNWS), but not for other parties (NWS), is analogously comparable to the domestic contracting context in which one party seeks to amend the terms of an existing contract to its advantage, and to persuade the other party to the contract to recognize those changes, even when there is no consideration flowing to the other party in the form of changed contractual provisions sought by that other party. In the common law tradition, such contractual amendments are generally forbidden by reference to the pre-existing duty rule, which states that a contract modification in which any party offers for consideration only that which they are already under contractual obligation to do, is void for want of consideration.[32] There is of course no requirement of consideration in treaty law, and I offer this domestic law reference only as a principled analogy to demonstrate the inequity of attempts to amend an agreement between two parties, or sets of parties, to benefit only one of them and cost only the other.

III. Disarmament

As reviewed in Chapter 3, during the target era NWS officials consistently marginalized the importance of the disarmament pillar of the NPT, codified in Article VI. They adopted a uniformly obfuscatory interpretive stance on the obligation contained in Article VI, and on the rare occasions when they did interpret the

---

[31] See Daniel H. Joyner, *International Law and the Proliferation of Weapons of Mass Destruction* (2009) ch 1.
[32] See E. Allan Farnsworth, *Contracts* (4th edn, 2004) p. 267.

terms of Article VI in some detail they maintained an interpretation which held that the Article VI obligation is one of very limited scope—in some cases approaching non-existence. This interpretation was most clearly expressed in the speeches and writings of U.S. representative Christopher Ford, who argued that the only legal obligation for NWS in Article VI is the minimal obligation to put forth good faith effort toward negotiations on disarmament.

The analysis given in both the non-proliferation and peaceful use sections of this chapter, recalling the conclusions reached in Chapter 2 regarding the context and object and purpose of the NPT, and in particular the principle of the juridical equality of the three pillars of the NPT which flowed from that analysis, applies with equal force to this undue marginalization by NWS of the disarmament pillar of the NPT. Disproportionate prioritization of the non-proliferation pillar of the NPT at the expense of the disarmament pillar of the NPT in NWS policy positions, led NWS to interpretive conclusions regarding the scope and meaning of NPT Article VI which were in disharmony with the plain meaning of the terms of Article VI as understood within the provision's proper context, and in the light of the NPT's correctly understood object and purpose.

As noted above, U.S. representative Christopher Ford was the most candid and thorough among NWS officials in declaring his interpretation of NPT Article VI, which interpretation was reflected in his official statements. In his 2007 article in the *Non-proliferation Review*, Ford argues for the limited interpretation of Article VI discussed above. He challenges the ICJ's 1996 Advisory Opinion head on and declares its 'twofold obligation' conclusion—and particularly the Court's conclusion that Article VI contains an 'obligation to achieve a precise result—nuclear disarmament in all its aspects'—to be erroneous. Rather, Ford looks to one paragraph in the preamble of the NPT, and to selected vignettes from the negotiating history of Article VI, to draw his interpretive conclusion of the minimalist obligation of Article VI.[33]

To give credit where it is due, Ford is right to challenge the interpretation of NPT Article VI adopted by the ICJ in its 1996 Advisory Opinion. In this section of the Court's opinion, the Court is not particularly methodical in its interpretive analysis, as it is in other sections of its opinion. Its interpretive conclusion regarding the scope and meaning of NPT Article VI is therefore rather brief and conclusory. The Court's consideration of Article VI occurs at the very end of the opinion, and is not directly connected to its conclusions regarding the question put to it. This fact leads Ford to suggest that the Court's consideration of NPT Article VI was *ultra vires* the Court's authority. However, as the Court itself states in paragraph 98 of its Opinion, the applicability of this consideration to the

---

[33] Christopher A. Ford, 'Debating Disarmament: Interpreting Article VI of the Treaty on the Non-Proliferation of Nuclear Weapons,' 14(3) *Non-proliferation Review* (November 2007). *Advisory Opinion on the Threat or Use of Nuclear Weapons*, ICJ Reports, 1996, p. 26.

question placed before the Court does appear legitimate when the question is 'seen in a broader context.' The questions of use of nuclear weapons and possession of nuclear weapons are, after all, inherently linked—one cannot use what one does not have.

Germane though the Court's consideration may be, with respect to the Court's substantive interpretation of Article VI and its finding in this provision an obligation on all NPT parties to achieve the result of nuclear disarmament, Ford is correct to argue that the Court almost certainly did stretch the meaning of the terms of Article VI past their plain meaning. Conversely, however, the extremely limited interpretation of the Article VI obligation which Ford advances in place of the Court's, almost certainly does not give the plain meaning of the terms of Article VI its full extent of scope and meaning.

Article VI states, in its entirety:

Each of the Parties to the Treaty undertakes to pursue negotiations in good faith on effective measures relating to cessation of the nuclear arms race at an early date and to nuclear disarmament, and on a treaty on general and complete disarmament under strict and effective international control.

Reading the terms of Article VI in their context within the article itself, we find an obligation 'to pursue negotiations in good faith on effective measures relating to [. . .]' and then a delineation of three results to which the effective measures spoken of should relate. These are:

1. cessation of the nuclear arms race at an early date;
2. nuclear disarmament; and
3. a treaty on general and complete disarmament under strict and effective international control.

The undertaking, or obligation, in Article VI is thus an obligation to pursue negotiations in good faith on effective measures relating to these three delineated end results. In his interpretive analysis, Ford places his focus on the term 'pursue.' He argues that this term cannot be said to comprise an obligation on NPT Parties to do anything other than to put forth good faith effort toward negotiations, as it inherently comprehends the fact that negotiations by definition involve more than one party, with the result that because negotiations are not within the control of any one state, no one state can be held liable for their not coming to pass.

But here I think Ford undervalues, or at least understates, the scope of individual accountability which the legal principle of 'good faith' in Article IV imposes upon each state party to the NPT. Again, the obligation is to pursue negotiations in good faith on effective measures related to the three delineated results. As the ICJ states in paragraph 102 of its 1996 Advisory Opinion, the principle of good faith is a long-established principle of international law with a justiciable legal meaning in the context of the creation and performance of legal obligations. It is a principle which has been frequently employed by the ICJ in its jurisprudence.[34]

In the context of NPT Article VI, each state party undertakes individually to pursue negotiations in good faith on effective measures related to the three delineated results. Ford makes much of the distinction between an obligation to pursue negotiations in good faith, and a counterfactual obligation to engage in negotiations in good faith.[35] To him, the term 'pursue negotiations' is somehow diluted in its obligatory scope as compared to the counterfactual term 'engage in negotiations.' I see much less of a distinction here than Ford does. Ford argues that the word 'pursue' is an important indication of the intent of the Article's drafters to acknowledge that negotiations may fail to commence or to produce an outcome, through no fault of one or a number of parties who are pursuing the commencement of negotiations in good faith. If, however, counterfactually the term employed in Article VI was 'engage in negotiations,' would the obligation thus phrased not admit of the same possibilities? And as Ford himself argues, an obligation to engage in negotiations would in some sense be logically inappropriate, as it would be inequitable to hold a state acting in good faith, and willing to negotiate, liable for the failure of negotiations to take place due to the acts of another state either not acting in good faith or otherwise unwilling to negotiate. Thus, the drafters of Article VI could not logically have constructed the term as an obligation to engage in negotiations, and the obligation to pursue negotiations in good faith was therefore the strongest phrasing logically left to them. A similar phrasing occurs, for example, in Article 33 of the United Nations Charter, which obligates all member states of the United Nations to 'seek a

---

[34] See generally David Koplow, 'Parsing Good Faith: Has the United States Violated Article VI of the Nuclear Non-Proliferation Treaty?' 1993 *Wisconsin Law Review* (2003) 301; UK Trident Replacement a 'Material Breach' of the NPT, Joint Opinion by Rabinder Singh QC and Professor Christine Chinkin, December 19, 2005, para. 69:

The Treaty obligation is thus not to disarm as such, but a positive obligation to pursue in good faith negotiations towards these ends, and to bring them to a conclusion. Good faith is the legal requirement for the process of carrying out of an existing obligation. In the *Nuclear Tests cases* the ICJ described the principle of good faith as '*one of the basic principles governing the creation and performance of legal obligations*' [...] The obligation of good faith has been described as not being one '*which obviously requires actual damage. Instead its violation may be demonstrated by acts and failures to act which, taken together, render the fulfilment of specific treaty obligations remote or impossible.*' In the context of an obligation to negotiate in good faith this would involve taking no action that would make a successful outcome impossible or unlikely [...]

quoting *Nuclear Tests cases* Australia v. France; New Zealand v. France, ICJ Reports, 1974, p. 253; p. 457, para. 46; and Guy Goodwin-Gill, 'State Responsibility and the "Good Faith" Obligation in International Law,' in M. Fitzmaurice and D. Sarooshi, eds, *Issues of State Responsibility before International Judicial Institutions* (2004) pp. 75, 84. See also 'Good Faith Negotiations Leading to the Total Elimination of Nuclear Weapons,' Legal Memorandum by the International Association of Lawyers Against Nuclear Arms and the International Human Rights Clinic at Harvard Law School (2009) ch 7. Available at <http://lcnp.org/disarmament/2009.05.ICJbooklet.pdf>.

[35] Christopher A. Ford, 'Debating Disarmament: Interpreting Article VI of the Treaty on the Non-Proliferation of Nuclear Weapons,' 14(3) *Non-proliferation Review* (November 2007) 403.

solution by negotiation [...]' to any dispute which endangers the maintenance of international peace and security.

If anything, it would appear that an obligation to pursue negotiations in good faith imposes an obligation of broader scope upon each state party than would an obligation merely to engage in negotiations in good faith, as it seems to reach to the pre-negotiation stage of diplomatic relations and impose the obligations of good faith not only upon the negotiations themselves once commenced, but also upon their active pursuit by each individual state party. Thus, I read the obligation to pursue negotiations in good faith not as a manifestation of intent of the drafters of Article VI to dilute or attenuate the obligation upon each individual NPT party, but rather by its plain meaning to comprise an obligation to proactively, diligently, sincerely, and consistently pursue good faith negotiations on effective measures relating to the three delineated results.[36]

The obligation to pursue negotiations in good faith contained in Article VI must be understood in its holistic entirety. It is not an obligation to pursue negotiations in good faith on effective measures relating to arms control or nuclear weapons regulation generally. It is a specifically phrased obligation to pursue negotiations in good faith on effective measures related to (1) cessation of the nuclear arms race at an early date, (2) nuclear disarmament, and (3) a treaty on general and complete disarmament. Reading the entirety of the provision thus provides further meaning to the obligation to pursue negotiations in good faith. The delineated results, to which the effective measures should relate, provide meaning to the kind of negotiations which NPT parties are obligated to pursue.

So, in Article VI each party to the NPT is under an individual obligation to pursue in good faith—i.e. proactively, diligently, sincerely, and consistently—negotiations in good faith on the specific subject of effective measures relating to the three delineated results.

Regarding the three specific results, Ford and other NWS officials have argued that there is a sequencing, or conditionality, implied by the terms and order of the delineation of these results, which serves to invalidate any argument that NWS are obligated to pursue negotiations in good faith on effective measures related to nuclear disarmament *before* the conclusion of a treaty on general and complete disarmament. Reading Article VI of the NPT itself, it is difficult to see any basis

---

[36] See, e.g., *Gabcikovo-Nagymaros Dam Project*, (Hungary v. Slovakia), ICJ Reports, 1997, p. 7, at para 142, where the court held: 'What is required in the present case by the rule *pucta sunt servanda*, as reflected in Article 26 of the Vienna Convention of 1969 on the Law of Treaties, is that the Parties find an agreed solution within the cooperative context of the Treaty. Article 26 combines two elements, which are of equal importance. It provides that "Every treaty in force is binding upon the parties to it and must be performed by them in good faith." This latter element, in the Court's view, implies that, in this case, it is the purpose of the Treaty, and the intentions of the parties in concluding it, which should prevail over its literal application. The principle of good faith obliges the Parties to apply it in a reasonable way and in such a manner that its purpose can be realized.'

in its terms for such an interpretation. And indeed, this interpretation by Ford and others is not based on the text of Article VI. Rather, it is based *solely* on a reading of one paragraph taken from the preamble of the NPT which reads:

The States concluding this Treaty, hereinafter referred to as the 'Parties to the Treaty' [...] Desiring to further the easing of international tension and the strengthening of trust between States in order to facilitate the cessation of the manufacture of nuclear weapons, the liquidation of all their existing stockpiles, and the elimination from national arsenals of nuclear weapons and the means of their delivery pursuant to a Treaty on general and complete disarmament under strict and effective international control [...]

Here, Ford places emphasis on the phrase 'the elimination from national arsenals of nuclear weapons and the means of their delivery *pursuant to* a Treaty on general and complete disarmament [...]'[37] This preamble paragraph, Ford argues, is an important context for the obligation in Article VI, and should imbue its terms with meaning.[38]

Firstly, as discussed in Chapter 2, the primary utility of the preamble of a treaty for interpretive purposes is its role in determining the object and purpose of the treaty. Provisions of a treaty may be read along with relevant sections of the preamble in order to clarify or add meaning where a provision or its terms are lacking in meaning. However, the preamble cannot be used to contradict the plain meaning of the terms of a treaty provision. This is precisely what Ford's interpretation of conditionality, using the preamble as his sole source of interpretation, would do.

Again viewing the actual text of Article VI, the obligation is to pursue negotiations in good faith on effective measures 'relating to cessation of the nuclear arms race at an early date and to nuclear disarmament, and on a treaty on general and complete disarmament under strict and effective international control.' There is no hint in the terms of this paragraph of any conditionality or prerequisite ordering of the type Ford argues for. Indeed, the plain meaning of the terms of Article VI, in their full context within the other provisions of the NPT, and in light of the object and purpose of the treaty, is quite clear and logically rendered. States are to pursue negotiations in good faith on effective measures relating to three delineated results. These results are listed in a perfectly logical sequential fashion. The first result to be the subject of negotiated effective measures is the cessation of the nuclear arms race. By any reasonable calculus, this result was accomplished by the ending of the Cold War and the dissolution of the Soviet Union, and the accomplishments in nuclear arms control which have occurred in the past twenty years. The second result to be the subject of negotiated effective measures is nuclear disarmament. As Randy Rydell and others have written, and

---

[37] Emphasis added.
[38] Christopher A. Ford, 'Debating Disarmament: Interpreting Article VI of the Treaty on the Non-Proliferation of Nuclear Weapons,' 14(3) *Non-proliferation Review* (November 2007) 403.

as simple logic dictates, nuclear disarmament is a lesser included concept and goal within the larger concept and goal of general and complete disarmament. Effective partial measures toward general and complete disarmament, one of which is nuclear disarmament, have long been understood to be prudently pursued concurrently with, and as a necessary part of, efforts toward the larger comprehensive goal.[39]

Employing the more sound interpretive method provided for in VCLT Article 31(3)(a), reference can be made to the subsequent interpretive agreements reached between the parties to the NPT, reflected in Review Conference final documents. In the 2000 Review Conference Final Document, NPT parties by consensus agreed upon a statement of thirteen 'practical steps for the systematic and progressive efforts to implement Article VI of the Treaty on the Non-Proliferation of Nuclear Weapons [...]' Among the thirteen steps thus agreed upon are the ratification of the Comprehensive Test Ban Treaty, the conclusion of the Fissile Material Cut-off Treaty, the principle of irreversibility to apply to nuclear disarmament, and a host of other disarmament measures including the conclusion of the START II and III agreements, 'the engagement as soon as appropriate of all the nuclear-weapon States in the process leading to the total elimination of their nuclear weapons,' and 'an unequivocal undertaking by the nuclear-weapon States to accomplish the total elimination of their nuclear arsenals leading to nuclear disarmament to which all States parties are committed under Article VI.'

It is only after all of these practical steps related directly to nuclear disarmament, which the conference agreed upon for the implementation of Article VI, that the following is included as practical step number eleven: 'Reaffirmation that the ultimate objective of the efforts of States in the disarmament process is general and complete disarmament under effective international control.' This sequencing in the 2000 Review Conference Final Document mirrors precisely the sequencing in Article VI itself.

There is simply no sound interpretive reason not to, and very sound interpretive reasons to read Article VI precisely as its terms and their logical sequencing dictate— that each NPT party is currently under an individual obligation to pursue negotiations in good faith on effective measures related to nuclear disarmament.[40] They are

---

[39] See Randy Rydell, 'Nuclear Disarmament and General and Complete Disarmament,' in David Krieger, ed., *The Challenge of Abolishing Nuclear Weapons* (2009). See also George Bunn and Roland Timerbaev, 'Nuclear Disarmament: How Much Have the Five Nuclear Powers Promised in the Non-Proliferation Treaty?' in John Rhinelander and Adam Scheinman, eds, *At the Nuclear Crossroads* (1995).

[40] See George Bunn and Roland Timerbaev, 'Nuclear Disarmament: How Much Have the Five Nuclear Powers Promised in the Non-Proliferation Treaty?' in John Rhinelander and Adam Scheinman, eds, *At the Nuclear Crossroads* (1995) p. 29:

But the plain meaning of Article VI, its negotiating history, and the parties' practice in implementing it all suggest that these pre-conditions do not need to be satisfied to trigger an obligation to negotiate in good faith toward zero nuclear weapons along the 'nuclear disarmament' route. After 25 years and an end to the Cold War, the time has been reached when Article VI requires all five

also under an individual obligation to pursue negotiations in good faith on effective measures relating to a treaty on general and complete disarmament (GCD). These are separate obligations with no conditionality or sequencing legally connecting them. Indeed, the only sequencing implied by the terms of Article VI itself, and reflected in the thirteen practical steps adopted by NPT parties in the 2000 Review Conference Final Document, is the opposite sequence to that argued for by Ford. In the text of Article VI, nuclear disarmament is mentioned as a result prior to the mentioning of a GCD treaty as a result, and again is a logical lesser included concept which would most reasonably be accomplished before the accomplishment of a negotiated GCD treaty.

So what does it mean to pursue negotiations in good faith on effective measures relating to nuclear disarmament? As discussed above in Chapter 3, nuclear disarmament is a term of art which has a meaning distinct from other related terms, including the term arms control. These two terms—arms control and disarmament—are often used interchangeably in discourse concerning nuclear weapons, but they are in fact quite different concepts. Again as discussed above, arms control efforts are efforts which seek and which are designed by policy to effect a limitation or reduction of their subject weapons technologies, but which do not intend nor are designed by policy to achieve complete elimination of those weapons. Arms control efforts are typically designed to decrease the cost and risk associated with stockpiling of weapons, but they maintain a conception of the continued presence of those weapons in military arsenals. They are not part of a policy program the object of which is the elimination of their subject weapons from national arsenals.

Disarmament efforts, on the other hand, are part of such a policy program whose stated object is the complete elimination of their subject weapons from national arsenals, even if that program is to be implemented through multiple, progressive steps. Thus, while arms control efforts and disarmament efforts may look similar, in that the short-term aim of both is to limit and reduce their subject weapons technologies, they are in fact quite different in that disarmament efforts are clearly framed within a policy program the object of which is complete elimination from national arsenals.

Thus, the obligation in NPT Article VI to pursue negotiations in good faith of effective measures relating to nuclear disarmament takes on meaning and scope from this definition of the term 'nuclear disarmament' as distinct from, *inter alia*, the term 'nuclear arms control'. *Effective measures relating to nuclear disarmament*

---

nuclear-weapon states to begin such talks. Article VI does not say whether negotiating toward zero means taking one step downward after another through one negotiation after another, or a 'phased programme' involving a package of steps agreed in one long negotiation. At the same time, Article VI does not authorize an avoidance of negotiations by any of the five just because the Americans and Russians have agreed to reduce to 3,500 strategic warheads. Indeed, all five nuclear powers have a present, pressing obligation to begin discussing proposals for moving in the direction of zero along one route or the other.

can therefore be interpreted as effective measures relating to the complete elimination of nuclear weapons from national arsenals, or at the least to effective measures which are part of a policy program whose stated object is the complete elimination of nuclear weapons from national arsenals, through progressive programmatic steps.[41] *Article VI therefore obligates all NPT parties to pursue negotiations in good faith specifically on such effective measures.*

Finally, when the negotiations referred to in Article VI do occur, the jurisprudence of the International Court of Justice and other international tribunals gives some illumination to the legal implications of the concept of good faith on such negotiations. In a word, negotiations pursued in good faith must be *meaningful.* In explaining the rules of law which applied principles of equity, including the principle of good faith, to the case of parties negotiating the delimitation of adjacent continental shelves, the ICJ stated in the 1969 *North Sea Continental Shelf* case that:

[t]he parties are under an obligation to enter into negotiations with a view to arriving at an agreement, and not merely to go through a formal process of negotiation as a sort of prior condition for the automatic application of a certain method of delimitation in the absence of agreement; they are under an obligation so to conduct themselves that the negotiations are meaningful, which will not be the case when either of them insists upon its own position without contemplating any modification of it.[42]

As the arbitral panel held in the *Lake Lanoux* arbitration of 1957, an obligation to seek agreement through negotiation can be breached, *inter alia*:

[…] in the event, for example, of an unjustified breaking off of the discussions, abnormal delays, disregard of the agreed procedures, systematic refusals to take into consideration adverse proposals or interests […][43]

Similarly, in the 1982 *Kuwait v. Aminoil* arbitration, the tribunal held that:

[a] scrutiny of the negotiations fails to reveal any conduct on either side that would constitute a shortcoming in respect of […] the general principles that ought to be observed in carrying out an obligation to negotiate—that is to say, good faith as properly to be understood; sustained upkeep of the negotiations over a period appropriate to the circumstances; awareness of the interests of the other party; and a persevering quest for an acceptable compromise.[44]

So, bringing all of these interpretive threads together, we can in summary interpret NPT Article VI to contain an individual legal obligation binding upon all NPT

---

[41] See George Bunn and Roland Timerbaev, 'Nuclear Disarmament: How Much Have the Five Nuclear Powers Promised in the Non-Proliferation Treaty?' in John Rhinelander and Adam Scheinman, eds, *At the Nuclear Crossroads* (1995) p. 13 ("'Disarmament' can sometimes mean reductions short of zero. However, the ordinary meaning of "nuclear disarmament" clearly *includes* zero even if it also includes reductions short of zero. Therefore, the obligation to negotiate measures "relating to […] nuclear disarmament" seems to include, among other things, zero.')

[42] (F.R.G. v. Den.; F.R.G. v. Neth.), ICJ Reports, 1969, p. 47, at para. 85.

[43] 24 I.L.R. 101, 128 (1957).   [44] 66 I.L.R. 519, 578 (1982).

parties, to proactively, diligently, sincerely, and consistently pursue meaningful nego-
tiations on effective measures relating to the complete elimination of nuclear weapons
from national arsenals, or at the least on effective measures which are part of a policy
program whose stated object is the complete elimination of nuclear weapons from
national arsenals, through progressive programmatic steps.

Having reached this interpretation of NPT Article VI, we can now proceed to consider the question of NWS compliance specifically with the Article VI obligation to pursue negotiations in good faith on effective measures relating to nuclear disarmament. As discussed in Chapter 3 above, during the target era NWS officials consistently argued that their accomplishments in reducing the number of nuclear warheads on operational readiness within their arsenals, through unilateral action and pursuant to bilateral agreements, in and of themselves constituted sufficient evidence of their progressive compliance with the obligations of NPT Article VI.

Right away, by reference to the interpretation of the Article VI obligation relating to nuclear disarmament reached herein, these oft-repeated arguments of compliance by NWS officials can be dismissed as erroneous. Evidence of arms control agreements and actions taken pursuant thereto, or of actions taken on a unilateral basis, to reduce the number of nuclear warheads in the national arsenals of NWS, without evidence (of which there is none) of negotiated national and/or international policy programs of nuclear disarmament of which such agreements and actions were a progressive part, is not alone sufficient to evidence compliance with the Article VI obligation relating to nuclear disarmament.[45] Thus, the primary arguments of NWS officials during the target era proffering evidence of NWS compliance with the obligations of Article VI can, unfortunately, be quickly dismissed as erroneous and obfuscatory.

However, this conclusion does not *per se* preclude a finding of NWS compliance with the Article VI obligation related to nuclear disarmament, as correctly interpreted. The question of whether there has been in the practice of the NWS the pursuit of negotiations in good faith on effective measures relating to nuclear disarmament, as properly interpreted, can be answered in two alternative ways. One way of answering this question is in the affirmative. The text of NPT Article VI does not specify a particular forum or mode for the pursuit of such negotiations. However, in Article VIII(3) the NPT does explicitly provide for the holding once every five years of NPT treaty review conferences, to be attended by all treaty parties. These review conferences are tasked in Article VIII(3) 'to review the operation of this Treaty with a view to assuring that the purposes of the Preamble and the provisions of the Treaty are being realized.' Thus, NPT review

---

[45] On NWS policies related to nuclear arms control during the target era see Christopher Chyba and Karthika Sasikumar, 'A World of Risk: The Current Environment for U.S. Nuclear Weapons Policy,' in George Bunn and Christopher Chyba, eds, *U.S. Nuclear Weapons Policy: Confronting Today's Threats* (2006) pp. 11–19; Roger Speed and Michael May, 'Assessing the United States' Nuclear Posture,' in ibid., pp. 248–286.

conferences would seem to be at least one natural forum whereat negotiations might be held, and agreement on effective measures relating to nuclear disarmament might be reached among NPT parties.

As has been noted previously, many but not all NPT review conferences have produced final documents, which are adopted by the consensus of the parties in attendance. There has been some debate over the juridical meaning and significance of these final documents. It is certainly true that different provisions in the text of these final documents may carry different juridical value. Thus, in the final documents the conference may simply 'note' or 'welcome' the existence of facts or developments. It may alternatively 'reaffirm' statements or principles. Such provisions are likely limited in their juridical or interpretive value. However, as the VCLT makes clear in Article 31(3), 'subsequent agreement[s] between the parties regarding the interpretation of the treaty or the application of its provisions,' may be 'taken into account, together with the context' of the treaty in authoritatively interpreting its terms. Thus, if NPT review conference final documents evidence agreement of the treaty parties on the interpretation of the treaty or the application of its provisions, then according to VCLT Article 31(3) this agreement is a significant source of treaty interpretation.[46]

Thus, when in the 2000 NPT Review Conference Final Document the conference of NPT parties by consensus 'agrees on the following practical steps for the systematic and progressive efforts to implement Article VI of the Treaty on the Non-Proliferation of Nuclear Weapons,' this agreement can be argued persuasively to constitute an instance of agreement on effective measures relating to nuclear disarmament, in at least partial or progressive fulfillment of the Article VI obligation.

Under this potential conclusion, i.e. that agreement on effective measures relating to nuclear disarmament has been achieved by the agreement on practical steps by the 2000 NPT Review Conference, the next step in the Article VI interpretive exercise is to conclude that, by reference to Article 31(3) of the VCLT, the agreed principles should be taken into account in interpreting the meaning of NPT Article VI. The thirteen steps for implementing Article VI adopted in the 2000 Review Conference Final Document thus become part of the 'yardstick' for determining state compliance with the obligation of Article VI. It has been argued that, even accepting the juridical meaning of the thirteen steps and their relevance for interpreting Article VI, this does not necessarily mean that they are the exclusive test for determining compliance with Article VI.[47] It may be correct to say that evidence of other efforts not contained in one of the thirteen steps might also be offered to prove at least partial compliance. However, the most

---

[46] See Burrus Carnahan, 'Treaty Review Conferences,' 81 *American Journal of International Law* (1987) 226, 229.

[47] See Christopher A. Ford, 'Debating Disarmament: Interpreting Article VI of the Treaty on the Non-Proliferation of Nuclear Weapons,' 14(3) *Non-proliferation Review* (November 2007) 412.

straightforward and clearest reading of the agreement on the thirteen steps in the 2000 NPT Review Conference Final Document is that these steps have been agreed upon by NPT parties as at least the primary means for complying with the obligations in Article VI relating to nuclear disarmament.

Carrying the analysis forward, under this interpretation of the obligation of Article VI relative to nuclear disarmament, agreement has been reached by NPT parties in good faith on effective measures relating to nuclear disarmament. These effective measures are the thirteen steps agreed upon in the 2000 NPT Review Conference Final Document. So interpreted, consideration can move on to an analysis of NWS compliance with this obligation, so defined. However, even a cursory review of the thirteen steps is sufficient to conclude that NPT NWS have not, in fact, complied in their actions with many if not most of the thirteen steps, and did not during the target era pursue policies in harmony with many if not most of them.[48] The United States, in particular, stated explicitly during the target era that it no longer supported all of the thirteen steps.[49]

Detailed analysis of NWS nuclear weapons policies during the target era has been undertaken by others, and the reader is referred to these in-depth studies.[50]

---

[48] See Jean du Preez, 'The 2005 NPT Review Conference: Can it Meet the Nuclear Challenge?' *Arms Control Today* (April 2005):

What should remain clear is that the 1995 package allowed all states-parties to support the indefinite extension while also providing several practical steps for achieving progress toward nuclear disarmament and non-proliferation. The 2000 Review Conference reaffirmed this program of action, including the 'unequivocal undertaking,' and agreed on a set of specific practical 'systematic and progressive' steps to implement Article VI. Although these undertakings are of a political binding nature, they certainly derive from and are linked to the legal commitments and undertakings provided for in the treaty. Most importantly, the treaty clearly would not have been indefinitely extended had it not been for the program of action on nuclear disarmament built into the package that allowed that decision to be taken. The trend by some nuclear-weapon states, such as the United States, to roll back or, in some cases, simply ignore many of these political commitments and undertakings points out yet another weakness in the way the treaty is being implemented. If the nuclear-weapon states are allowed to cherry-pick which commitments they consider applicable, then why are non-nuclear-weapon states refused the same privilege?

See also Lawrence Scheinman, 'Disarmament: Have the Five Nuclear Powers Done Enough?' *Arms Control Today* (Jan/Feb 2005); Daniel H. Joyner, *International Law and the Proliferation of Weapons of Mass Destruction* (2009) pp. 60–66; Christopher Chyba and Karthika Sasikumar, 'A World of Risk: The Current Environment for U.S. Nuclear Weapons Policy,' in George Bunn and Christopher Chyba, eds, *U.S. Nuclear Weapons Policy: Confronting Today's Threats* (2006) pp. 11–19; Roger Speed and Michael May, 'Assessing the United States' Nuclear Posture,' in ibid., pp. 248–286.

[49] Statement by J. Sherwood McGinnis, Deputy U.S. Representative to the Conference on Disarmament, to the Second Session of the Preparatory Committee for the 2005 NPT Review Conference, May 1, 2003.

[50] See Joseph Cirincione et al., *Deadly Arsenals, Nuclear, Biological and Chemical Threats* (2nd edn, Carnegie Endowment, 2005); Christopher Chyba and Karthika Sasikumar, 'A World of Risk: The Current Environment for U.S. Nuclear Weapons Policy,' in George Bunn and Christopher Chyba, eds, *U.S. Nuclear Weapons Policy: Confronting Today's Threats* (2006) pp. 11–19; Roger Speed and Michael May, 'Assessing the United States' Nuclear Posture,' in ibid., pp. 248–286; David A. Koplow, *Death by Moderation: The U.S. Military's Quest for Useable Weapons* (2009); Ivo Daalder and Jan Lodal, 'The Logic of Zero: Toward a World Without Nuclear Weapons,' 87(6) *Foreign Affairs* (Nov.–Dec. 2008) 80.

In summary, however, all NWS states kept and maintained their nuclear weapons stockpiles during the target era. The quantity of nuclear weapons in operational readiness in NWS arsenals did decline significantly during the target era. However, as noted above there were no instances of international negotiations or undertakings by or among NWS on a complete and irreversible elimination of national nuclear weapons arsenals, even in a progressive programmatic fashion, as prescribed in the 2000 NPT Review Conference Final Document's thirteen steps. Furthermore, a number of NWS undertook research and development programs aimed at qualitative improvements to their nuclear weapons arsenals, and actually increased the role of nuclear weapons in their security policies, in disharmony with the thirteen steps.[51] NWS policies during the target era uniformly provided for a retention of nuclear weapons in their national arsenals and strategic policies for the foreseeable future, with no near, mid-term or even long-term policy objective of complete and irreversible nuclear disarmament.[52]

Thus, if agreement was reached by NPT parties in good faith on effective measures relating to nuclear disarmament through the adoption of the thirteen steps agreed upon in the 2000 NPT Review Conference Final Document, it is clear that each and all of the NPT NWS are in noncompliance with the Article VI obligation relating to nuclear disarmament, thus interpreted.

However, it is alternatively possible to argue that the question of whether there has been in the practice of the NWS the pursuit of negotiations in good faith on effective measures relating to nuclear disarmament, as properly interpreted, should be answered in the negative. Essentially, if one does not accept the argument that the thirteen steps agreed in the 2000 Review Conference Final Document constituted such negotiations and agreement produced thereby, then there is no other evidence for the type of negotiations required of all states, including particularly NWS as possessors of nuclear weapons, under Article VI. Indeed, as noted above, the actions of NWS during the target era were in clear disharmony with such a policy of negotiation.

Thus, under this alternative potential conclusion as well, it is clear that each and all of the NPT NWS are in noncompliance with the Article VI obligation relating to nuclear disarmament, thus interpreted.

So in summary on the question of NWS compliance with the NPT Article VI obligation relating to nuclear disarmament, as correctly interpreted, the evidence proffered by NWS themselves to establish their compliance with this obligation has been determined to be incomplete and erroneously offered.

---

[51] See Christopher Chyba and Karthika Sasikumar, 'A World of Risk: The Current Environment for U.S. Nuclear Weapons Policy,' in George Bunn and Christopher Chyba, eds, *U.S. Nuclear Weapons Policy: Confronting Today's Threats* (2006) pp. 11–19; Roger Speed and Michael May, 'Assessing the United States' Nuclear Posture,' in ibid., pp. 248–286; David A. Koplow, *Death by Moderation: The U.S. Military's Quest for Useable Weapons* (2009) ch 5.

[52] The one arguable exception to this blanket statement, at least in terms of its rhetoric, is China, which often declared its policy or at least vision of full nuclear disarmament.

Furthermore, even proceeding to an objective analysis of the question of whether there has been in the practice of the NWS the pursuit of negotiations in good faith on effective measures relating to nuclear disarmament, as properly interpreted, both possible alternative answers to this question yield a conclusion, when compared to the actual state practice of NWS during the target period, that each and all of the NPT NWS are in noncompliance with the Article VI obligation relating to nuclear disarmament.

As concluded in this chapter's consideration of NWS legal arguments in the context of both the non-proliferation pillar and the peaceful use pillar of the NPT, the interpretive errors of NWS in the context of the disarmament pillar of the NPT, codified in NPT Article VI, are at their core the result of NWS officials disproportionately prioritizing the non-proliferation pillar of the NPT and incorrectly marginalizing the disarmament pillar of the NPT, and in so doing failing to interpret the provisions of the NPT in their proper context and in the light of the treaty's correctly understood object and purpose.

And again, as concluded particularly in the context of the peaceful use pillar of the NPT in this chapter, the nuclear disarmament policies—or more accurately the lack thereof—maintained by NWS in reliance on these erroneous legal interpretations during the target era, were illegally prejudicial to the legitimate legal interests of NNWS under the NPT's *quid pro quo* grand bargain. As reviewed above in Chapter 2, in the case of a contract treaty such as the NPT, because of the *quid pro quo* reciprocal structure of the treaty's commitments, a material breach by one or a group of parties will almost certainly strike at the heart of the treaty's object and purpose, and persuasively be argued to 'specially affect' the non-breaching parties, and to 'radically change [...] the position of every party with respect to the further performance of its obligations under the treaty.' Thus, a material breach by one party, and *a fortiori* an entire category of states parties to a contract treaty (e.g. the NWS in the NPT Article VI context) will provide strong arguments for the aggrieved category of parties to the treaty (e.g. the NNWS in the NPT Article VI context) pursuant to VCLT Article 60, to suspend the operation of the treaty as between themselves and the breaching state(s).[53]

---

[53] Yael Ronen comes to essentially the same legal conclusion regarding VCLT Article 60 in her book *The Iran Nuclear Issue* (2010).

5

Developments after 2008: Change and Continuity

It is against this backdrop of the policies and treaty interpretations particularly of NPT NWS during the target period of this volume's primary study, that we can lastly move on to consider patterns of change and continuity in the policies and actions of NPT NWS since the end of the target era in 2008. As this volume is being finished in the summer of 2010, this latter period constitutes only approximately eighteen months, which in other areas of international legal inquiry might not constitute a sufficiently long duration of time to justify an entire final chapter. However, the past eighteen months have witnessed such significant developments in international law and politics regarding nuclear energy and nuclear weapons, that to not include a review of this relatively short yet eventful period in this study's consideration would leave the study incomplete and untimely.

The changes that have occurred in the direction of NWS nuclear policies and approaches toward the NPT since the end of 2008 can be traced primarily to the change in government administration in the United States from the Presidency of George W. Bush to the Presidency of Barack Obama. President Obama has not only changed U.S. policy in significant ways, but has also provided a leadership role, looked to by other NWS, for facilitation of changes to the nuclear policies of other NWS as well.

I. 2009

The first sign of a change in U.S. policy on nuclear weapons came in dramatic fashion in a speech given by President Obama on April 5, 2009 in Prague, Czech Republic:

So today, I state clearly and with conviction America's commitment to seek the peace and security of a world without nuclear weapons. I'm not naive. This goal will not be reached quickly—perhaps not in my lifetime. It will take patience and persistence [...] Now, let me describe to you the trajectory we need to be on. First, the United States will take concrete steps towards a world without nuclear weapons. To put an end to Cold War thinking, we will reduce the role of nuclear weapons in our national security strategy, and urge others to do the same [...] To reduce our warheads and stockpiles, we will negotiate a new Strategic Arms Reduction Treaty with the Russians this year [...] And this will set the stage for further cuts, and we will seek to include all nuclear weapons states in this endeavor. To achieve a global ban on nuclear testing, my administration will immediately and aggressively pursue U.S. ratification of the Comprehensive Test Ban Treaty [...] And to cut off the building blocks needed for a bomb, the United States will seek a new treaty that verifiably ends the production of fissile materials intended for use in state nuclear weapons.[1]

Obama's formally stated commitment to a policy of nuclear disarmament—the actual complete elimination of nuclear weapons from its national arsenal—was the first time a U.S. President had made such a commitment.[2] As Obama then proceeds to spell out the steps the United States will take, some of which (e.g. a diminished role for nuclear weapons in military policy) were in fact changes of course and some of which (e.g. a new START treaty) were continuations of older initiatives, these actions are fundamentally re-contextualized as parts of a progressive, programmatic move toward this ultimate policy end. In his Prague speech and in later speeches, Obama essentially changed U.S. nuclear weapons policy to a disarmament posture, in contrast to its longstanding arms control posture.

Shortly after the Prague speech, in May of 2009, NPT parties met in New York City for the third and final session of the Preparatory Committee for the 2010 NPT Review Conference. This was the first NPT meeting at which officials of the Obama administration would be in attendance on behalf of the United States. U.S. Representative Rose Gottemoeller's statement to the 2009 PrepCom was undeniably more balanced in the attention it gave to each of the three principled pillars of the NPT than U.S. statements during the previous decade had been. Its tone was less aggressive on non-proliferation issues, and it gave more serious consideration to disarmament issues in particular, following on from President Obama's policy statements in Prague.

On Article IV peaceful use issues, Gottemoeller's statement was more of a mixed bag, with language more clearly recognizing 'the right of all states to benefit from the peaceful use of nuclear energy,' but at the same time supporting policy initiatives such as a multilateral fuel bank which had been championed by the

---

[1] Remarks by U.S. President Barack Obama, Hradcany Square, Prague, Czech Republic, April 5, 2009.

[2] Catherine M. Kelleher and Scott L. Warren, 'Getting to Zero Starts Here: Tactical Nuclear Weapons,' 39(8) *Arms Control Today* (October 2009) 6; ('Although President Ronald Reagan declared an end goal of zero nuclear weapons, it never became a formal policy position. The Obama administration has stated that all arms control agreements will be based on the premise of getting to zero.') See also Randy Rydell, 'The Future of Nuclear Arms: A World United and Divided by Zero,' 39(3) *Arms Control Today* (April 2009) 21–25.

previous administration. There was some change to the U.S. position on fuel banks, however. Instead of envisioning a multilateral fuel bank as a requisite condition of supply, as it had been envisioned by President Bush, Gottemoeller's statement seemed to abandon that conditional link, and said only that such a fuel bank could:

reassure countries embarking on or expanding nuclear power programs and complying fully with their non-proliferation obligations that they could reliably purchase reactor fuel in the event of commercial supply disruption. It could also demonstrate to them that it is not necessary to pursue expensive enrichment and reprocessing facilities to exploit nuclear energy for peaceful purposes.[3]

Other states participating in the PrepCom voiced their recognition and appreciation of the new policy direction of the U.S. particularly on disarmament. The representative of Cuba, speaking on behalf of the Non-Aligned Movement stated:

We meet at a challenging time, one in which opportunity to achieve progress in the disarmament pillar—long neglected by key states—is now in sight. The U.S. and the Russian Federation are increasingly willing to reconsider the number and type of nuclear weapons that they harbor and to reduce their stockpiles, building on previous agreements. Their announcement to work towards implementation of Article Vi of the NPT is indeed a welcome gesture. Concrete steps towards total elimination of nuclear weapons by nuclear weapons states should follow in an irreversible, verifiable and transparent manner.[4]

These statements and other statements by NWS and NNWS at the 2009 PrepCom raised hopes significantly for a successful Review Conference in 2010—hopes which had not been high after the divisive failure of the 2005 Review Conference.

In September of 2009, President Obama himself chaired a meeting of the U.N. Security Council—the first time a U.S. President has ever chaired a meeting of the Security Council—at which the Council unanimously approved a U.S.-drafted resolution on nuclear security and disarmament. Resolution 1887, which was not adopted under the Council's Chapter VII authority, resolves 'to create the conditions for a world without nuclear weapons,' and to that end encourages states to engage in a number of efforts related to nuclear disarmament

[3] Statement by Rose Gottemoeller, Assistant Secretary of State for Verification, Compliance and Implementation, on Behalf of the United States of America, to the General Debate of the Third Session of the Preparatory Committee for the 2010 Review Conference of the States Parties to the Treaty on the Non-proliferation of Nuclear Weapons, May 5, 2009.

[4] Statement by H.E. Ambassador Abelardo Moreno, Permanent Representative of Cuba to the United Nations on Behalf of the group of Non-Aligned States Parties to the Treaty on the Non-proliferation of Nuclear Weapons, to the General Debate of the Third Session of the Preparatory Committee for the 2010 Review Conference of the States Parties to the Treaty on the Non-proliferation of Nuclear Weapons, May 4, 2009.

and nuclear security. Resolution 1887 does not itself create any particularly new legal obligations in the area of nuclear disarmament. It essentially restates and supports a number of already existing legal obligations, and identifies and supports efforts to create new obligations. However, Resolution 1887 is important, and may mark a significant re-orientation of the work of the Security Council from its work over the previous decade in the nuclear area, which focused almost exclusively on dealing with non-proliferation-related 'problem cases' like North Korea and Iran.[5] Resolution 1887 is rather a unanimous statement by the Security Council supporting nuclear disarmament and calling upon U.N. member states to redouble their efforts to achieve this goal.

In its treatment of NPT Article IV peaceful use issues, however, Resolution 1887 again displays essential continuity from the policy positions espoused by NPT NWS (who are also of course the permanent five members of the U.N. Security Council) over the previous decade. The resolution '[c]alls upon states to adopt stricter national controls for the export of sensitive goods and technologies of the nuclear fuel cycle' and encourages further work on establishing multilateral fuel banks. Even more disturbingly from an NPT interpretation perspective, Resolution 1887:

Encourages States to require as a condition of nuclear exports that the recipient State agree that, in the event that it should terminate, withdraw from, or be found by the IAEA Board of Governors to be in non-compliance with its IAEA safeguards agreement, the supplier state would have a right to require the return of nuclear material and equipment provided prior to such termination, non-compliance or withdrawal, as well as any special nuclear material produced through the use of such material or equipment; [and]

Encourages States to consider whether a recipient State has signed and ratified an additional protocol based on the model additional protocol in making nuclear export decisions [...]

The restrictions and conditions on nuclear supply which the Security Council here encourages states to adopt would appear to be based upon interpretations of both Article III and Article IV of the NPT which had been maintained by NWS and particularly U.S. officials during the previous decade, and which have been demonstrated in the previous chapters of this book, to be erroneous.

On October 9, 2009 came the surprising news that President Obama would be awarded the Nobel Peace Prize. In its official statement of award, the Nobel Committee explained that in awarding the prize, it 'attached special importance to Obama's vision of and work for a world without nuclear weapons [...] [which has] powerfully stimulated disarmament and arms control negotiations.'

---

[5] See Daniel H. Joyner, 'Can International Law Protect States from the Security Council?: Nuclear Non-proliferation and the U.N. Security Council in a Multipolar World,' in Matthew Happold, ed., *International Law in a Multipolar World* (2010).

II. 2010

The significant changes in U.S. policy particularly on the subject of nuclear weapons disarmament in 2009 set the stage for three separate, yet interrelated, high-profile events in 2010.

A. Nuclear Posture Review

First, on April 6, 2010 the United States released a new Nuclear Posture Review (NPR). This was the first comprehensive statement of U.S. policy regarding nuclear weapons since the previous NPR was released in 2002, and the policy changes reflected in the 2010 NPR were significant.[6] The 2010 NPR further formalized in U.S. policy a progressive disarmament posture with regard to the existing U.S. nuclear weapons arsenal. It explained the rationale behind this policy change thus:

The massive nuclear arsenal we inherited from the Cold War era of bipolar military confrontation is poorly suited to address the challenges posed by suicidal terrorists and unfriendly regimes seeking nuclear weapons. Therefore, it is essential that we better align our nuclear policies and posture to our most urgent priorities—preventing nuclear terrorism and nuclear proliferation [...] [F]undamental changes in the international security environment in recent years—including the growth of unrivaled U.S. conventional military capabilities, major improvements in missile defenses, and the easing of Cold War rivalries—enable us to fulfill those objectives at significantly lower nuclear force levels and with reduced reliance on nuclear weapons. Therefore, without jeopardizing our traditional deterrence and reassurance goals, we are now able to shape our nuclear weapons policies and force structure in ways that will better enable us to meet our most pressing security challenges.[7]

Further, it recognized, as officials from the previous administration had been reluctant to do, the inherent link between nuclear disarmament and nuclear non-proliferation:

By reducing the role and numbers of U.S. nuclear weapons—meeting our NPT Article VI obligation to make progress toward nuclear disarmament—we can put ourselves in a much stronger position to persuade our NPT partners to join with us in adopting the measures needed to reinvigorate the non-proliferation regime and secure nuclear materials worldwide [...] By working to reduce the salience of nuclear weapons in international affairs and moving step-by-step toward eliminating them, we can reverse the growing expectation that we are destined to live in a world with more nuclear-armed states, and decrease incentives for additional countries to hedge against an uncertain future by pursuing nuclear options of their own.[8]

---

[6] For more on the 2002 NPR, see Daniel H. Joyner, *International Law and the Proliferation of Weapons of Mass Destruction* (2009) ch 1.
[7] At p. v.   [8] At pp. v–vi.

Not to be overlooked, this excerpt also contains language which constitutes a significant change in legal interpretation of Article VI from that maintained by Christopher Ford and other Bush-era U.S. officials. Here the obligation in NPT Article VI is termed to be an obligation 'to make progress toward nuclear disarmament.' A far cry from Ford's 'good faith effort toward negotiations' on disarmament.[9]

Perhaps the most important sections of the NPR are those devoted to a revision of U.S. policy regarding the role of nuclear weapons in U.S. security strategy. As the NPR states:

The fundamental role of U.S. nuclear weapons, which will continue as long as nuclear weapons exist, is to deter nuclear attack on the United States, our allies, and partners. During the Cold War, the United States reserved the right to use nuclear weapons in response to a massive conventional attack by the Soviet Union and its Warsaw Pact allies. Moreover, after the United States gave up its own chemical and biological weapons (CBW) pursuant to international treaties (while some states continue to possess or pursue them), it reserved the right to employ nuclear weapons to deter CBW attack on the United States and its allies and partners. Since the end of the Cold War, the strategic situation has changed in fundamental ways. With the advent of U.S. conventional military preeminence and continued improvements in U.S. missile defenses and capabilities to counter and mitigate the effects of CBW, the role of U.S. nuclear weapons in deterring non-nuclear attacks—conventional, biological, or chemical—has declined significantly. The United States will continue to reduce the role of nuclear weapons in deterring non-nuclear attacks. To that end, the United States is now prepared to strengthen its long-standing 'negative security assurance' by declaring that the United States will not use or threaten to use nuclear weapons against non-nuclear weapons states that are party to the NPT and in compliance with their nuclear non-proliferation obligations.[10]

Disarmament advocates had hoped that the 2010 NPR would revise the U.S. negative security assurance to provide for a commitment by the U.S. not to use nuclear weapons except in response to an actual or imminent nuclear attack. And while the NPR did recognize this as the 'fundamental role' of U.S. nuclear weapons, the actual commitment expressed in the report was rather more nuanced and enigmatic. It is a commitment by the U.S. not to threaten or use nuclear weapons against non-nuclear weapon states 'that are party to the NPT and in compliance with their nuclear non-proliferation obligations.' And in fact there are further caveats to this commitment:

Given the catastrophic potential of biological weapons and the rapid pace of bio-technology development, the United States reserves the right to make any adjustment in the assurance that may be warranted by the evolution and proliferation of the biological weapons threat and U.S. capacities to counter that threat. In the case of

---

[9] Christopher A. Ford, 'Debating Disarmament: Interpreting Article VI of the Treaty on the Non-Proliferation of Nuclear Weapons,' 14(3) *Non-proliferation Review* (November 2007) 403, 411.
[10] At pp. vii–viii.

countries not covered by this assurance—states that possess nuclear weapons and states not in compliance with their nuclear non-proliferation obligations—there remains a narrow range of contingencies in which U.S. nuclear weapons may still play a role in deterring a conventional or CBW attack against the United States or its allies and partners. The United States is therefore not prepared at the present time to adopt a universal policy that deterring nuclear attack is the sole purpose of nuclear weapons, but will work to establish conditions under which such a policy could be safely adopted.[11]

With regard to the primary terms of the commitment—that of no-first-use against non-nuclear weapon states 'that are party to the NPT and in compliance with their nuclear non-proliferation obligations'—the most problematic element is clearly the latter clause requiring compliance with 'nuclear non-proliferation obligations.' The NPR does not provide any further meaning to this term. One must assume that the provisions of the NPT themselves would be contained within the term 'nuclear non-proliferation obligations.' Another almost certainly intended inclusion is the provision of NPT NNWS safeguard agreements with the IAEA. More questionable is whether subsidiary arrangement agreements entered into between the IAEA and NNWS, pursuant to Article 39 of a standard INFCIRC/153 safeguards agreement, are contemplated for inclusion in this term's scope.[12]

Determining which legal provisions are included in the term 'nuclear non-proliferation obligations' is not the only challenging aspect of this stipulation in the U.S. no-first-use commitment. By far the more challenging is the question of the evidence to which U.S. authorities would look to determine that the limiting force of this stipulation has been triggered. There are also unresolved semantic questions regarding the term 'compliance.'

The essential question on evidence is simply, who gets to decide when an NPT NNWS is not in compliance with the NPT? Is this to be a unilateral judgment made by U.S. authorities? Or one only recognized by the U.S. once a competent international judicial body has made the determination? One can only assume that the former is contemplated. Next, what about compliance with IAEA safeguards agreements? Here, there is, as discussed in detail in Chapter 4, authority given in the IAEA Statute to the IAEA Board of Governors to determine that an NNWS party to a safeguards agreement is in noncompliance with the terms of that agreement. But here is the question of semantics. When the NPR uses the term 'compliance,' does it intend to refer to compliance as defined in the IAEA Statute? Or does it rather intend to refer to compliance in the sense of treaty compliance *à la* Article 60 of the VCLT—i.e. the absence of material breach of a treaty?

---

[11] At p. viii.

[12] For more on subsidiary arrangements, see Daniel Joyner 'The Qom Enrichment Facility: Was Iran Legally Bound to Disclose?' JURIST (jurist.law.pitt.edu), March 5, 2010. Available at <http://jurist.law.pitt.edu/forumy/2010/03/qom-enrichment-facility-was-iran.php>.

It will be recalled that in Chapter 4 above, I concluded that a determination by the IAEA that a NNWS is in noncompliance with its safeguards agreement is not *per se* equivalent to or constitutive of a determination of material breach of the safeguards agreement. I concluded rather that a determination of safeguards agreement noncompliance by the IAEA is better interpreted to comprise a preliminary technical finding of treaty noncompliance, short of material breach, which results in explicitly detailed rights and responsibilities of the IAEA under Article XII of its Statute.

So, again, who gets to decide when a state is in noncompliance with its IAEA safeguards agreement such that the U.S. commitment of no-first-use no longer applies to it? The IAEA? The ICJ? The U.S. unilaterally? The NPR does not tell us, and we are thus left with a great deal of uncertainty as to the contours and means of determination of the principal condition to the 2010 U.S. NPR's no-first-use commitment.[13]

Finally, the 2010 NPR is noteworthy for its position on tactical nuclear weapons. The regulation and reduction of tactical, or battlefield usable, nuclear weapons has never been addressed through non-proliferation treaties. All reductions in tactical nuclear weapons have been accomplished through unilateral undertakings, with the expectation of reciprocity. The Bush administration in the U.S. pursued programs for the development of new and more effective generations of tactical nuclear weapons, even as it was signing and implementing agreements, including the 2002 Moscow Treaty, for the progressive elimination of its strategic nuclear stockpile.[14] The primary military usefulness of these new tactical nuclear weapons was perceived to be their ability to defeat hard and deeply buried targets (HDBT) which even the most sophisticated 'bunker buster' conventional bombs could not reach.[15]

The 2010 NPR appears to change this policy direction of qualitative improvement to the U.S. tactical nuclear weapons arsenal when it states:

The United States will not develop new nuclear warheads. Life Extension Programs (LEPs) will use only nuclear components based on previously tested designs, and will not support new military missions or provide for new military capabilities.[16]

However, this change may not be as unambiguous or as sweeping as it first appears. Much will depend upon how the Obama administration interprets the terms 'new nuclear warheads' and 'new military capabilities' in implementation of this new policy. As Tom Collina has explained:

---

[13] There is also of course the serious question of whether, with all of its caveats and stipulations, this new U.S. policy statement is in line with international law on the question of the use of nuclear weapons. This area of law was rather infamously treated by the ICJ in its primary holding in its 1996 Advisory Opinion, *Advisory Opinion on the Threat or Use of Nuclear Weapons*, ICJ Reports, 1996.

[14] See David A. Koplow, *Death by Moderation: The U.S. Military's Quest for Useable Weapons* (2009) ch 5.

[15] See ibid. at 111.   [16] At p. xiv.

Another issue is how the administration defines a 'nuclear weapon' in the context of its no-new-nuclear-weapons pledge. For example, the Air Force plans to begin work in fiscal year 2011 on a new, nuclear-capable long-range cruise missile, according to Department of Defense budget documents. The new missile would replace the current B-52 bomber-delivered air-launched cruise missile (ALCM) that is now in service but slated for retirement by 2030. ALCMs are armed with W80-1 nuclear warheads. Would the new missile count as a new nuclear weapon? According to an administration source, Obama's reference to 'nuclear weapons' was specific to nuclear warheads, not delivery systems such as missiles and airplanes. Indeed, in addition to the new cruise missile, the administration is moving ahead with a variety of nuclear-capable delivery systems, such as the F-35 Joint Strike Fighter, a replacement for the Ohio-class nuclear-armed submarine, and the modernization of existing strategic ballistic missiles such as the land-based Minuteman III and submarine-based Trident II.[17]

B. 2010 Prague Treaty

The second event, which occurred on April 8, 2010, only two days after the release of the NPR, was the signing by the U.S. and Russia of a new arms reduction treaty to replace the 1991 START I Treaty, which had expired in 2009. This new treaty has so far been referred to interchangeably as 'the New START Treaty' or as 'the Prague Treaty.'

The most important provisions of the Prague Treaty are those which legally obligate both the U.S. and Russia to reduce the number of deployed strategic warheads in their arsenals to 1550 warheads each. As the official White House fact sheet boasts, this limit on warheads is '74% lower than the limit of the 1991 START Treaty and 30% lower than the deployed strategic warhead limit of the 2002 Moscow Treaty.'[18] The treaty further provides for a legal limit for both parties of 800 ICBM launchers, SLBM launchers, and nuclear-equipped heavy bombers. Finally, it provides for a separate limit of 700 deployed ICBMs, deployed SLBMs, and deployed nuclear-equipped heavy bombers. Under the treaty, which has at the time of writing not yet been ratified by either state, the parties are to achieve these limits on their arsenals by 2017.

While the above-quoted statement by the White House regarding the warhead limits agreed to in the Prague Treaty, and their relationship to the limits agreed to in previous treaties, is technically correct, there has been a good deal of criticism regarding the accounting terms in the treaty which allow such statements to be made. As Hans Kristensen has observed:

[W]hile the treaty reduces the legal *limit* for deployed strategic warheads, it doesn't actually reduce the *number* of warheads. Indeed, the treaty does not require destruction of a single nuclear warhead and actually permits the United States and Russia to deploy almost

---

[17] 'What is a "New" Nuclear Weapon?' 40(3) *Arms Control Today* (April 2010) 30, 32.
[18] Available at <http://www.whitehouse.gov/the-press-office/key-facts-about-new-start-treaty>.

the same number of strategic warheads that were permitted by the 2002 Moscow Treaty.[19]

Kristensen is referring here to the new counting rule in the Prague Treaty which fictitiously attributes only one deployed nuclear weapon to each nuclear-equipped heavy bomber. Thus, an American B-52 bomber counts as only one deployed nuclear weapon under the treaty's counting method, even though a B-52 can, depending on its configuration, carry more than twenty nuclear weapons at a time. Similarly, Russian heavy bombers can carry up to sixteen nuclear weapons at a time.

This is a new counting rule under the Prague Treaty, which broke from the formula used in the 2002 Moscow Treaty. One implication of this new counting rule, according to Kristensen, is that:

with the 'fake' bomber counting rule the United States and Russia could, if they chose to do so, deploy more strategic warheads under the New START Treaty by 2017 than would have been allowed by the Moscow Treaty by 2012.[20]

While conceding that Kristensen's calculations are correct, Jeffrey Lewis argues that, when viewed holistically, the Prague Treaty's limiting provisions are a modest yet significant step forward from previous agreements including START I and the 2002 Moscow Treaty. Lewis argues that warhead-accounting rules under all three of these treaties have been fictitious in one way or another. He argues that the real value of the Prague Treaty is that, while it doesn't definitively limit nuclear warheads themselves, it does put a clear cap on the number of delivery units for nuclear weapons. As Lewis states:

While the number of warheads is important, the real key to the Prague Treaty is the numerical limit on deployed delivery vehicles—700. Seven hundred is the number of Minuteman III missiles, Trident missiles and B1, B2 and B52 bombers. The United States wanted a much lower warhead number than did the Russians, who were only willing to budge on warhead numbers if the US came down on delivery vehicles. So, the two numbers are tightly integrated.[21]

Lewis's arguments are compelling that the overall significance of the Prague Treaty is in providing for modest yet significant reductions to the nuclear arsenals of the U.S. and Russia, and as importantly in constituting a continuation of diplomatic and legal engagement between the Cold War rivals in furthering the agenda of progressive nuclear arms reduction.

---

[19] 'New START Treaty Has New Counting,' FAS Strategic Security Blog (<http://www.fas.org>), March 29, 2010. Available at <http://www.fas.org/blog/ssp/2010/03/newstart.php>.
[20] 'New START Treaty Has New Counting,' FAS Strategic Security Blog (<http://www.fas.org>), March 29, 2010. Available at <http://www.fas.org/blog/ssp/2010/03/newstart.php>.
[21] 'Prague Treaty Cuts are Modest, Real,' ArmsControlWonk.com, April 5, 2010. Available at <http://www.armscontrolwonk.com/2682/prague-treaty-cuts-are-modest-real>.

C. NPT Review Conference

With the April release of the U.S. Nuclear Posture Review and its amended policy positions particularly on nuclear weapons disarmament, and the signing days later of the Prague Treaty apparently actualizing these policies in part, there appeared to be considerable momentum for a successful NPT Review Conference in May, 2010. This positive momentum was welcome, as all delegates to the Review Conference remembered only too well the unsuccessful and acrimonious 2005 Review Conference, which failed to produce a consensus final document.

The Review Conference lasted for twenty-four days, between May 4 and May 28, 2010. In the end, a consensus final document was agreed to by the conference, to the relief of many. Before moving on to an analysis of the final document itself, we should first take note of the statements made by NWS officials during the course of the Review Conference. Overall, these statements were uniformly more balanced in their prioritization as between the three principled pillars of the NPT than NWS statements had typically been during the 1998–2008 decade. Disproportionate prioritization of the non-proliferation pillar was not clearly evident in any of the NWS statements, or in their combined statement.

The statements adopted a more positive tone and a more encouraging message regarding peaceful uses of nuclear energy generally, often taking note of the 'virtues' of the peaceful atom. Particular examples of this include the joint statement of the NWS to the Review Conference which states:

We note the increasing demand for nuclear energy and stress its potential in addressing climate change, in facilitating achievement of the Millenium Development Goals and sustainable development, in providing energy security and in addressing vital non-power applications such as nuclear medicine, agriculture and industry.[22]

Similarly, in Russia's opening statement to the Review Conference, the Russian representative read a message from Russian President Dmitry Medvedev in which he notes:

'The peaceful atom' is playing the growing role in satisfying energy demand of the world economy. Existing and future nuclear power plants are instrumental to the economic growth, raising living standards of the millions of people.[23]

These laudatory statements are a far cry indeed from Russian Representative Anatoly Antonov's statement to the 2008 NPT PrepCom, in which he made the following observation, cited previously, with regard to the maintenance and spread of indigenous enrichment capabilities by developing states:

---

[22] Statement by the People's Republic of China, France, the Russian Federation, the United Kingdom of Great Britain and Northern Ireland, and the United States of America to the 2010 Non-Proliferation Treaty Review Conference.

[23] Statement by the Deputy Minister of Foreign Affairs of the Russian Federation, Sergey A Ryabkov, at the 2010 Review Conference of the Parties to the Treaty on the Non-Proliferation of Nuclear Weapons, May 4, 2010.

We can see today that countries are increasingly interested in developing nuclear energy as a reliable resource ensuring their energy security [...] First of all, those should be taken to supply countries developing their own atomic energy with nuclear fuel in a reliable and assured manner. One way is that every country can establish its own facilities to enrich uranium, produce fuel and further reprocess it. Yet, it is a very complicated process not only in terms of funds, but also in terms of intellectual, scientific, physical and technical resources. Is moving along this path justified when the world market is capable of meeting both current and future needs in this area? It is unlikely so.[24]

The most important change present in the statements of NWS officials at the 2010 RevCon, however, is in the area of the disarmament pillar of the NPT. Here, there is a sea change in both tone and substance from NWS statements made during the target decade of this study. Not without irony, this change was led by the United States. U.S. Secretary of State Hillary Clinton stated in her opening address to the conference:

We also recognize our responsibility as a nuclear weapons state to move toward disarmament, and that is exactly what we are doing.[25]

Expressing the same sentiment, but with more detail and clarity, the joint statement of the NWS to the 2010 RevCon states:

As nuclear-weapon States, we reaffirm our enduring commitment to the fulfillment of our obligations under Article VI of the NPT and our continuing responsibility to take concrete and credible steps towards irreversible disarmament, including provisions for verification.[26]

This is a truly remarkable statement in light of the minimalist interpretations of the obligation in Article VI that were evident in NWS statements during the 1998–2008 decade, as reviewed above. Recognizing that Article VI establishes an obligation 'to take concrete and credible steps towards irreversible disarmament,' is nothing less than a sea change from interpretations of Article VI espoused by NWS officials like John Bolton, Andrew Semmel, and Christopher Ford.

However, perhaps the most noteworthy of the statements of NWS officials to the 2010 RevCon is the statement by the representative of the United Kingdom, John Duncan. It is a statement like no other among NWS statements since 2000. The statement begins with the following paragraph:

The Final Document of the 2000 Review Conference set out thirteen practical steps for the systematic and progressive efforts to implement Article VI of the NPT. The following

[24] Statement by H.E. Ambassador Anatoly Antonov, Head of the Delegation of the Russian Federation at the Second Session of the Preparatory Committee for the 2010 Review Conference of the Parties to the Treaty on the Non-Proliferation of Nuclear Weapons, April 28, 2008.

[25] United States Statement to the NPT Review Conference, May 3, 2010, by U.S. Secretary of State Hillary Clinton.

[26] Statement by the People's Republic of China, France, the Russian Federation, the United Kingdom of Great Britain and Northern Ireland, and the United States of America to the 2010 Non-Proliferation Treaty Review Conference.

table sets out the UK's *progress to date* against the Thirteen Steps towards nuclear disarmament.[27]

The rest of the statement consists in its entirety of a tabulated representation, wherein the left column of the table lists the thirteen steps in order from the 2000 Review Conference Final Document, and corresponding rows in the right column give information on the efforts of the U.K. to comply with each respective step in turn.

Why is this so remarkable? First, it is a general statement by an NWS party wholly devoted to the issue of disarmament. Second, the substance and format of the statement implicitly and quite clearly accepts the thirteen steps from the 2000 Final Document as having interpretive meaning in the context of NPT Article VI. This is a singular effort on the part of the U.K., and one to be complimented for its clarity of organization, and accuracy of interpretation.

The Final Document itself is long and complex, and deciphering its often coded provisions to produce meaning and identify change or continuity is challenging. However, the 2010 Review Conference Final Document does contain some remarkable language manifesting progress and dynamic change on a number of key issues. Before reviewing these passages, it is important to remember that, as reviewed above, this document in its manifestations of 'subsequent agreement between the parties regarding the interpretation of the treaty or the application of its provisions,' has legal significance for the interpretation of the provisions of the NPT.[28] In the specific context of the 2010 Review Conference Final Document, the portion of the text which represents the fully negotiated, consensus agreement of the parties to the NPT is the section entitled 'Conclusions and recommendations for follow-on actions,' which begins at page nineteen of the Final Document. Pages one through eighteen of the document comprise a report by the President of the conference, Ambassador Libran Cabactulan of the Philippines, on the discussions which took place in conference sessions. While the entirety of the final document was adopted by the conference by consensus, only the section entitled 'Conclusions and recommendations for follow-on actions' represents the consensus agreements of the parties to the NPT.

On NPT Article IV and peaceful use issues, the Final Document calls on all states to:

Respect each country's choices and decisions in the field of peaceful uses of nuclear energy without jeopardizing its policies or international cooperation agreements and arrangements for peaceful uses of nuclear energy and its fuel cycle policies.[29]

This is an important statement of interpretation of the right to peaceful use in Article IV, recognizing that every NPT party has the essential freedom to

---

[27] U.K. Statement to the 2010 Non-Proliferation Treaty Review Conference by Ambassador John Duncan, Ambassador for Multilateral Arms Control and Disarmament, May 19, 2010.
[28] VCLT Article 31(3)(a). See Burrus Carnahan, 'Treaty Review Conferences,' 81 *American Journal of International Law* (1987) 226, 229.   [29] Action 47.

determine how it wishes to exercise this right, in a manner most in keeping with its sovereign interests, apparently including the indigenous development and maintenance of the full nuclear fuel cycle. It further recognizes that other NPT parties, and in particular supplier states, should respect those determinations and not restrict peaceful nuclear cooperation with a developing state simply because that state's determination of the means of exercising its Article IV rights is not the determination that the supplier state wishes it would be.

In addressing the subject of multilateral fuel bank proposals, the Final Document calls on all NPT parties to:

Continue to discuss further [...] the development of multilateral approaches to the nuclear fuel cycle, including the possibilities of creating mechanisms for assurance of nuclear fuel supply, as well as possible schemes dealing with the back-end of the fuel cycle without affecting rights under the Treaty and without prejudice to national fuel cycle policies [...][30]

The importance of this paragraph lies in its explicit caveat that multilateral approaches to peaceful nuclear fuel supply should not attempt to circumscribe in any way the right of all states to indigenously develop and maintain full nuclear fuel cycle capability. This interpretive statement should be seen as disharmonious with and corrective of the extreme interpretations of the conditionality of the Article IV right maintained by NWS officials during the target decade of this study, and used by them to justify exclusive-source multilateral fuel bank proposals.

On Article VI and disarmament, there is interpretive gold to be found in the 2010 Review Conference Final Document. There are statements of interpretation in this document which should put to conclusive rest many of the arguments of the limited nature of the Article VI obligation, and the juridical/interpretive irrelevance of the thirteen steps from the 2000 Review Conference Final Document, that were previously maintained by NWS officials notably including Christopher Ford. As the 2010 Final Document states by consensus agreement:

The Conference reaffirms the unequivocal undertaking of the nuclear-weapon States to accomplish the total elimination of their nuclear arsenals leading to nuclear disarmament, to which all States parties are committed under Article VI.[31]

In the same section the conference 'agrees on the following Action Plan on nuclear disarmament which includes concrete steps for the total elimination of nuclear weapons [...]' In this Action Plan are listed, *inter alia*, the following 'principles and objectives':

iii. The Conference reaffirms the continued validity of the practical steps agreed to in the Final Document of the 2000 NPT Review Conference.

---

[30] Action 58.   [31] Principles and Objectives I(A)ii, p. 19.

v. The Conference expresses its deep concern at the catastrophic humanitarian consequences of any use of nuclear weapons, and reaffirms the need for all States at all times to comply with applicable international law, including international humanitarian law.

The Final Document goes on to note:

The Conference reaffirms the urgent need for the nuclear-weapon States to implement the steps leading to nuclear disarmament agreed to in the Final Document of the 2000 NPT Review Conference [...]

The Conference affirms the need for the nuclear-weapon States to reduce and eliminate all types of their nuclear weapons and encourages in particular those States with the largest nuclear arsenals to lead efforts in this regard.

The Conference recognizes the legitimate interests of non-nuclear-weapon States in the constraining by the nuclear weapon States of the development and qualitative improvement of nuclear weapons and ending the development of advanced new types of nuclear weapons.

Finally, in Action 5 of the agreed Action Plan, the NWS themselves specifically

commit to accelerate concrete progress on the steps leading to nuclear disarmament, contained in the Final Document of the 2000 NPT Review Conference, in a way that promotes international stability, peace and undiminished and increased security.

The remainder of Action 5 is a list of activities with a view to which the NWS are 'called upon to promptly engage [...]' At the end of this list, the NWS are 'called upon to report the above undertakings to the Preparatory Committee at 2014.' The Action Plan concludes by stating that '[t]he 2015 Review Conference will take stock and consider the next steps for the full implementation of Article VI.'

III. Summary Analysis of Change and Continuity Post-2008

Since the end of 2008, there has undeniably been very significant and welcome change in the policy of NWS parties generally, and the United States in particular, on the subject of nuclear weapons disarmament and the interpretation of NPT Article VI. U.S. President Obama deserves the lion's share of credit for this dramatic turnaround and, in my opinion, deserves the Nobel Peace Prize for the reasons cited by the Nobel Committee, among which was particularly mentioned his 'vision of and work for a world without nuclear weapons.' These changes in policy have brought the U.S., in particular, much closer into compliance with the thirteen steps agreed upon in the 2000 Review Conference Final Document.

Even more fundamentally, as one author has observed, the events of 2009–2010 may well constitute a historical pivot point, or paradigm shift in the way we collectively think and talk about nuclear weapons, and from now on all nuclear weapons regulation and reduction efforts will be more clearly contextualized within the communal policy goal of the complete elimination of nuclear weapons from national arsenals.[32] This would indeed be a Nobel-worthy achievement.

However, while not taking anything away from these accomplishments in para-digm shifting with regard to nuclear weapons disarmament, it must also be noted that there has been a more mixed record of change and continuity in the past eighteen months on the subject of the peaceful use of nuclear energy and the interpretation of NPT Article IV. At the 2009 PrepCom and the 2010 RevCon, the statements of NWS officials have adopted a much more positive and encouraging tone on issues of peaceful nuclear energy, and on its spread and its virtues for helping humanity and in particular developing countries. These statements represent a welcome rhetorical return to the Atoms for Peace principles enunciated by U.S. President Eisenhower in 1953, which underpin the Statute of the IAEA and the NPT.

And in terms of interpretation of Article IV, the 2010 Review Conference Final Document does appear in places to correct some of the erroneous legal interpretations maintained by NWS officials during the target era of this study. This has been combined with statements by NWS officials in the past eighteen months which have seemed to drop the exclusive sourcing requirement with regard to multilateral fuel cycle sources.

However, along with these changes there has also been significant continuity in the statements and actions of NWS since 2008 on other aspects of Article IV interpreta-tion and related policy. A number of NWS, including the United States, continue to push for the creation of multilateral fuel banks to supply NNWS with nuclear fuel. As President Obama himself said in his 2009 Prague speech, such a fuel bank will allow countries to access peaceful power 'without increasing the risk of proliferation.'[33] This is code which can be paraphrased as 'without those countries needing indigen-ous fuel cycle capability.' While the tone of NWS officials toward peaceful nuclear energy has turned more positive and encouraging over the past eighteen months, the message of internationalizing the sourcing of nuclear fuel (read: sourcing fuel from the West) and the nuclear fuel cycle in order to provide an alternative to NNWS domestic development of fuel cycle capabilities, has not changed.

For their part, NNWS developing countries continue to be suspicious of inter-national fuel bank proposals, and generally in opposition to them, for a number of reasons. First, they have memories. They know the conceptual provenance of multilateral fuel bank proposals and their origin in the Bush administration. They remember the original and clearly stated aspect of exclusive sourcing that accompanied these proposals. They fear that the new tone of the Obama administration only puts sheep's clothing on the original wolfish idea.[34]

---

[32] See Jeffrey Lewis, 'The Pivot,' ArmsControlWonk.com, April 7, 2010. Available at <http://www.armscontrolwonk.com/2686/the-pivot>.

[33] Remarks by U.S. President Barack Obama, Hradcany Square, Prague, Czech Republic, April 5, 2009.

[34] See Patricia Lewis, 'Prospects for the NPT and the 2010 Review Conference,' 40(2) *Arms Control Today* (March 2010) 19 ('The various proposals for multinational approaches to the nuclear

Second, and relatedly, they fear that, once established, multilateral fuel banks could provide a powerful *de facto* rhetorical argument to NWS. Even if exclusive sourcing is not formally attached to the fuel bank agreements, NWS could argue once fuel banks and multinational enrichment centers are up and running that it is now truly unnecessary for developing NNWS to maintain indigenous fuel cycle capability, and that NNWS of good will wishing to aid in the cause of non-proliferation will exclusively source their fuel from these international sources. This argument could eventually be issue-linked with other trade and economic decisions to pressure NNWS into 'voluntarily' giving up their indigenous fuel cycle capabilities. This argument might find traction in the Nuclear Suppliers Group, and NWS adherents to the NSG may convince the group of supplier states to adopt stricter standards for export of enrichment and other fuel cycle technology.

This is not mere speculation. In June of 2009, well into the Obama administration, the United States proposed just such a set of revised and tightened standards for adoption by the NSG. The proposal was defeated after concern was expressed by developing state NSG members Turkey, Brazil, South Korea, and South Africa, among others.[35] However, the United States appears committed to continuing the push for more restrictive NSG standards on export of enrichment technologies—a position which does not sit easily with recent NWS statements extolling the potential benefits to humanity to be realized from the spread of peaceful nuclear energy production capacity.[36]

Furthermore, on the subject of the IAEA Additional Protocol, both the U.S. Nuclear Posture Review and U.N. Security Council Resolution 1887 call specifically for the IAEA Additional Protocol to be made a condition of peaceful nuclear supply.

Finally, there are still problematic policy positions maintained by NWS which betray the continuance of erroneous legal interpretations of NPT Article IV, and in particular the relationship between Article IV and Article III. For example, in her opening statement to the 2010 NPT Review Conference, U.S. Secretary of State Hillary Clinton stated:

fuel cycle and assurance of supply are having a difficult time gaining traction in the developing world. There are persistent fears that the nuclear supplier countries are plotting price-fixing cartels and that they have a long term aim of infringing on Article 4 rights.')

[35] 'Accord on New Rules Eludes Nuclear Suppliers,' 39(6) *Arms Control Today* (July/August 2009) 29.

[36] For the most recent developments on this issue at the NSG, see Elaine Grossman, 'Turkish Opposition Prolongs Deadlock on Proposed Nuclear Trade Guidelines,' *Global Security Newswire*, July 2, 2010; Daniel Horner, 'NSG Makes Little Headway at Meeting,' 40(6) *Arms Control Today* (July/August 2010) 45:

Meanwhile, at their June 25–26 meeting in Muskoka, Canada, the Group of Eight (G-8) industrialized countries extended their policy to adopt on a national basis the proposed NSG guidelines on enrichment and reprocessing transfers. The leaders of Canada, France, Germany, Italy, Japan, Russia, the United Kingdom, and the United States said in their summit communiqué, 'We reiterate our commitment as found in paragraph 8 of the L'Aquila Statement on Non-Proliferation.' Paragraph 8 of the L'Aquila statement, issued at the July 2009 G-8 summit in Italy, said the eight countries

Potential violators must know that they will pay a high price if they break the rules, and that is certainly not the case today. The international community's record of enforcing compliance in recent years is unacceptable. So we need to consider automatic penalties for the violation of safeguards agreements such as suspending all international nuclear cooperation or IAEA technical cooperation projects until compliance has been restored.[37]

Linking safeguards noncompliance to cooperation on peaceful nuclear supply in this way is an essential continuance of Bush-era policies found in the previous chapters herein to be based upon erroneous legal interpretations of NPT Articles III and IV, and to constitute actions unlawfully prejudicial to the legitimate legal interests of NNWS under the NPT grand bargain.[38]

Earlier, in July 2009, while discussing recommendations the U.K. would make for discussion at the NPT Review Conference in 2010, Prime Minister Gordon Brown said:

I think we will probably want to have a more tough regime, that the onus will be on the countries that don't have nuclear weapons to prove that they don't have nuclear weapons […] At the moment, one of the problems that we've had with Iran is the question of whether you can prove or not if someone is developing a nuclear weapon.[39]

This sort of burden shifting is, again, an essential continuance of legally erroneous and prejudicial policies maintained during the pre-2009 target decade, and manifests a continuing unbalanced policy position on the three NPT pillars.

Erroneous interpretations of NPT Articles III and IV have unfortunately become widespread, among non-NWS officials and even within the legal academy.[40] It is my hope that the analysis in this book will aid in correcting these and other misinterpretations of the NPT, and in restoring balance to the three principled pillars of the NPT, which together comprise the NPT's grand bargain.

would implement as 'national policy' for a year the draft NSG guidelines on enrichment and reprocessing and urged the NSG 'to accelerate its work and swiftly reach consensus this year to allow for global implementation of a strengthened mechanism on transfers of enrichment and reprocessing facilities, equipment, and technology.'

[37] United States Statement to the NPT Review Conference, May 3, 2010, by U.S. Secretary of State Hillary Clinton.

[38] The July 2010 report issued by the U.S. State Department, entitled *Adherence to and Compliance with Arms Control, Nonproliferation, and Disarmament Agreements and Commitments*, is replete with interpretive errors regarding Iran and the NPT. On pp. 3 and 62, it makes the bald assertion that Iran is in breach of NPT Article III, without providing any compelling arguments establishing this allegation. It even, quite enigmatically, argues on p. 67 that alleged noncompliance by Iran with its Subsidiary Arrangements agreement with the IAEA constitutes a violation of NPT Article III. Again, no legal argument supporting this assertion (indeed, in my opinion there could be none) is attempted in the report.

[39] 'UK PM to Set Out Plan for Nuclear Talks,' Jane Wardell, Associated Press, July 9, 2009.

[40] See, e.g., John Carlson, 'Defining Noncompliance: NPT Safeguards Agreements,' 39(4) *Arms Control Today* (May 2009) 22 ('Noncompliance with an NPT safeguards agreement constitutes violation of Article III of the NPT, the obligation to accept safeguards on all nuclear material […]'); N. Jansen Calamita, 'Sanctions, Countermeasures, and the Iranian Nuclear Issue,' 42 *Vanderbilt Journal of Transnational Law* (2009) 1393, 1397; 'Taking Stock of the NPT: An Interview with U.S. Special Representative Susan Burk,' *Arms Control Today* (March 2010) 10.

ANNEX I

Treaty on the Non-Proliferation of Nuclear Weapons

Treaty on the Non-Proliferation of Nuclear Weapons

Signed at Washington, London, and Moscow July 1, 1968

Entered into force March 5, 1970

The States concluding this Treaty, hereinafter referred to as the 'Parties to the Treaty',

Considering the devastation that would be visited upon all mankind by a nuclear war and the consequent need to make every effort to avert the danger of such a war and to take measures to safeguard the security of peoples,

Believing that the proliferation of nuclear weapons would seriously enhance the danger of nuclear war,

In conformity with resolutions of the United Nations General Assembly calling for the conclusion of an agreement on the prevention of wider dissemination of nuclear weapons,

Undertaking to cooperate in facilitating the application of International Atomic Energy Agency safeguards on peaceful nuclear activities,

Expressing their support for research, development and other efforts to further the application, within the framework of the International Atomic Energy Agency safeguards system, of the principle of safeguarding effectively the flow of source and special fissionable materials by use of instruments and other techniques at certain strategic points,

Affirming the principle that the benefits of peaceful applications of nuclear technology, including any technological by-products which may be derived by nuclear-weapon States from the development of nuclear explosive devices, should be available for peaceful purposes to all Parties of the Treaty, whether nuclear-weapon or non-nuclear weapon States,

Convinced that, in furtherance of this principle, all Parties to the Treaty are entitled to participate in the fullest possible exchange of scientific information for, and to contribute alone or in cooperation with other States to, the further development of the applications of atomic energy for peaceful purposes,

Declaring their intention to achieve at the earliest possible date the cessation of the nuclear arms race and to undertake effective measures in the direction of nuclear disarmament,

Urging the cooperation of all States in the attainment of this objective,

Recalling the determination expressed by the Parties to the 1963 Treaty banning nuclear weapon tests in the atmosphere, in outer space and under water in its Preamble to seek to achieve the discontinuance of all test explosions of nuclear weapons for all time and to continue negotiations to this end,

Desiring to further the easing of international tension and the strengthening of trust between States in order to facilitate the cessation of the manufacture of nuclear weapons, the liquidation of all their existing stockpiles, and the elimination from national arsenals of nuclear weapons and the means of their delivery pursuant to a Treaty on general and complete disarmament under strict and effective international control,

Recalling that, in accordance with the Charter of the United Nations, States must refrain in their international relations from the threat or use of force against the territorial integrity or political independence of any State, or in any other manner inconsistent with the Purposes of the United Nations, and that the establishment and maintenance of international peace and security are to be promoted with the least diversion for armaments of the world's human and economic resources,

Have agreed as follows:

Article I

Each nuclear-weapon State Party to the Treaty undertakes not to transfer to any recipient whatsoever nuclear weapons or other nuclear explosive devices or control over such weapons or explosive devices directly, or indirectly; and not in any way to assist, encourage, or induce any non-nuclear weapon State to manufacture or otherwise acquire nuclear weapons or other nuclear explosive devices, or control over such weapons or explosive devices.

Article II

Each non-nuclear-weapon State Party to the Treaty undertakes not to receive the transfer from any transferor whatsoever of nuclear weapons or other nuclear explosive devices or of control over such weapons or explosive devices directly, or indirectly; not to manufacture or otherwise acquire nuclear weapons or other nuclear explosive devices; and not to seek or receive any assistance in the manufacture of nuclear weapons or other nuclear explosive devices.

Article III

1. Each non-nuclear-weapon State Party to the Treaty undertakes to accept safeguards, as set forth in an agreement to be negotiated and concluded with the International Atomic Energy Agency in accordance with the Statute of the International Atomic Energy Agency and the Agency's safeguards system, for the exclusive purpose of verification of the fulfillment of its obligations assumed under this Treaty with a view to preventing diversion of nuclear energy from peaceful uses to nuclear weapons or other nuclear explosive devices. Procedures for the safeguards required by this article shall be followed with respect to source or special fissionable material whether it is being produced, processed, or used

in any principal nuclear facility or is outside any such facility. The safeguards required by this article shall be applied to all source or special fissionable material in all peaceful nuclear activities within the territory of such State, under its jurisdiction, or carried out under its control anywhere.

2. Each State Party to the Treaty undertakes not to provide: (a) source or special fissionable material, or (b) equipment or material especially designed or prepared for the processing, use or production of special fissionable material, to any non-nuclear-weapon State for peaceful purposes, unless the source or special fissionable material shall be subject to the safeguards required by this article.

3. The safeguards required by this article shall be implemented in a manner designed to comply with article IV of this Treaty, and to avoid hampering the economic or technological development of the Parties or international cooperation in the field of peaceful nuclear activities, including the international exchange of nuclear material and equipment for the processing, use or production of nuclear material for peaceful purposes in accordance with the provisions of this article and the principle of safeguarding set forth in the Preamble of the Treaty.

4. Non-nuclear-weapon States Party to the Treaty shall conclude agreements with the International Atomic Energy Agency to meet the requirements of this article either individually or together with other States in accordance with the Statute of the International Atomic Energy Agency. Negotiation of such agreements shall commence within 180 days from the original entry into force of this Treaty. For States depositing their instruments of ratification or accession after the 180-day period, negotiation of such agreements shall commence not later than the date of such deposit. Such agreements shall enter into force not later than eighteen months after the date of initiation of negotiations.

Article IV

1. Nothing in this Treaty shall be interpreted as affecting the inalienable right of all the Parties to the Treaty to develop research, production and use of nuclear energy for peaceful purposes without discrimination and in conformity with articles I and II of this Treaty.

2. All the Parties to the Treaty undertake to facilitate, and have the right to participate in, the fullest possible exchange of equipment, materials and scientific and technological information for the peaceful uses of nuclear energy. Parties to the Treaty in a position to do so shall also cooperate in contributing alone or together with other States or international organizations to the further development of the applications of nuclear energy for peaceful purposes, especially in the territories of non-nuclear-weapon States Party to the Treaty, with due consideration for the needs of the developing areas of the world.

Article V

Each party to the Treaty undertakes to take appropriate measures to ensure that, in accordance with this Treaty, under appropriate international observation and through appropriate international procedures, potential benefits from any peaceful applications of nuclear explosions will be made available to non-nuclear-weapon States Party to the Treaty on a nondiscriminatory basis and that the charge to such Parties for the explosive devices used will be as low as possible and exclude any charge for research and development. Non-nuclear-weapon States Party to the Treaty shall be able to obtain such benefits, pursuant to a special international agreement or agreements, through an appropriate international body with adequate representation of non-nuclear-weapon States. Negotiations on this subject shall commence as soon as possible after the Treaty enters into force. Non-nuclear-weapon States Party to the Treaty so desiring may also obtain such benefits pursuant to bilateral agreements.

Article VI

Each of the Parties to the Treaty undertakes to pursue negotiations in good faith on effective measures relating to cessation of the nuclear arms race at an early date and to nuclear disarmament, and on a Treaty on general and complete disarmament under strict and effective international control.

Article VII

Nothing in this Treaty affects the right of any group of States to conclude regional treaties in order to assure the total absence of nuclear weapons in their respective territories.

Article VIII

1. Any Party to the Treaty may propose amendments to this Treaty. The text of any proposed amendment shall be submitted to the Depositary Governments which shall circulate it to all Parties to the Treaty. Thereupon, if requested to do so by one-third or more of the Parties to the Treaty, the Depositary Governments shall convene a conference, to which they shall invite all the Parties to the Treaty, to consider such an amendment.

2. Any amendment to this Treaty must be approved by a majority of the votes of all the Parties to the Treaty, including the votes of all nuclear-weapon States Party to the Treaty and all other Parties which, on the date the amendment is circulated, are members of the Board of Governors of the International Atomic Energy Agency. The amendment shall enter into force for each Party that deposits its instrument of ratification of the amendment upon the deposit of such instruments of ratification by a majority of all the Parties, including the instruments of ratification of all nuclear-weapon States Party to the Treaty and all other Parties which, on the date the amendment is circulated, are members of the Board of Governors of the International Atomic Energy Agency. Thereafter, it shall enter into force for any other Party upon the deposit of its instrument of ratification of the amendment.

3. Five years after the entry into force of this Treaty, a conference of Parties to the Treaty shall be held in Geneva, Switzerland, in order to review the operation of this Treaty with a view to assuring that the purposes of the Preamble and the provisions of the Treaty are being realized.

At intervals of five years thereafter, a majority of the Parties to the Treaty may obtain, by submitting a proposal to this effect to the Depositary Governments, the convening of further conferences with the same objective of reviewing the operation of the Treaty.

Article IX

1. This Treaty shall be open to all States for signature. Any State which does not sign the Treaty before its entry into force in accordance with paragraph 3 of this article may accede to it at any time.

2. This Treaty shall be subject to ratification by signatory States. Instruments of ratification and instruments of accession shall be deposited with the Governments of the United States of America, the United Kingdom of Great Britain and Northern Ireland and the Union of Soviet Socialist Republics, which are hereby designated the Depositary Governments.

3. This Treaty shall enter into force after its ratification by the States, the Governments of which are designated Depositaries of the Treaty, and forty other States signatory to this Treaty and the deposit of their instruments of ratification. For the purposes of this Treaty, a nuclear-weapon State is one which has manufactured and exploded a nuclear weapon or other nuclear explosive device prior to January 1, 1967.

4. For States whose instruments of ratification or accession are deposited subsequent to the entry into force of this Treaty, it shall enter into force on the date of the deposit of their instruments of ratification or accession.

5. The Depositary Governments shall promptly inform all signatory and acceding States of the date of each signature, the date of deposit of each instrument of ratification or of accession, the date of the entry into force of this Treaty, and the date of receipt of any requests for convening a conference or other notices.

6. This Treaty shall be registered by the Depositary Governments pursuant to article 102 of the Charter of the United Nations.

Article X

1. Each Party shall in exercising its national sovereignty have the right to withdraw from the Treaty if it decides that extraordinary events, related to the subject matter of this Treaty, have jeopardized the supreme interests of its country. It shall give notice of such withdrawal to all other Parties to the Treaty and to the United Nations Security Council three months in advance. Such notice shall include a statement of the extraordinary events it regards as having jeopardized its supreme interests.

2. Twenty-five years after the entry into force of the Treaty, a conference shall be convened to decide whether the Treaty shall continue in force indefinitely, or shall be extended for an additional fixed period or periods. This decision shall be taken by a majority of the Parties to the Treaty.

Article XI

This Treaty, the English, Russian, French, Spanish and Chinese texts of which are equally authentic, shall be deposited in the archives of the Depositary Governments. Duly certified copies of this Treaty shall be transmitted by the Depositary Governments to the Governments of the signatory and acceding States.

IN WITNESS WHEREOF the undersigned, duly authorized, have signed this Treaty.

DONE in triplicate, at the cities of Washington, London and Moscow, this first day of July one thousand nine hundred sixty-eight.

ANNEX II

Atoms for Peace

U.S. President Dwight Eisenhower's 'Atoms for Peace' Speech
December 8, 1953

Before the General Assembly of the United Nations on Peaceful
Uses of Atomic Energy

Madame President, Members of the General Assembly:

When Secretary General Hammarskjold's invitation to address this General Assembly reached me in Bermuda, I was just beginning a series of conferences with the Prime Ministers and Foreign Ministers of Great Britain and of France.

Our subject was some of the problems that beset our world.

During the remainder of the Bermuda Conference, I had constantly in mind that ahead of me lay a great honor. That honor is mine today as I stand here, Privileged to address the General Assembly of the United Nations.

At the same time that I appreciate the distinction of addressing you, I have a sense of exhilaration as I look upon this Assembly.

Never before in history has so much hope for so many people been gathered together in a single organization. Your deliberations and decisions during these somber years have already realized part of those hopes.

But the great test and the great accomplishments still lie ahead. And in the confident expectation of those accomplishments, I would use the office which, for the time being, I hold, to assure you that the Government of the United States will remain steadfast in its support of this body. This we shall do in the conviction that you will provide a great share of the wisdom, the courage, and the faith which can bring to this world lasting peace for all nations, and happiness and well-being for all men.

Clearly, it would not be fitting for me to take this occasion to present to you a unilateral American report on Bermuda. Nevertheless, I assure you that in our deliberations on that lovely island we sought to invoke those same great concepts of universal peace and human dignity which are so clearly etched in your Charter.

Neither would it be a measure of this great opportunity merely to recite, however hopefully, pious platitudes.

I therefore decided that this occasion warranted my saying to you some of the things that have been on the minds and hearts of my legislative and executive associates and on mine for a great many months—thoughts I had originally planned to say primarily to the American people.

I know that the American people share my deep belief that if a danger exists in the world, it is a danger shared by all—and equally, that if hope exists in the mind of one nation, that hope should be shared by all.

Finally, if there is to be advanced any proposal designed to ease even by the smallest measure the tensions of today's world, what more appropriate audience could there be than the members of the General Assembly of the United Nations?

I feel impelled to speak today in a language that in a sense is new—one which I, who has spent so much of my life in the military profession, would have preferred never to use. That new language is the language of atomic warfare.

The atomic age has moved forward at such a pace that every citizen of the world should have some comprehension, at least in comparative terms, of the extent of this development of the utmost significance to every one of us. Clearly, if the people of the world are to conduct an intelligent search for peace, they must be armed with the significant facts of today's existence.

My recital of atomic danger and power is necessarily stated in United States terms, for these are the only incontrovertible facts that I know. I need hardly point out to this Assembly, however, that this subject is global, not merely national in character.

On July 16, 1945, the United States set off the world's first atomic explosion. Since that date in 1945, the United States of America has conducted 42 test explosions.

Atomic bombs today are more than 25 times as powerful as the weapons with which the atomic age dawned, while hydrogen weapons are in the ranges of millions of tons of TNT equivalent.

Today, the United States' stockpile of atomic weapons, which, of course, increases daily, exceeds by many times the explosive equivalent of the total of all bombs and all shells that came from every plane and every gun in every theatre of war in all of the years of World War II.

A single air group, whether afloat or land-based, can now deliver to any reachable target a destructive cargo exceeding in power all the bombs that fell on Britain in all of World War II.

In size and variety, the development of atomic weapons has been no less remarkable. The development has been such that atomic weapons have virtually achieved conventional status within our armed services. In the United States, the Army, the Navy, the Air Force, and the Marine Corps are all capable of putting this weapon to military use.

But the dread secret, and the fearful engines of atomic might, are not ours alone.

In the first place, the secret is possessed by our friends and allies, Great Britain and Canada, whose scientific genius made a tremendous contribution to our original discoveries, and the designs of atomic bombs.

The secret is also known by the Soviet Union. The Soviet Union has informed us that, over recent years, it has devoted extensive resources to atomic weapons. During this period, the Soviet Union has exploded a series of atomic devices, including at least one involving thermo-nuclear reactions.

If at one time the United States possessed what might have been called a monopoly of atomic power, that monopoly ceased to exist several years ago. Therefore, although our earlier start has permitted us to accumulate what is today a great quantitative advantage, the atomic realities of today comprehend two facts of even greater significance.

First, the knowledge now possessed by several nations will eventually be shared by others—possibly all others.

Second, even a vast superiority in numbers of weapons, and a consequent capability of devastating retaliation, is no preventive, of itself, against the fearful material damage and toll of human lives that would be inflicted by surprise aggression.

The free world, at least dimly aware of these facts, has naturally embarked on a large program of warning and defense systems. That program will be accelerated and expanded.

But let no one think that the expenditure of vast sums for weapons and systems of defense can guarantee absolute safety for the cities and citizens of any nation. The awful arithmetic of the atomic bomb does not permit any such easy solution. Even against the most powerful defense, an aggressor in possession of the effective minimum number of atomic bombs for a surprise attack could probably place a sufficient number of his bombs on the chosen targets to cause hideous damage.

Should such an atomic attack be launched against the United States, our reactions would be swift and resolute. But for me to say that the defense capabilities of the United States are such that they could inflict terrible losses upon an aggressor—for me to say that the retaliation capabilities of the United States are so great that such an aggressor's land would be laid waste—all this, while fact, is not the true expression of the purpose and the hope of the United States.

To pause there would be to confirm the hopeless finality of a belief that two atomic colossi are doomed malevolently to eye each other indefinitely across a trembling world. To stop there would be to accept helplessly the probability of civilization destroyed—the annihilation of the irreplaceable heritage of mankind handed down to us generation from generation—and the condemnation of mankind to begin all over again the age-old struggle upward from savagery toward decency, and right, and justice.

Surely no sane member of the human race could discover victory in such desolation. Could anyone wish his name to be coupled by history with such human degradation and destruction.

Occasional pages of history do record the faces of the 'Great Destroyers' but the whole book of history reveals mankind's never-ending quest for peace, and mankind's God-given capacity to build.

It is with the book of history, and not with isolated pages, that the United States will ever wish to be identified. My country wants to be constructive, not destructive. It wants agreement, not wars, among nations. It wants itself to live in freedom, and in the confidence that the people of every other nation enjoy equally the right of choosing their own way of life.

So my country's purpose is to help us move out of the dark chamber of horrors into the light, to find a way by which the minds of men, the hopes of men, the souls of men everywhere, can move forward toward peace and happiness and well-being.

In this quest, I know that we must not lack patience. I know that in a world divided, such as ours today, salvation cannot be attained by one dramatic act.

I know that many steps will have to be taken over many months before the world can look at itself one day and truly realize that a new climate of mutually peaceful confidence is abroad in the world.

But I know, above all else, that we much start to take these steps—now.

The United States and its allies, Great Britain and France, have over the past months tried to take some of these steps. Let no one say that we shun the conference table.

On the record has long stood the request of the United States, Great Britain, and France to negotiate with the Soviet Union the problems of a divided Germany.

On that record has long stood the request of the same three nations to negotiate the problems of Korea.

Most recently, we have received from the Soviet Union what is in effect an expression of willingness to hold a Four Power meeting. Along with our allies, Great Britain and France, we were pleased to see that this note did not contain the unacceptable preconditions previously put forward.

As you already know from our joint Bermuda communiqué, the United States, Great Britain, and France have agreed promptly to meet with the Soviet Union.

The Government of the United States approaches this conference with hopeful sincerity. We will bend every effort of our minds to the single purpose of emerging from that conference with tangible results toward peace—the only true way of lessening international tension.

We never have, we never will, propose or suggest that the Soviet Union surrender what is rightfully theirs. We will never say that the people of Russia are an enemy with whom we have no desire ever to deal or mingle in friendly and fruitful relationship.

On the contrary, we hope that this coming Conference may initiate a relationship with the Soviet Union which will eventually bring about a free intermingling of the peoples of the east and of the west—the one sure, human way of developing the understanding required for confident and peaceful relations.

Instead of the discontent which is now settling upon Eastern Germany, occupied Austria, and countries of Eastern Europe, we seek a harmonious family of free European nations, with none a threat to the other, and least of all a threat to the peoples of Russia.

Beyond the turmoil and strife and misery of Asia, we seek peaceful opportunity for these peoples to develop their natural resources and to elevate their lives.

These are not idle words or shallow visions. Behind them lies a story of nations lately come to independence, not as a result of war, but through free grant or peaceful negotiation. There is a record, already written, of assistance gladly given by nations of the west to needy peoples, and to those suffering the temporary effects of famine, drought, and natural disaster.

These are deeds of peace. They speak more loudly than promises or protestations of peaceful intent. But I do not wish to rest either upon the reiteration of past proposals or the restatement of past deeds. The gravity of the time is such that every new avenue of peace, no matter how dimly discernible, should be explored.

These is at least one new avenue of peace which has not yet been well explored—an avenue now laid out by the General Assembly of the United Nations.

In its resolution of November 18th, 1953 this General Assembly suggested—and I quote—'that the Disarmament Commission study the desirability of establishing a sub-committee consisting of representatives of the Powers principally involved, which should seek in private an acceptable solution...and report on such a solution to the General Assembly and to the Security Council not later than 1 September 1954.'

The United States, heeding the suggestion of the General Assembly of the United Nations, is instantly prepared to meet privately with such other countries as may be 'principally involved,' to seek 'an acceptable solution' to the atomic armaments race which overshadows not only the peace, but the very life, of the world.

We shall carry into these private or diplomatic talks a new conception.

The United States would seek more than the mere reduction or elimination of atomic materials for military purposes.

It is not enough to take this weapon out of the hands of the soldiers. It must be put into the hands of those who will know how to strip its military casing and adapt it to the arts of peace.

The United States knows that if the fearful trend of atomic military build-up can be reversed, this greatest of destructive forces can be developed into a great boon, for the benefit of all mankind.

The United States knows that peaceful power from atomic energy is no dream of the future. That capability, already proved, is here—now—today. Who can doubt, if the entire body of the world's scientists and engineers had adequate amounts of fissionable material with which to test and develop their ideas, that this capability would rapidly be transformed into universal, efficient, and economic usage.

To hasten the day when fear of the atom will begin to disappear from the minds of people, and the governments of the East and West, there are certain steps that can be taken now.

I therefore make the following proposals:

The Governments principally involved, to the extent permitted by elementary prudence, to begin now and continue to make joint contributions from their stockpiles of normal uranium and fissionable materials to an international Atomic Energy Agency. We would expect that such an agency would be set up under the aegis of the United Nations.

The ratios of contributions, the procedures and other details would properly be within the scope of the 'private conversations' I have referred to earlier.

The United States is prepared to undertake these explorations in good faith. Any partner of the United States acting in the same good faith will find the United States a not unreasonable or ungenerous associate.

Undoubtedly initial and early contributions to this plan would be small in quantity. However, the proposal has the great virtue that it can be undertaken without the irritations and mutual suspicions incident to any attempt to set up a completely acceptable system of world-wide inspection and control.

The Atomic Energy Agency could be made responsible for the impounding, storage, and protection of the contributed fissionable and other materials. The ingenuity of our scientists will provide special safe conditions under which such a bank of fissionable material can be made essentially immune to surprise seizure.

The more important responsibility of this Atomic Energy Agency would be to devise methods whereby this fissionable material would be allocated to serve the peaceful pursuits of mankind. Experts would be mobilized to apply atomic energy to the needs of agriculture, medicine, and other peaceful activities. A special purpose would be to provide abundant electrical energy in the power-starved areas of the world. Thus the contributing powers would be dedicating some of their strength to serve the needs rather than the fears of mankind.

The United States would be more than willing—it would be proud to take up with others 'principally involved' the development of plans whereby such peaceful use of atomic energy would be expedited.

Of those 'principally involved' the Soviet Union must, of course, be one.

I would be prepared to submit to the Congress of the United States, and with every expectation of approval, any such plan that would:

First—encourage world-wide investigation into the most effective peacetime uses of fissionable material, and with the certainty that they had all the material needed for the conduct of all experiments that were appropriate;

Second—begin to diminish the potential destructive power of the world's atomic stockpiles;

Third—allow all peoples of all nations to see that, in this enlightened age, the great powers of the earth, both of the East and of the West, are interested in human aspirations first, rather than in building up the armaments of war;

Fourth—open up a new channel for peaceful discussion, and initiate at least a new approach to the many difficult problems that must be solved in both private and public conversations, if the world is to shake off the inertia imposed by fear, and is to make positive progress toward peace.

Against the dark background of the atomic bomb, the United States does not wish merely to present strength, but also the desire and the hope for peace.

The coming months will be fraught with fateful decisions. In this Assembly; in the capitals and military headquarters of the world; in the hearts of men everywhere, be they governors, or governed, may they be decisions which will lead this work out of fear and into peace.

To the making of these fateful decisions, the United States pledges before you—and therefore before the world—its determination to help solve the fearful atomic dilemma—to devote its entire heart and mind to find the way by which the miraculous inventiveness of man shall not be dedicated to his death, but consecrated to his life.

I again thank the delegates for the great honor they have done me, in inviting me to appear before them, and in listening to me so courteously. Thank you.

ANNEX III

Selected US Statements 1998–2009

Contents

Statement by
Dr Andrew K. Semmel
Alternative Representative of the United States of America
To the Second Session of the Preparatory Committee
For the 2005 NPT Review Conference

Peaceful Nuclear Cooperation
NPT Article IV

Geneva, Switzerland May 7, 2003

The United States is strongly committed to the goals of Article IV. Through both multi-lateral and bilateral programs we seek to promote the numerous beneficial peaceful appli-cations of nuclear techniques. One of the most important avenues for peaceful nuclear development is the Technical Cooperation Program of the International Atomic Energy Agency (IAEA).

IAEA Technical-Cooperation

For the past decade the Technical Cooperation Program of the IAEA has focussed increasingly on matching nuclear techniques to the development needs of its Member States. The United States has worked closely with the IAEA Secretariat and other Member States to establish a program of sustainable development activities building on estab-lished and emerging nuclear techniques. We place high priority on maximizing the effec-tive and timely delivery of technical cooperation. Toward that end, we support IAEA's work to strengthen the design of technical cooperation projects, improve the delivery of assistance, and match assistance to the genuine needs of recipients. The U.S. provides substantial financial and technical support to many IAEA technical cooperation initia-tives. We are the single largest donor to the Technical Cooperation Program, providing over twenty-five percent of its funding. In the last two years, we have contributed an additional $1.7 million to IAEA's work on the so-called "Sterile Insect Technique" in Africa, Latin America, and the Mediterranean. We have also assisted IAEA's work in landmine detection in Europe, water resource improvements in Latin America, and rind-erpest eradication in Africa, thereby improving food security in rural African economies.

U.S. Bilateral Cooperation

Complementing our work with the IAEA, the U.S. also engages in numerous bilateral cooperative activities around the world. We currently have twenty-five bilateral agree-ments for peaceful nuclear cooperation with individual states and Euratom—bringing our cooperation partners to forty NPT Parties in all. These agreements provide the necessary legal basis for our peaceful nuclear cooperation with other states. They promote the transfer of significant civil nuclear material, equipment and components under appropriate nonproliferation conditions and controls. Through the U.S.

Agreement for Peaceful Nuclear Cooperation with the IAEA, we carry out similar cooperation activities with a number of other States Parties to the NPT.

Many countries can trace the origins of their peaceful nuclear programs to equipment, material, and technology supplied by the United States under Article IV of the NPT. Much cooperation takes place pursuant to commercial arrangements. Last year alone, our Nuclear Regulatory Commission licensed U.S. companies to transfer equipment, material and components to seventeen countries, all NPT parties in good standing.

A major focus of our Article IV efforts has long been the creation and support of effective nuclear safety infrastructures in recipient countries. Various U.S. government agencies work closely with the IAEA and its Member States to operate scores of safety projects worldwide. In the realm of emergency response, for example, our Department of Energy provides advice to states and international organizations to ensure that nuclear emergency planning meets international standards and provides all necessary protection to workers, the public, and the environment.

Similarly, the U.S. has worked with our Asian colleagues to promote the Asian Extrabudgetary Program, which is improving the safety of nuclear installations in China, Malaysia, Indonesia, Thailand, Philippines, and Vietnam. We have funded projects on reactor accident analysis, assistance in anti-corrosion cracking efforts, and the safety of life extension and decommissioning of reactors. We have also participated in "train-the-trainer" workshops in radiation and waste safety. Ensuring that all national nuclear programs possess a strong foundation of sound nuclear safety principles is an enduring U.S. priority.

Our Nuclear Regulatory Commission also participates in information exchange and cooperative safety research programs with thirty-three other countries. These programs provide communication channels for use in the event of problems at U.S. or other nuclear power plants. They encourage the identification of possible precursor events warranting further investigation. They also encourage interaction among states that are improving their regulatory infrastructures, and represent building blocks for bilateral cooperation on a variety of other safety and security issues.

Adequate national and international liability regimes are also necessary for peaceful nuclear cooperation. We urge all states to sign the Convention on Supplementary Compensation for Nuclear Damage (CSC). This Convention will help establish a global regime to facilitate peaceful nuclear commerce and assure that resources will be available to help compensate victims in the event of a nuclear incident.

The safe transportation of radioactive materials has always been an important priority. The U.S. has worked closely with the IAEA, the International Maritime Organization (IMO) and other international organizations to ensure that a strong international regime with rigorous standards governs such transport. We look forward to the upcoming International Conference on Safety of Transport of Radioactive Materials in Vienna this July. The Conference will be an excellent forum for experts to conduct a technical discussion of current transport safety standards.

Cooperation and Responsibility

Article IV of the NPT provides for the "inalienable right" of all Parties to develop nuclear energy for peaceful purposes. This right is grounded firmly by the Treaty in the clear understanding that such development must be in conformity with the nonproliferation undertakings of Articles I and II. Thus, Article IV does not stand alone or in isolation. *The inalienable right to develop nuclear energy is not an entitlement but rather flows from demonstrable and verifiable compliance with Articles I, II, and III of the Treaty.*

Every NPT Review Conference has explicitly noted the link between peaceful nuclear cooperation and the nonproliferation goals of the NPT. These two pillars of the NPT are closely joined and should be. Fulfillment of nuclear nonproliferation norms and behavior not only is a prerequisite for peaceful nuclear cooperation but also is the paramount concern of the Treaty regime. All of our previous statements have made it clear that our concerns regarding compliance with nonproliferation norms have intensified and deepened. They are central to our views on making the NPT work effectively.

No one could seriously maintain that a country not complying with its NPT nonproliferation obligations should nonetheless have a "right" to benefit from nuclear cooperation. No such unconditional right exists. Regrettably a few NPT parties have clearly abused the Treaty by maintaining the facade of a peaceful nuclear program while secretly acquiring capabilities to produce nuclear weapons. Iraq obtained peaceful nuclear assistance up to the time of the 1990 Gulf War. North Korea built nuclear facilities it claimed were for peaceful energy needs, but which were, as we all know, clearly designed for a nuclear weapons program. In the past year, while constantly professing "transparency," Iran surprised the world with the suddenly-disclosed advanced nature of its nuclear fuel cycle program. This includes facilities with direct application to the production of fissile material for nuclear weapons. The IAEA is now scrutinizing those facilities. In light of the serious unresolved issues posed by Iran's nuclear program, we strongly disagree with Iran's assertion that it has an inherent "right" under Article IV to its program or to receive foreign assistance or cooperation with it.

In all three cases,—Iraq, North Korea, and Iran—NPT parties used apparent compliance with the Treaty to present a peaceful public image. That image and the claimed "right" to a peaceful nuclear program were used to mask access to foreign help in building fissile material production facilities that could support a nuclear weapons capability. In all three cases, the secret programs have been exposed. But for many years, each of these countries was able to use its status as an NPT member "in good standing" to divert attention from its real motivations and to facilitate foreign nuclear assistance.

Responsible NPT parties must not accept such practices. Abuse of the NPT undermines confidence in the Treaty as an effective framework for peaceful nuclear cooperation. It undermines all of our interests. It can lead to enormous losses to development and electricity needs currently met by nuclear power. At the same time, the ability of states to gain peaceful nuclear benefits in the face of legitimate concerns about violations of their NPT obligations devalues the Treaty for the vast majority of parties that honor their Treaty obligations.

All NPT parties in good standing need to reinforce the fundamental principle that Article IV benefits are extended only to NPT parties that are clearly in compliance with Articles I, II, and III. Supplier states must forego assistance to states with suspect nuclear programs until the suspicions are resolved. The mere claim of peaceful intent is not sufficient. We all know that IAEA safeguards can never be an absolute guarantee, but states—especially those with ambitious nuclear programs—must back up their claims of peaceful intent and "transparency" by fully implementing the IAEA's Strengthened Safeguards Additional Protocol.

Nuclear supplier states recognized over twenty-five years ago the sensitivity of enrichment and reprocessing facilities. The first public version of the Nuclear Suppliers Group (NSG) Guidelines urged restraint in the transfer of technology for such facilities, even if they were under IAEA safeguards. The NSG also recommended that when supplying such technology or facilities, full transparency should be incorporated through IAEA or other international involvement in order to eliminate possible misuse. The Guidelines also urged consultations on sensitive cases to ensure a proposed transfer would not contribute to risks of conflict or instability.

These provisions were the direct result of a judgement that enrichment or reprocessing facilities presented a serious proliferation risk, given their direct application to producing fissile material for nuclear weapons. In states where such facilities have dubious economic justification, where nonproliferation credentials are suspect, where covert procurement techniques are used, and especially where IAEA inspections or other disclosures reveal attempts to keep sensitive technology programs secret, the pursuit of enrichment or reprocessing capability sends a strong signal that a state may be seeking nuclear weapons. All responsible NPT parties should recognize the danger inherent in such states possessing the means to produce nuclear weapons material. The DPRK recently illustrated the case for us all.

The unpredictability of the international security environment stands as a stark reminder of the critical need for a strong NPT regime now, and in the future. Article IV is a vital part of a viable NPT regime that the U.S. has actively supported for more than three decades. But Article IV does not exist in a vacuum. To make the NPT's benefits a reality, we must work together to insist that all states fully meet their fundamental obligations under the Treaty.

Thank you Mr. Chairman.

STATEMENT BY
UNITED STATES UNDER SECRETARY OF STATE
FOR ARMS CONTROL AND INTERNATIONAL
SECURITY
JOHN R. BOLTON

to the

THIRD SESSION OF THE PREPARATORY
COMMITTEE FOR THE 2005 REVIEW
CONFERENCE OF THE TREATY ON THE
NON-PROLIFERATION OF NUCLEAR WEAPONS

"The NPT: A Crisis of Non-Compliance"

New York

April 27, 2004

Good morning, Mr. Chairman

It is a pleasure to address the third Preparatory Meeting of the Non-Proliferation Treaty Review Conference. I would like to take this opportunity to congratulate the Chairman on assuming his responsibilities.

The United States supports the Non-Proliferation Treaty and is committed to its goals. But despite our strong support, the support of many NPT countries and the best intentions of most of you here, at least four NPT non-nuclear member countries were or are using the NPT as cover for the development of nuclear weapons. States like Iran are actively violating their treaty obligations, and have gained access to technologies and materials for their nuclear weapons programs. North Korea violated its NPT obligations while a party, and then proved its strategic decision to seek nuclear weapons by withdrawing from the Treaty entirely. Two states in the past—Iraq and Libya—had also violated the NPT. Libya took the important decision to disclose and eliminate its weapons of mass destruction programs, a paradigm that other nations now seeking nuclear weapons should emulate.

There is a crisis of NPT noncompliance, and the challenge before us is to devise ways to ensure full compliance with the Treaty's nonproliferation objectives. Without such compliance by all members, confidence in the security benefits derived from the NPT will erode. To address this serious problem, President Bush recently announced a series of proposals that are aimed at strengthening compliance with the obligations we all undertook when we signed the Treaty. These proposals will address a fundamental problem that has allowed nations like Iran and North Korea to exploit the benefits of NPT membership to develop their nuclear weapons programs. The President is determined to stop rogue states from gaining nuclear weapons under cover of supposed peaceful nuclear technology. As President Bush said on February 11, "Proliferators must not be allowed to cynically manipulate the NPT to acquire the material and infrastructure necessary for manufacturing illegal weapons."

We must resolve to deal firmly and swiftly with countries whose nuclear programs pose a serious threat to the NPT. We must resolve to send a signal to potential Treaty violators that their actions will not be tolerated. We must resolve to take action now or more and more states could be emboldened to follow the lead of Iran and North Korea, and could hide behind the cover of NPT legitimacy while pursuing nuclear weapons technology. As President Bush said, "There is a consensus among nations that proliferation cannot be tolerated. Yet this consensus means little unless it is translated into action. Every civilized nation has a stake in preventing the spread of weapons of mass destruction."

President Bush's Proposals

The U.S. remains strongly committed to its Article VI obligations, and President Bush has made major contributions to the goals of Article VI. The transformation of our relationship with Russia led quickly to a commitment by President Bush to undertake reductions in deployed nuclear weapons to historically low levels. A similar pledge by President Putin soon followed, and both commitments were later codified in the Treaty of Moscow. There are many similar accomplishments, such as the establishment of the Global

Partnership against the spread of WMD, which President Bush has proposed expanding, and which will accomplish much toward ridding the world of WMD materials and equipment. Overall, it is a very impressive record of action that is making the world a safer place.

In order to address loopholes and the crisis of noncompliance with the NPT, President Bush announced four proposals that would strengthen the Treaty and the governance structures of the International Atomic Energy Agency ("IAEA"). The first proposal would close the loophole in the Treaty that allows states such as Iran and North Korea to pursue fissile material for nuclear weapons under peaceful cover. Enrichment and reprocessing plants would be limited to those states that now possess them. Members of the Nuclear Suppliers Group would refuse to sell enrichment and reprocessing equipment and technologies to any state that does not already possess full-scale, functioning enrichment and reprocessing plants. Nuclear fuel supplier states would ensure a reliable supply of nuclear fuel at reasonable prices to all NPT parties in full compliance with the NPT that agreed to forego such facilities. In this way, nations could use peaceful nuclear power as anticipated by the Treaty but not to produce fissile material for nuclear weapons. The Treaty provides no right to such sensitive fuel cycle technologies.

Second, President Bush proposed creating a special committee of the IAEA Board of Governors, to "focus intensively on safeguards and…ensure that nations comply with their international obligations." The Bush Administration is committed to working with the IAEA and its members to ensure that clandestine nuclear activity is uncovered and reported to the United Nations Security Council. As the President said when announcing these proposals, "For international norms to be effective, they must be enforced."

As a third step, the President urged states that are serious about fighting proliferation to approve and implement the Additional Protocol and proposed that, as of the end of 2005, the Additional Protocol be a condition of supply for Nuclear-Suppliers Group-controlled items. While the Additional Protocol is not foolproof, if implemented and rigorously enforced, it would give the IAEA important new tools to detect undeclared nuclear activity. As President Bush said: "Nations that are serious about fighting proliferation will approve and implement the Additional Protocol." There are no excuses; if you wish to be considered a responsible partner and leader in strengthening nuclear nonproliferation, you must be willing to do your share by demonstrating a willingness to assume the obligations of this important new tool. The IAEA has demonstrated over the years that it is able to devise approaches that can protect sensitive or proprietary technology. I urge all states that have not concluded an Additional Protocol to do so at the earliest possible date.

Fourth, the President proposed that we stop states under investigation for NPT and IAEA violations from holding seats on the IAEA Board of Governors or on the new IAEA special committee. As it now stands, states under investigation by the IAEA are allowed to sit in judgment of their own covert nuclear weapons programs as well as those of other rogue states. Violators thus can get a platform to impede effective IAEA action and enforcement against their own secret nuclear weapons efforts. It was outrageous that Iran actually was a member of the Board last year while that body was deliberating how to deal with Iran's nuclear weapons effort. Ensuring that suspect states do not sit on the IAEA Board is particularly important given the Board's tradition of trying to reach decisions by consensus. As the President said, 'The integrity and mission of the IAEA depends on this simple principle: Those actively breaking the rules should not be entrusted with enforcing the rules.'

The Inherent Linkage between Articles II & IV of the NPT

The central bargain of the NPT is that if non-nuclear weapons states renounce the pursuit of nuclear weapons, they may gain assistance in developing civilian nuclear power. This bargain is clearly set forth in Article IV of the Treaty, which states that the Treaty's "right" to develop peaceful nuclear energy is clearly conditioned upon parties complying with Treaty Articles I & II. If a state party seeks to acquire nuclear weapons and thus fails to conform with Article II, then under the Treaty that party forfeits its right to develop peaceful nuclear energy.

To determine whether states are in conformity with Article II, we must be able to verify rigorously compliance with the Treaty. All parties to the NPT should have comprehensive laws and regulations in force to ensure compliance with their obligation not to seek or acquire assistance in developing nuclear weapons. It is our view that non-nuclear weapons states also share the Article I requirement not to assist others to acquire nuclear weapons or the means for their development.

This is even more important after the revelations of the extent of the A.Q. Khan black market network. Khan's network made enormous sums of money selling nuclear designs and equipment to countries with clandestine nuclear programs. The network operated in countries all over the world, including many NPT member states, for purposes of manufacturing, brokering, and transiting nuclear technology. Many of the countries in which the network operated did not even know that nuclear-related black market activities were taking place in their countries.

The United States is willing to work with nations that need to set up efficient export control systems. But nations must also be willing to enforce those controls. President Bush proposed a new Security Council resolution last fall requiring all states to criminalize WMD proliferation, enact strict export controls, and secure all sensitive materials within their borders. And last month, the five Permanent Members of the Security Council circulated a draft resolution. We hope that the Council will adopt that resolution this very week. Once it is passed, we are prepared to assist other governments in drafting and enforcing the new laws that will help stem WMD proliferation.

But verification is not enough. The most air-tight verification regime in the world is worthless if confirmed violations are ignored.

Enforcement is critical. We must increase the costs and reduce the benefits to violators, in ways such as the proliferation Security Initiative now being pursued actively around the world, and which President Bush has proposed strengthening further. We cannot look the other way, out of fear or concern that the cost of enforcement will be borne by those objecting to the violation. We cannot hope the problem will go away. We cannot leave it to "the other guy" to carry the full measure of the challenge of demanding full compliance. We cannot divert attention from the violations we face by focusing on Article VI issues that do not exist. If a party cares about the NPT, then there is a corresponding requirement to care about violations and enforcement.

Iran

We face significant challenges from terrorist-sponsoring regimes that are developing weapons of mass destruction in many forms. Today, I would like to focus on three very different cases, one a major success story for nonproliferation, and two where the nuclear proliferation threat to international peace and security continues to grow.

First, Iran, one of the most fundamental challenges to the non-proliferation regime, which has concealed a large-scale covert nuclear weapons program for over eighteen years. It is clear that Iran draws from many of the same networks that supplied Libya with nuclear technology, components, and materials, including the A.Q. Khan network, as Khan himself has confessed.

It is no surprise that the IAEA has uncovered much evidence of Iran's undeclared activity. There is as yet, however, no reason to believe that Iran has made a strategic decision to abandon its nuclear weapons program and its violation of its NPT Article II obligations. Iran's recent failures to disclose work on uranium enrichment centrifuges of an advanced design and on Polonium-210, and to explain the presence of highly enriched uranium, are clear indicators that Iran continues its quest for nuclear weapons. Following an all-too-familiar pattern, Iran omitted this information from its October 2003 declaration to the IAEA—a declaration that Iran said provided the "full scope of Iranian nuclear activities" and a "complete centrifuge R&D chronology."

Iran has expressed interest in the purchase of up to six additional nuclear power plants, and has told the IAEA that it is pursuing a heavy-water research reactor at Arak—a type of reactor that might be well suited for plutonium production. This ambitious reactor program is a remarkable venture for a country whose oil and gas reserves will last several hundred years. There is no conceivable economic justification for Iran to build costly nuclear fuel cycle facilities to support a small "nuclear power" program. It is clear that the primary role of Iran's "nuclear power" program is to serve as a cover and a pretext for the import of nuclear technology and expertise that can be used to support nuclear weapons development.

Iran's continued deception and delaying tactics have not gone unnoticed by the international community. Despite Iran's massive deception and denial campaign, the IAEA has uncovered a large amount of information indicating numerous major violations of Iran's treaty obligations under its NPT Safeguards Agreement. On the basis of the evidence collected by IAEA inspectors and exhaustively documented in his reports, the Director General has concluded that, "it is clear that Iran has failed in a number of instances over an extended period of time to meet its obligations under its Safeguards Agreement...."

The IAEA Statute requires that the IAEA Board of Governors report noncompliance with safeguards obligations to the United Nations Security Council. In the U.S. view, this standard was clearly met as early as June of last year. Iranian noncompliance with safeguards obligations has been manifest for many months, and both the Board and the Director General have noted Iran's multiple breaches and failures in this regard. We did not press for such a report at the recent March meeting. The IAEA Board will at some point, however, need to fulfill its responsibility under the IAEA Statute to report the safeguards failures found in Iran to the Security Council, as it did in the case of Libya. If Iran continues its unwillingness to comply with the NPT, the Council can then take up this issue as a threat to international peace and security. If the Council is unable to do so, it will not only be a blow to our efforts to hold Iran accountable, but also a blow to the effectiveness of the Council itself and to the credibility of the entire NPT regime.

Iran's oil rich environment, grudging cooperation with the IAEA, its deception, and its 18-year record of clandestine activity leads us to the inevitable conclusion that Iran is lying and that its goal is to develop a nuclear weapon in violation of its Article II commitments. We believe that Iran's stalling tactics clearly indicate that it has not fulfilled even the minimal steps it agreed to last September and again in February. If we permit Iran's deception to go on much longer, it will be too late. Iran will have nuclear weapons.

If Iran wants to restore international confidence in its civilian nuclear program, it must "come clean" and answer satisfactorily all unresolved IAEA questions. Iran must make a clear decision to open up its nuclear program to transparent inspections, including full access under the Additional Protocol, and comply with all of its NPT and IAEA responsibilities. If Iran does not do this, it will remain in violation of Article II of the Treaty and, according to Article IV, will forfeit any right to civilian nuclear power assistance.

North Korea

North Korea's use of the NPT as a cover to hide its nuclear weapons ambitions and its subsequent withdrawal from the Treaty constitute the clearest example of a state cynically manipulating the NPT to threaten the international community with its nuclear weapons program. We now face the danger not only of a North Korea in possession of nuclear weapons, but the risk that it will export fissile material or weapons to other rogue states or to terrorists. Continuous international pressure is essential to ensure the complete, verifiable, and irreversible dismantlement of its nuclear weapons program, including both its plutonium and uranium enrichment programs. The United States continues to support the Six-Party Process, but we have long said that we will measure success in the talks through concrete progress. Simply continuing to talk, however, is not progress. And as Vice President Cheney recently stated in China, "Time is not necessarily on our side." We urge all member states to support the Six-Party talks aimed at achieving a peaceful, diplomatic end to North Korea's nuclear programs.

Libya

On December 19, 2003, Libya announced that it would voluntarily rid itself of its WMD equipment and programs. Libya declared its intention to comply in full with the NPT and to sign the Additional Protocol. All of these remarkable steps, Libya announced, would be undertaken "in a transparent way that could be proved, including accepting immediate international inspection."

Libya has made enormous progress toward fulfilling these commitments. In cooperation with the United States, the United Kingdom, and the IAEA, Libya has dismantled its known nuclear weapons program. In cooperation with the United Kingdom, Libya and the IAEA, we removed nuclear weapon design documents, gas centrifuge components designed to enrich uranium, containers of uranium hexafluoride (UF6), a uranium conversion facility, and 15 kilograms of fresh high-enriched uranium reactor fuel which was removed to Russia.

As Colonel Qadaffi said recently in his speech to the Organization of African Unity, "The security of Libya does not come from the nuclear bomb, the nuclear bomb represents a danger to the country which has them." If they wish to rejoin the community of civilized nations, states like Iran and North Korea could learn from Libya's recent example. On December 19, 2003, when Libya made its WMD commitment, the President of the United States indicated that fulfillment of Libya's commitment would open the way for better relations with the United States. We meant exactly that. Last week the President decided to terminate application of the Iran and Libya Sanctions Act ("ILSA") on Libya. The President is changing the Executive Order sanctions under the International Emergency Economic Powers Act that will enable trade with Libya. The United States will not be the only nation that seeks to improve its relations with Libya, but based upon changed behavior by the Libyan regime, we believe that these steps toward better relations are warranted. As President Bush said in February, "Abandoning the pursuit of illegal weapons can lead to better relations with the United States, and other free nations. Continuing to seek those weapons will not bring security or international prestige, but only political isolation, economic hardship, and other unwelcome consequences."

Conclusion

As I said at the outset, the United States is committed to a strong and effective nuclear non-proliferation regime. But the time for business as usual is over. An irresponsible handful of nations not living up to their Treaty commitments are undermining the NPT's mission. Without full compliance by all NPT members, confidence in the NPT as a non-proliferation instrument erodes. What will eventually result is a world with an ever-growing number of states possessing nuclear weapons, where terrorists and rogue states would have expanded access to nuclear technology and expertise. In such a world, the risk of catastrophic attacks against civilized nations would be far greater.

The President's initiatives aim to prevent such a scenario, and I urge you to lend your full support to them. We must be mindful that only transparency, rigorous verification, and firm political resolve against violators can shore up confidence in the NPT. After all, the Treaty can only be as strong as our will to insist that states comply with it.

President Announces New Measures to Counter the Threat of WMD

Remarks by the President on Weapons of Mass Destruction Proliferation
Fort Lesley J. McNair—National Defense University Washington, D.C.

2:30 P.M. EST

THE PRESIDENT: Thanks for the warm welcome. I'm honored to visit the National Defense University. For nearly a century, the scholars and students here have helped to prepare America for the changing threats to our national security. Today, the men and women of our National Defense University are helping to frame the strategies through which we are fighting and winning the war on terror. Your Center for Counterproliferation Research and your other institutes and colleges are providing vital insight into the dangers of a new era. I want to thank each one of you for devoting your talents and your energy to the service of our great nation.

I want to thank General Michael Dunn for inviting me here. I used to jog by this facility on a regular basis. Then my age kicked in. (Laughter.) I appreciate Ambassador Wolfgang Ischinger, from Germany. Mr. Ambassador, thank you for being here today. I see my friend, George Shultz, a distinguished public servant and true patriot, with us. George, thank you for coming; and Charlotte, it's good to see you. I'm so honored that Dick Lugar is here with us today. Senator, I appreciate you taking time and thanks for bringing Senator Saxby Chambliss with you, as well. I appreciate the veterans who are here and those on active duty. Thanks for letting me come by.

On September the 11th, 2001, America and the world witnessed a new kind of war. We saw the great harm that a stateless network could inflict upon our country, killers armed with box cutters, mace, and 19 airline tickets. Those attacks also raised the prospect of even worse dangers—of other weapons in the hands of other men. The greatest threat before humanity today is the possibility of secret and sudden attack with chemical or biological or radiological or nuclear weapons.

In the past, enemies of America required massed armies, and great navies, powerful air forces to put our nation, our people, our friends and allies at risk. In the Cold War, Americans lived under the threat of weapons of mass destruction, but believed that deterrents made those weapons a last resort. What has changed in the 21st century is that, in the hands of terrorists, weapons of mass destruction would be a first resort—the preferred means to further their ideology of suicide and random murder. These terrible weapons are becoming easier to acquire, build, hide, and transport. Armed with a single vial of a biological agent or a single nuclear weapon, small groups of fanatics, or failing states, could gain the power to threaten great nations, threaten the world peace.

America, and the entire civilized world, will face this threat for decades to come. We must confront the danger with open eyes, and unbending purpose. I have made clear to all the policy of this nation: America will not permit terrorists and dangerous regimes to threaten us with the world's most deadly weapons. (Applause.)

Meeting this duty has required changes in thinking and strategy. Doctrines designed to contain empires, deter aggressive states, and defeat massed armies cannot fully protect us from this new threat. America faces the possibility of catastrophic attack from ballistic missiles armed with weapons of mass destruction. So that is why we are developing and deploying missile defenses to guard our people. The best intelligence is necessary to win the war on terror and to stop proliferation. So that is why I have established a commission that will examine our intelligence capabilities and recommend ways to improve and adapt them to detect new and emerging threats.

We're determined to confront those threats at the source. We will stop these weapons from being acquired or built. We'll block them from being transferred. We'll prevent them from ever being used. One source of these weapons is dangerous and secretive regimes that build weapons of mass destruction to intimidate their neighbors and force their influence upon the world. These nations pose different challenges; they require different strategies.

The former dictator of Iraq possessed and used weapons of mass destruction against his own people. For 12 years, he defied the will of the international community. He refused to disarm or account for his illegal weapons and programs. He doubted our resolve to enforce our word—and now he sits in a prison cell, while his country moves toward a democratic future. (Applause.)

To Iraq's east, the government of Iran is unwilling to abandon a uranium enrichment program capable of producing material for nuclear weapons. The United States is working with our allies and the International Atomic Energy Agency to ensure that Iran meets its commitments and does not develop nuclear weapons. (Applause.)

In the Pacific, North Korea has defied the world, has tested long-range ballistic missiles, admitted its possession of nuclear weapons, and now threatens to build more. Together with our partners in Asia, America is insisting that North Korea completely, verifiably, and irreversibly dismantle its nuclear programs.

America has consistently brought these threats to the attention of international organizations. We're using every means of diplomacy to answer them. As for my part, I will continue to speak clearly on these threats. I will continue to call upon the world to confront these dangers, and to end them. (Applause.)

In recent years, another path of proliferation has become clear, as well. America and other nations are learning more about black-market operatives who deal in equipment and expertise related to weapons of mass destruction. These dealers are motivated by greed, or fanaticism, or both. They find eager customers in outlaw regimes, which pay millions for the parts and plans they need to speed up their weapons programs. And with deadly technology and expertise going on the market, there's the terrible possibility that terrorists groups could obtain the ultimate weapons they desire most.

The extent and sophistication of such networks can be seen in the case of a man named Abdul Qadeer Khan. This is the story as we know it so far.

A.Q. Khan is known throughout the world as the father of Pakistan's nuclear weapons program. What was not publicly known, until recently, is that he also led an extensive international network for the proliferation of nuclear technology and know-how.

For decades, Mr. Khan remained on the Pakistani government payroll, earning a modest salary. Yet, he and his associates financed lavish lifestyles through the sale of nuclear technologies and equipment to outlaw regimes stretching from North Africa to the Korean Peninsula.

A.Q. Khan, himself, operated mostly out of Pakistan. He served as director of the network, its leading scientific mind, as well as its primary salesman. Over the past decade, he made frequent trips to consult with his clients and to sell his expertise. He and his associates sold the blueprints for centrifuges to enrich uranium, as well as a nuclear design stolen from the Pakistani government. The network sold uranium hexafluoride, the gas that the centrifuge process can transform into enriched uranium for nuclear bombs. Khan and his associates provided Iran and Libya and North Korea with designs for Pakistan's older centrifuges, as well as designs for more advanced and efficient models. The network also provided these countries with components, and in some cases, with complete centrifuges.

To increase their profits, Khan and his associates used a factory in Malaysia to manufacture key parts for centrifuges. Other necessary parts were purchased through network operatives based in Europe, the Middle East, and Africa. These procurement agents saw the trade in nuclear technologies as a shortcut to personal wealth, and they set up front companies to deceive legitimate firms into selling them tightly controlled materials.

Khan's deputy—a man named B.S.A. Tahir—ran SMB computers, a business in Dubai. Tahir used that computer company as a front for the proliferation activities of the A.Q. Khan network. Tahir acted as both the network's chief financial officer and money launderer. He was also its shipping agent, using his computer firm as cover for the movement of centrifuge parts to various clients. Tahir directed the Malaysia facility to produce these parts based on Pakistani designs, and then ordered the facility to ship the components to Dubai. Tahir also arranged for parts acquired by other European procurement agents to transit through Dubai for shipment to other customers.

This picture of the Khan network was pieced together over several years by American and British intelligence officers. Our intelligence services gradually uncovered this network's reach, and identified its key experts and agents and money men. Operatives followed its transactions, mapped the extent of its operations. They monitored the travel of A.Q. Khan and senior associates. They shadowed members of the network around the world, they recorded their conversations, they penetrated their operations, we've uncovered their secrets. This work involved high risk, and all Americans can be grateful for the hard work and the dedication of our fine intelligence professionals. (Applause.)

Governments around the world worked closely with us to unravel the Khan network, and to put an end to his criminal enterprise. A.Q. Khan has confessed his crimes, and his top associates are out of business. The government of Pakistan is interrogating the network's members, learning critical details that will help them prevent it from ever operating again. President Musharraf has promised to share all the information he learns about the Khan network, and has assured us that his country will never again be a source of proliferation.

Mr. Tahir is in Malaysia, where authorities are investigating his activities. Malaysian authorities have assured us that the factory the network used is no longer producing centrifuge parts. Other members of the network remain at large. One by one, they will be found, and their careers in the weapons trade will be ended.

As a result of our penetration of the network, American and the British intelligence identified a shipment of advanced centrifuge parts manufactured at the Malaysia facility. We followed the shipment of these parts to Dubai, and watched as they were transferred to the *BBC China*, a German-owned ship. After the ship passed through the Suez Canal, bound for Libya, it was stopped by German and Italian authorities. They found several containers, each forty feet in length, listed on the ship's manifest as full of 'used machine parts.' In fact, these containers were filled with parts of sophisticated centrifuges.

The interception of the *BBC China* came as Libyan and British and American officials were discussing the possibility of Libya ending its WMD programs. The United States and Britain confronted Libyan officials with this evidence of an active and illegal nuclear program. About two months ago, Libya's leader voluntarily agreed to end his nuclear and chemical weapons programs, not to pursue biological weapons, and to permit thorough inspections by the International Atomic Energy Agency and the Organization for the Prohibition of Chemical Weapons. We're now working in partnership with these organizations and with the United Kingdom to help the government of Libya dismantle those programs and eliminate all dangerous materials.

Colonel Ghadafi made the right decision, and the world will be safer once his commitment is fulfilled. We expect other regimes to follow his example. Abandoning the pursuit of illegal weapons can lead to better relations with the United States, and other free nations. Continuing to seek those weapons will not bring security or international prestige, but only political isolation, economic hardship, and other unwelcome consequences. (Applause.)

We know that Libya was not the only customer of the Khan network. Other countries expressed great interest in their services. These regimes and other proliferators like Khan should know: We and our friends are determined to protect our people and the world from proliferation. (Applause.)

Breaking this network is one major success in a broad-based effort to stop the spread of terrible weapons. We're adjusting our strategies to the threats of a new era. America and the nations of Australia, France and Germany, Italy and Japan, the Netherlands, Poland, Portugal, Spain and the United Kingdom have launched the Proliferation Security Initiative to interdict lethal materials in transit. Our nations are sharing intelligence information, tracking suspect international cargo, conducting joint military exercises. We're prepared to search planes and ships, to seize weapons and missiles and equipment that raise proliferation concerns, just as we did in stopping the dangerous cargo on the *BBC China* before it reached Libya. Three more governments—Canada and Singapore and Norway—will be participating in this initiative. We'll continue to expand the core group of PSI countries. And as PSI grows, proliferators will find it harder than ever to trade in illicit weapons.

There is a consensus among nations that proliferation cannot be tolerated. Yet this consensus means little unless it is translated into action. Every civilized nation has a stake in preventing the spread of weapons of mass destruction. These materials and technologies, and the people who traffic in them, cross many borders. To stop this trade, the nations of the world must be strong and determined. We must work together, we must act effectively. Today, I announce seven proposals to strengthen the world's efforts to stop the spread of deadly weapons.

First, I propose that the work of the Proliferation Security Initiative be expanded to address more than shipments and transfers. Building on the tools we've developed to fight terrorists, we can take direct action against proliferation networks. We need greater cooperation not just among intelligence and military services, but in law enforcement, as well. PSI participants and other willing nations should use the Interpol and all other means to bring to justice those who traffic in deadly weapons, to shut down their labs, to seize their materials, to freeze their assets. We must act on every lead. We will find the middlemen, the suppliers and the buyers. Our message to proliferators must be consistent and it must be clear: We will find you, and we're not going to rest until you are stopped. (Applause.)

Second, I call on all nations to strengthen the laws and international controls that govern proliferation. At the U.N. last fall, I proposed a new Security Council resolution requiring all states to criminalize proliferation, enact strict export controls, and secure all sensitive materials within their borders. The Security Council should pass this proposal quickly. And when they do, America stands ready to help other governments to draft and enforce the new laws that will help us deal with proliferation.

Third, I propose to expand our efforts to keep weapons from the Cold War and other dangerous materials out of the wrong hands. In 1991, Congress passed the Nunn-Lugar legislation, Senator Lugar had a clear vision, along with Senator Nunn, about what to do with the old Soviet Union. Under this program, we're helping former Soviet states find productive employment for former weapons scientists. We're dismantling, destroying and securing weapons and materials left over from the Soviet WMD arsenal. We have more work to do there.

And as a result of the G-8 Summit in 2002, we agreed to provide $20 billion over 10 years—half of it from the United States—to support such programs. We should expand this cooperation elsewhere in the world. We will retain [sic] WMD scientists and technicians in countries like Iraq and Libya. We will help nations end the use of weapons-grade uranium in research reactors. I urge more nations to contribute to these efforts. The nations of the world must do all we can to secure and eliminate nuclear and chemical and biological and radiological materials.

As we track and destroy these networks, we must also prevent governments from developing nuclear weapons under false pretenses. The Nuclear Non-Proliferation Treaty was designed more than 30 years ago to prevent the spread of nuclear weapons beyond those states which already possessed them. Under this treaty, nuclear states agreed to help non-nuclear states develop peaceful atomic energy if they renounced the pursuit of nuclear weapons. But the treaty has a loophole which has been exploited by nations such as North Korea and Iran. These regimes are allowed to produce nuclear material that can be used to build bombs under the cover of civilian nuclear programs.

So today, as a fourth step, I propose a way to close the loophole. The world must create a safe, orderly system to field civilian nuclear plants without adding to the danger of weapons proliferation. The world's leading nuclear exporters should ensure that states have reliable access at reasonable cost to fuel for civilian reactors, so long as those states renounce enrichment and reprocessing. Enrichment and reprocessing are not necessary for nations seeking to harness nuclear energy for peaceful purposes.

The 40 nations of the Nuclear Suppliers Group should refuse to sell enrichment and reprocessing equipment and technologies to any state that does not already possess full-scale, functioning enrichment and reprocessing plants. (Applause.) This step will prevent new states from developing the means to produce fissile material for nuclear bombs. Proliferators must not be allowed to cynically manipulate the NPT to acquire the material and infrastructure necessary for manufacturing illegal weapons.

For international norms to be effective, they must be enforced. It is the charge of the International Atomic Energy Agency to uncover banned nuclear activity around the world and report those violations to the U.N. Security Council. We must ensure that the IAEA has all the tools it needs to fulfill its essential mandate. America and other nations support what is called the Additional Protocol, which requires states to declare a broad range of nuclear activities and facilities, and allow the IAEA to inspect those facilities.

As a fifth step, I propose that by next year, only states that have signed the Additional Protocol be allowed to import equipment for their civilian nuclear programs. Nations that are serious about fighting proliferation will approve and implement the Additional Protocol. I've submitted the Additional Protocol to the Senate. I urge the Senate to consent immediately to its ratification.

We must also ensure that IAEA is organized to take action when action is required. So, a sixth step, I propose the creation of a special committee of the IAEA Board which will focus intensively on safeguards and verification. This committee, made up of governments in good standing with the IAEA, will strengthen the capability of the IAEA to ensure that nations comply with their international obligations.

And, finally, countries under investigation for violating nuclear non-proliferation obligations are currently allowed to serve on the IAEA Board of Governors. For instance, Iran—a country suspected of maintaining an extensive nuclear weapons program—recently completed a two-year term on the Board. Allowing potential violators to serve on the Board creates an unacceptable barrier to effective action. No state under investigation for proliferation violations should be allowed to serve on the IAEA Board of Governors—or on the new special committee. And any state currently on the Board that comes under investigation should be suspended from the Board. The integrity and mission of the IAEA depends on this simple principle: Those actively breaking the rules should not be entrusted with enforcing the rules. (Applause.)

As we move forward to address these challenges we will consult with our friends and allies on all these new measures. We will listen to their ideas. Together we will defend the safety of all nations and preserve the peace of the world.

Over the last two years, a great coalition has come together to defeat terrorism and to oppose the spread of weapons of mass destruction—the inseparable commitments of the war on terror. We've shown that proliferators can be discovered and can be stopped. We've shown that for regimes that choose defiance, there are serious consequences. The way ahead is not easy, but it is clear. We will proceed as if the lives of our citizens depend on our vigilance, because they do. Terrorists and terror states are in a race for weapons of mass murder, a race they must lose. (Applause.) Terrorists are resourceful; we're more resourceful. They're determined; we must be more determined. We will never lose focus or resolve. We'll be unrelenting in the defense of free nations, and rise to the hard demands of dangerous times.

May God bless you all. (Applause.)

End 3:07 P.M. EST

The Delegation of the United States of America to the
2005 Review Conference of the
Treaty on the Non-Proliferation of Nuclear Weapons
2–27 May, 2005

STATEMENT BY
STEPHEN G. RADEMAKER
UNITED STATES ASSISTANT SECRETARY OF STATE
FOR ARMS CONTROL

to the

2005 REVIEW CONFERENCE OF THE
TREATY ON THE NON-PROLIFERATION
OF NUCLEAR WEAPONS

New York
May 2, 2005

Thank you, Mr. President.

The Nuclear Non-Proliferation Treaty is a key legal barrier against the spread of nuclear weapons and material related to the production of such weapons. That we can meet today, thirty-five years after the Treaty entered into force, and not count twenty or more nuclear weapon states—as some predicted in the 1960s—is a sign of the Treaty's success. NPT parties can be justly proud of the NPT's contribution to global security.

Nearly 190 states are now party to the Treaty the greatest number of parties to any multi-lateral security agreement, save the United Nations Charter. We are pleased that so many of the states party have gathered in this great hall for the Seventh Review Conference of the NPT.

The NPT is fundamentally a treaty for mutual security. It is clear that the security of all member states depends on unstinting adherence to the Treaty's nonproliferation norms by all other parties. The Treaty's principal beneficiaries are those member states that do *not* possess nuclear weapons because they can be assured that their neighbors also do not possess nuclear weapons. Strict compliance with nonproliferation obligations is essential to regional stability, to forestalling nuclear arms races, and to preventing resources needed for economic development from being squandered in a destabilizing and economically unproductive pursuit of weapons.

There has been important progress in advancing the NPT's objectives. One clear success is the recent Libyan decision to abandon its clandestine nuclear weapons program, a program aided by the A.Q. Khan network. Libya should be commended for making the strategic decision to return to NPT compliance, to voluntarily give up its nuclear weapons program, and to cooperate with the IAEA and others. In doing so, it moved to end its damaging international isolation and paved the way for improved relations with the international community.

Libya has joined other states, including South Africa, Ukraine, Belarus and Kazakhstan, that have wisely concluded that their security interests are best served by turning away from nuclear weapons and coming into full compliance with the NPT as non-nuclear weapon states. This demonstrates that, in a world of strong nonproliferation norms, it is never too late to make the decision to become a fully compliant NPT state. In all of these cases, including the most recent case of Libya, such a decision was amply rewarded.

We have also had success in designing new tools outside of the NPT that complement the Treaty. The Proliferation Security Initiative (PSI) is one such important new tool. First proposed by President Bush in Krakow, Poland on May 31, 2003, over 60 nations have now associated themselves with this effort against the international outlaws that traffic in deadly materials. We are pleased that the PSI was endorsed by Security Council Resolution 1540 and by the Secretary General's High Level Panel on Threats, Challenges and Change, and we reaffirm our determination not to shrink from using this important new tool.

We cannot simply celebrate these successes, however. While these successes are important, more must be done. Today, the Treaty is facing the most serious challenge in its history due to instances of noncompliance. Although the vast majority of member states have lived up to their NPT nonproliferation obligations that constitute the Treaty's most important contribution to international peace and security, some have not.

Indeed, Mr. President, some continue to use the pretext of a peaceful nuclear program to pursue the goal of developing nuclear weapons. We must confront this challenge in order to ensure that the Treaty remains relevant. This Review Conference provides an opportunity for us to demonstrate our resolve in reaffirming our collective determination that noncompliance with the Treaty's core nonproliferation norms is a clear threat to international peace and security.

I want to take a few minutes to outline the major issues facing the NPT.

By secretly pursuing reprocessing and enrichment capabilities in order to produce nuclear weapons, North Korea violated both its safeguards obligations and its nonproliferation obligations under the NPT before announcing its intention to withdraw from the Treaty in 2003. In recent months, it has claimed to possess nuclear weapons.

For almost two decades Iran has conducted a clandestine nuclear weapons program, aided by the illicit network of A.Q. Khan. After two and a half years of investigation by the IAEA and adoption of no fewer than seven decisions by the IAEA Board of Governors calling on Iran to cooperate fully with the IAEA in resolving outstanding issues with its nuclear program, many questions remain unanswered. Even today, Iran persists in not cooperating fully. Iran has made clear its determination to retain the nuclear infrastructure it secretly built in violation of its NPT safeguards obligations, and is continuing to develop its nuclear capabilities around the margins of the suspension it agreed to last November, for example, by continuing construction of the heavy water reactor at Arak, along with supporting infrastructure.

Pursuit of nuclear weapons by noncompliant states is not the only threat to the NPT. New challenges have emerged from non-state actors.

One category of problematic non-state actors consists of individuals acting in their own self-interest who have helped facilitate proliferation. For many years the A.Q. Khan nuclear smuggling network provided nuclear technology and materials—even weapon designs—to NPT violators through a widespread, illicit procurement network. While this network has been disbanded, we are still uncovering and repairing the damage it has wrought upon the nuclear nonproliferation regime. It is imperative that no other networks take its place.

A second category of problematic non-state actors consists of terrorist organizations who magnify the threat of proliferation by potentially placing nuclear weapons in the hands of those determined to use them. It is no secret that terrorists want to acquire weapons of mass destruction, including nuclear weapons. The consequences if they succeed would be catastrophic. We must take every possible step to thwart their efforts. This means improving the security of nuclear materials, stopping illicit nuclear trafficking, strengthening safeguards, establishing and enforcing effective export controls, and acting decisively to dismantle terrorist networks everywhere.

Last year, President Bush proposed an action plan to prevent further nuclear proliferation and to address each of these needs. This plan included seven specific initiatives, including the need to criminalize proliferation-related activities. In response, the UN Security Council adopted Resolution 1540, which requires states to: criminalize proliferation of weapons of mass destruction and their means of delivery by non-state actors;

enact and enforce effective export controls; and secure proliferation-sensitive equipment. This is an essential step in reducing the dangers of illicit proliferation networks and of terrorist efforts to acquire weapons of mass destruction.

The United States continues to work with others to advance other elements of the President's action plan, including:

- universalizing adherence to the Additional Protocol and making it a condition of nuclear supply, which will strengthen the means to verify NPT compliance;
- restricting the export of sensitive technologies, particularly the spread of enrichment and reprocessing technology, which will close a key loophole in the NPT;
- creating a special safeguards committee of the IAEA Board of Governors, which will focus the attention of the Board on issues central to the purpose of the Treaty;
- strengthening the Proliferation Security Initiative to intercept and prevent illicit shipments of weapons of mass destruction, their delivery systems, and related materials, which is a critical adjunct to the work of the Treaty undertaken by nations acting to defeat proliferation threats; and
- expanding the "Global Partnership" to eliminate and secure sensitive materials, including weapons of mass destruction, which broadens U.S. and Russian efforts aimed at cooperative threat reduction.

Although most of these activities call for action outside the formal framework of the NPT, they are grounded or the norms and principles of nuclear nonproliferation laid down by the Treaty. If adopted, they will each answer directly real threats to the vitality of the Treaty. Accordingly, we hope the deliberations at this Conference will lend political support to these initiatives, and we encourage all states participating in this Conference to join us in supporting these steps.

U.S. support for the NPT extends far beyond our determined efforts to reinforce the Treaty's core nonproliferation norms. The benefits of peaceful nuclear cooperation comprise an important element of the NPT. Through substantial funding and technical cooperation, the United States fully supports peaceful nuclear development in many states, bilaterally and through the IAEA. But the language of Article IV is explicit and unambiguous: states asserting their right to receive the benefits of peaceful nuclear development must be in compliance with their nonproliferation obligations under Articles I and II of the NPT. No state in violation of Articles I or II should receive the benefits of Article IV. All nuclear assistance to such a state, bilaterally or through the IAEA, should cease. Again, we hope the deliberations at this Review Conference will endorse this proposition.

Which brings us back to the compliance challenges of North Korea and Iran. On North Korea, we are attempting to bring together the regional players in the Six Party Talks to convince Pyongyang that its only viable option is to negotiate an end to its nuclear ambitions. We have tabled a proposal that addresses the North's stated concerns and also provides for the complete, verifiable, and irreversible elimination of North Korean nuclear programs.

As to Iran, Britain, France, and Germany, with our support, are seeking to reach a diplomatic solution to the Iranian nuclear problem, a solution that given the history of clandestine nuclear weapons work in that country, must include permanent cessation of Iran's enrichment and reprocessing efforts, as well as dismantlement of equipment and facilities related to such activity. Iran must provide such objective and verifiable guarantees in order to demonstrate that it is not using a purportedly peaceful nuclear program to hide a nuclear weapons program or to conduct additional clandestine nuclear work elsewhere in the country.

Handling the proliferation challenges we face requires a robust IAEA safeguards system that not only helps to protect our common security against nuclear proliferation, but also builds confidence that peaceful nuclear development is not being abused. Safeguards are therefore essential to facilitating peaceful nuclear programs. As President Bush stated last year, "we must ensure the IAEA has all the tools it needs to fulfill its essential mandate." Making the Additional Protocol the verification standard and establishing a special safeguards committee of the IAEA Board of Governors are two key ways to strengthen international safeguards and provide the IAEA with much needed support and access.

An effective, transparent export control regime also helps build confidence among states that assistance provided for peaceful nuclear development will not be diverted to illegal weapons purposes. Yet, recent developments and revelations are troubling. The spread of enrichment and reprocessing technology poses a particularly dangerous risk. Collectively, we need to address urgently the very real security implications of the further spread of these technologies. Some countries, such as Iran, are seeking these facilities, either secretly or with explanations that cannot withstand scrutiny. We dare not look the other way. As President Bush has proposed, tighter controls should be adopted on enrichment and reprocessing technologies. We must close the loopholes in the Treaty that allow the unnecessary spread of such technologies. This can be accomplished without compromising truly peaceful nuclear programs, and in a manner which ensures that NPT parties that have no such facilities and are in full compliance with the Treaty are able to acquire nuclear fuel at a reasonable price.

The United States remains fully committed to fulfilling our obligations under Article VI. Since the last review conference the United States and the Russian Federation concluded our implementation of START I reductions, and signed and brought into force the Moscow Treaty of 2002. Under the Moscow Treaty, we have agreed to reduce our operationally deployed strategic nuclear warheads to 1,700–2,200, about a third of the 2002 levels, and less than a quarter of the level at the end of the Cold War. When this Treaty is fully implemented by the end of 2012, the United States will have reduced the number of strategic nuclear warheads it had deployed in 1990 by about 80%. In addition, we have reduced our non-strategic nuclear weapons by 90% since the end of the Cold War, dismantling over 3,000 such weapons pursuant to the Presidential Nuclear Initiatives of 1991 and 1992. We have also reduced the role of nuclear weapons in our deterrence strategy and are cutting our nuclear stockpile almost in half, to the lowest level in decades.

Mr. President and fellow delegates, we have eliminated thousands of nuclear weapons, eliminated an entire class of intermediate-range ballistic missiles, taken B-1 bombers out of nuclear service, reduced the number of ballistic missile submarines, drastically reduced our nuclear weapons-related domestic infrastructure, and are now eliminating our most modern and sophisticated land-based ballistic missile. We have also spent billions of dollars, through programs such as Nunn-Lugar, to help other countries control and eliminate their nuclear materials. We are proud to have played a leading role in reducing nuclear arsenals.

More can be done, of course. For example, we have called upon the Conference on Disarmament to initiate negotiations on a Fissile Material Cut-off Treaty (FMCT). We believe that ar. FMCT would help to promote nuclear nonproliferation by establishing the universal norm that no state should produce fissile material for weapons. For its part, the United States ceased production of fissile material for weapons purposes nearly two decades ago. Today we reiterate the call we issued last year at the Conference on Disarmament for all nations committed to the FMCT to join us in declaring a moratorium on fissile material production for weapons purposes until a binding FMCT has been concluded and entered into force.

We intend to provide much more detailed information about the steps we have taken in accordance with Article VI at a later point during this Conference. The full record will leave no doubt about the commitment of the United States to fulfillment of its Article VI obligations.

In conclusion, Mr. President, the NPT is a critical tool in the global struggle against proliferation. The United States remains committed to universal adherence to the NPT, and we hope that countries still outside will join the Treaty, which they can do only as non-nuclear weapon states. However, we must remain mindful that the Treaty will not continue to advance our security in the future if we do not successfully confront the current proliferation challenges. Our common obligation is clear. This Conference offers us the opportunity to expand our understanding of these critical challenges and to seek common ground on ways to respond. In the interest of world peace and security, let us work together to preserve and strengthen the NPT.

Thank you, Mr. President.

A Recipe for Success at the 2010 Review Conference

Dr Christopher A. Ford
United States Special Representative for Nuclear Nonproliferation

Opening Remarks to the 2008 NPT Preparatory Committee
Palais des Nations, Geneva, Switzerland
(April 28, 2008)
P.M.

Thank you, Mr. Chairman.

The Treaty on the Non-Proliferation of Nuclear Weapons (NPT) was opened for signature four decades ago this summer. It stands today not just as a landmark treaty—the most widely adhered-to nonproliferation or arms control agreement in human history—but, much more importantly, as an important contributor to international peace and security. The NPT, and the broader nonproliferation regime of which it forms a vital part, powerfully serves the security interests of all its States Party by helping combat the further spread of nuclear weapons. This helps reduce the risk of catastrophic nuclear warfare, prevent the emergence of new nuclear arms races, and ensure that ongoing regional rivalries are not inflamed by States Party possessing nuclear weapons. By accomplishing its core nonproliferation purpose, the NPT also powerfully serves the interest of the other goals to which States Party committed themselves in the Treaty's text, including promotion of the peaceful uses of nuclear technology, and progress toward nuclear disarmament.

The world today is vastly safer and more secure than the one in which the NPT was opened for signature, and part of the reason for this has been the success of States Party in ensuring compliance with the nonproliferation obligations that during the NPT's negotiation were referred to as "the core of the Treaty."[1]

States' commitments to preventing the further spread of nuclear weapons have led to profound successes. Even during the height of the Cold War—when the NPT nuclear weapons states (NWS) possessed vast arsenals of nuclear weapons, and the danger of nuclear warfare on a global scale loomed large over all mankind—States Party to the Treaty recognized their strong shared interests in preventing further nuclear proliferation. Despite the tensions of that period—and predictions by U.S. President John Kennedy that the world would probably have between 15 and 20 nuclear weapons states even by the end of the 1960s—several nascent nuclear weapons efforts in various countries around the world were quietly shut down. Despite such predictions, a clear commitment to nonproliferation ensured that proliferation was slowed from its anticipated sprint to a mere crawl. Such successes helped prevent a perilous Cold War world from becoming much

---

[1] See, e.g., U.S. Arms Control and Disarmament Agency, *International Negotiations on the Treaty on the Nonproliferation of Nuclear Weapons* (Washington, D.C., 1969), at 81 quoting Canadian representative Burns, in ENDC/PV. 338, at 5-01; see also Conference of the Eighteen-Nation Committee on Disarmament *process verbal*. ENDC/PV. 378. March 13, 1982, at 11.

more dangerous still. They also helped preserve the foundation for progress on other significant Treaty goals, most prominently peaceful uses and disarmament.

But while remembering these successes, we must not be complacent. After all, treaties' effectiveness depends upon the collective willpower and commitment of their sovereign States Party to their goals. Despite tremendous progress in fulfilling other key goals of the NPT—in slashing the nuclear arsenals of almost all the NWS, including the two former superpower adversaries, and in widely sharing the benefits of peaceful nuclear technology—the international community has been struggling with proliferation challenges from Iranian and North Korean nuclear weapons ambitions that so far do *not* yet seem to have been abandoned. To be sure, the nonproliferation regime recently had a notable success in Libya's decision in 2003 to abandon its weapons of mass destruction (WMD) programs—which helped that country end its damaging isolation from the international community. So far, however, the jury is still out on whether the NPT regime will be able to meet today's challenges. It is imperative for States Party to work together more effectively to fulfill the Treaty's central purpose of preventing nuclear weapons proliferation. Upon this hinges the prospects for continuing peaceful nuclear technology cooperation, and for achieving both Treaty universality and eventual nuclear disarmament.

Mr. Chairman, as we approach the half-way point of this NPT Review Cycle, what can be said about the progress States Party have been making? How can we all work together to help the Treaty survive the challenges it faces and live up to the hopes invested in it by governments around the world? Let me first summarize the progress that the United States sees occurring in key issue areas, before outlining what we believe to be the best road ahead.

Peaceful Uses. With respect to peaceful uses of nuclear energy, the period since the end of the 2005 NPT Review Cycle has seen some real progress. Specifically, there has been an increasing recognition of two critical points—and a growing understanding of how to resolve the apparent tension between them. First, there is wide international understanding that the proliferation of the capability to produce fissile material usable in nuclear weapons poses grave dangers to the nonproliferation regime. The difficulty in obtaining fissile material is the principal obstacle to developing nuclear weapons, and the unchecked or unsafeguarded acquisition of material-production capabilities by countries with potential nuclear weapons ambitions is antithetical to the cause of nonproliferation. The spread of such capabilities would also require more resources and capabilities for the safeguards regime, which would need to provide warning of diversion timely enough to permit effective responses, and to ensure against the absence of undeclared nuclear material production in countries that possess the requisite technology

Second, there is wide international appreciation that it is not enough for the current level of international nuclear energy cooperation to continue. It must actually be *intensified* in order to help mankind meet its skyrocketing energy needs in ways that minimize further damage to the environment while increasing energy security. This, too, will present resource and technological challenges to the safeguards system, as larger and larger numbers of nuclear facilities come on line around the world. More importantly, however, because reactors require fuel, and because fuel production has to occur somewhere, these two factors might seem to create a tension—dividing the NPT against itself on an article-by-article basis with peaceful use concerns pitted against the interests of the Treaty's nonproliferation core.

This, however, need not be the case, for promoting peaceful nuclear cooperation need not entail subverting the central object of the Treaty. In fact, recent progress on these fronts highlights the very real possibility that States Party will be able—as U.S. President Bush and Russian President Putin put it in July 2007—to expand nuclear energy in a way that strengthens the nuclear nonproliferation regime. Building upon President Bush's 2004 initiative, the United States has been moving forward with programs such as the Global Nuclear Energy Partnership (GNEP)—efforts designed to *expand* international nuclear cooperation in proliferation-responsible ways, and to provide such attractive and responsible cooperative alternatives that countries offered the chance to participate will not choose to pursue enrichment and reprocessing technology (ENR). Closely linked to such undertakings have been multilateral proposals by many of the major nuclear fuel suppliers, working with the IAEA, to develop an even more robust and reliable international system of fuel supply that will help remove any perceived need for more countries to develop ENR capabilities of their own. The United States looks forward to working with all countries, along with the IAEA, to develop further the concept of reliable fuel supply.

Moreover, efforts by Iran to play upon some countries' sincere concerns about technology access to justify its own activities in violation of safeguards and the NPT have been encountering increasing resistance during this Review Cycle. In contrast to the end of the 2005 Review Cycle, there is less rhetoric about the alleged "denial of inalienable rights" and more legitimate debate about the concrete benefits and technical merits of fuel-supply programs and GNEP-style cooperation predicated upon countries' voluntary forbearance with respect to fuel-cycle technology. The NPT forum thus may be moving from a deliberately polarized and misleading discourse about "denial of rights" to a more constructive one focusing upon the *availability of proliferation-responsible alternatives*. That is indeed progress—and a potential path to the resolution of much of the seeming tension between Articles II and IV.

Disarmament. At the end of the 2005 Review Cycle, some NPT States Party apparently held the belief—promoted by Iran and others—that the NPT nuclear weapons states (NWS) somehow had backtracked on their commitment to the ultimate goal of nuclear disarmament, and that they were in violation of their obligations under Article VI. With respect to United States nuclear posture and policy, any such beliefs are patently false. By simply laying out the facts, we believe we have made progress in correcting misperceptions and allaying concerns.

Happily, Mr. Chairman, States Party today better understand the United States' exemplary progress. The numbers speak for themselves: we now have reduced our operationally-deployed strategic nuclear weapons from over 10,000 to under 3,000 today. We have accelerated our rates of warhead dismantlement, and are on our way toward dismantling *three out of every four* of all the many thousands of U.S. nuclear weapons that were in existence at the end of the Cold War, bringing our arsenal down to its lowest levels since the 1950s. We continue to: reduce the number of delivery systems; eliminate entire classes of weapons such as intermediate-range missiles and nuclear artillery shells; remove many hundreds of tons of fissile material from our weapons programs; maintain our moratorium on underground nuclear testing; help peacefully dispose of hundreds of tons of fissile material from former Soviet nuclear weapons; fulfill our promises to slash non-strategic nuclear forces; build a new plant to convert large quantities of plutonium from former U.S. nuclear weapons into nuclear reactor fuel: refrain from producing new uranium or plutonium for nuclear weapons; and work to bring about the complete, global prohibition of fissile material production for use in nuclear weapons.

States Party also better understand that the United States' story of disarmament progress is not just about numbers. They know we have been moving to reduce reliance upon nuclear weapons by improving our means to accomplish strategic deterrence through a "New Triad" that includes the development of *non*-nuclear capabilities, active and passive defenses, and a responsive production capability that will allow the United States to adopt its weapons needs based on evolving requirements—and which is already helping us move toward a posture in which we can reduce the number of nuclear warheads in existence as we feel less need to maintain as many of them as a "hedge" against unforeseen changes in the strategic threat environment or technical surprise. States Party know that the United States remains firmly and unequivocally committed to the disarmament goals of the Preamble and Article VI of the NPT, and indeed that we have become a leading contributor to international discussions of how to move forward toward those ends. Through these efforts, we are creating the conceptual and infrastructural foundations for meeting the shared goal of a future world that is not merely free of nuclear weapons, but that can *remain* so because would-be proliferators are unlikely to win significant strategic benefits by "breaking out" of a disarmament regime.

Thanks to these efforts and to those of some of the other NWS, Article VI discourse is now gradually arriving at the place where disarmament debate *should* have been all along. In short, astonishing progress has already been achieved and is continuing, most of the NWS are becoming increasingly accustomed to a constructive degree of voluntary transparency about nuclear matters, and there seems to be a growing interest in realistic and practical discussions about the possibility of nuclear disarmament. Accordingly, the first portion of the 2010 NPT Review Cycle should be counted as a success for anyone who is serious about the cause of disarmament.

Nonproliferation. With regard to non-proliferation—the overarching purpose of the NPT, and the foundation upon which of the objectives of peaceful uses and disarmament rest—the record is mixed. It is not clear that all States Party in the NPT regime are as strongly committed to nonproliferation today than at the end of the 2005 Review Cycle, and some may be less so.

To be sure, the unchecked spread of ENR technology would create the risk of "latent" or "virtual" nuclear weapons programs in countries of concern, and is a focus of growing worry. The world has become appropriately alarmed about Iran's rush to produce fissile materials for reactors it does not have in order to prevent an "energy crisis" it does not face—particularly given that Iran lacks the domestic uranium reserves to support the "Independent" commercial program it claims to desire. There is also a growing appreciation for the importance of ensuring that nuclear safeguards will provide warning of fissile material diversion in time to permit an effective response by members of a fractious and cumbersome multilateral regime—a task that will require special attention as the use of nuclear energy for civil power generation expands worldwide, and if any additional countries acquire ENR.

But the Iranian and North Korean nuclear programs continue to pose serious challenges to the international nuclear nonproliferation regime. It is encouraging that the international community has just adopted a third resolution in the United Nations Security Council, requiring that Iran suspend its enrichment and reprocessing activities and imposing additional sanctions in the wake of that regime's continued contempt for international law and for the multilateral institutions in which the United States and so many other countries have placed their hopes for meeting proliferation challenges.

With regard to North Korea, much additional work still needs to be done to achieve the vision of the September 2005 Joint Statement, under which the DPRK committed to abandon all nuclear weapons and existing nuclear programs and return, at an early date, to the NPT and to IAEA safeguards as a non-nuclear weapons state. One can only be alarmed, for instance, that North Korea collaborated with a State Party to the NPT—a country, Mr. Chairman, subject to the nonproliferation obligations of Article II and Article III of the Treaty—to construct a nuclear reactor in that country, a reactor *not* intended for peaceful purposes and which was developed covertly and in violation of the very procedures designed to reassure the world of the peaceful intent of nuclear activities. Nonetheless, the Six-Party process has resulted in important initial steps toward the denuclearization of the Korean Peninsula, and we are working with our partners to achieve the verifiable denuclearization of the Korean Peninsula. The United States is committed to ensuring that North Korea does not further engage in proliferation activities, and we will work with our partners to establish in the Six-Party Framework a rigorous verification mechanism to ensure that such conduct and other nuclear activities have ceased.

While we have seen evidence that sustained international solidarity in compliance enforcement can produce changes in a proliferator's behavior, however, the international nonproliferation regime clearly needs to do better in the future. If delegations to the 2010 Review Conference cannot look back and conclude that the Treaty regime contributed to the successful resolution of these proliferation challenges, the future of the NPT will dim.

What Next for 2010? As we all work to ensure that the 2010 Review Conference represents a successful conclusion to this cycle, we should build upon the model presented by last year's ably-chaired Preparatory Committee (PrepCom) meeting. At the first PrepCom, the States Party demonstrated admirable solidarity in the face of cynical efforts by one country to impede multilateral responses to proliferation challenges by sidetracking and obstructing NPT deliberations. The meeting even enjoyed a period, however brief, of valuable substantive debate, which laid the foundation for further constructive discussions here this year.

With regard to the next Review Conference, the United States in 2007 outlined an ambitious work plan that we believe should help all States Party structure their approaches to achieving a constructive Final Document in 2010. I encourage you to review it, for the United States believes that the substantive proposals set out in that work plan still remain the strongest foundation upon which to build consensus for an effective Final Document in 2010.

As we all work toward agreement, however, we should remember that it may not be possible to reach consensus in 2010 upon a comprehensive text that covers every detail of every issue currently confronting the NPT regime. If we make the "perfect the enemy of the good," as the saying goes, we will have only ourselves to blame if the Review Conference is accounted a "failure." The United States believes we can reach agreement on some very significant issues in a Final Document of more limited scope *and* debate issues upon which Treaty parties continue to *disagree* (for indeed it is important to have such debate).

The United States believes that the best recipe for success in 2010 is for us at this meeting—and in 2009—to develop areas that are (or can become) "ripe" for agreement at the Review Conference. Certain issues, we believe, already stand out in this regard.

- All States Party should be able to agree in 2010 upon the critical importance of ensuring strict compliance with all articles of the NPT. The adoption of the agenda at last year's Preparatory Committee indicates that the basis for such agreement already exists.
- We believe most States Party can agree upon the importance of promoting and indeed expanding international nuclear cooperation for peaceful purposes in ways consistent with nonproliferation principles. In this way, the integrity of the nonproliferation regime can be preserved, while helping mankind better enjoy the benefits of nuclear power in a world of staggering energy demand and increasing environmental degradation through the use of fossil fuels. Many different detailed proposals have been advanced as to how best to do this—particularly with respect to ensuring an even more robust and reliable supply of nuclear fuel—but we believe that there is broad agreement on the *principle* that some such solution is necessary.
- We believe that most States Party can agree upon the importance of taking steps to deter—and, if necessary, to respond to—withdrawal from the NPT by states that are in violation of its provisions. This is not an issue of denying them their right to withdraw, for that is enshrined in Article X, but rather of making it more difficult for violators to use the withdrawal mechanism to escape accountability for their violations.
- We believe that States Party can agree upon the importance of swift and effective responses to Treaty violations. What those mechanisms will be may be the subject of debate and discussion, but it is clear that we need to develop more effective approaches so that the delay between detection and reaction is minimized, the cost to the violator is increased, and the anticipated benefits of noncompliance to the violator are reduced.
- We also believe that all would agree with a strong statement on the importance of ensuring strong and viable nuclear safeguards including the Additional Protocol— safeguards capable of providing warning of the diversion of nuclear material or technology in sufficient time to permit effective responses—even as a global "renaissance" in nuclear power generation expands the number of facilities operating worldwide. Facilities must be adequately safeguarded, and all nuclear technology and material must be protected against theft or misuse by non-state actors such as terrorists.
- In light of the great importance placed upon the issue in NPT fora, we believe it may be possible, and would be valuable, for States Party to reaffirm well-established principles—expressed, for instance, in the 1995 Resolution on the Middle East—regarding the importance of bringing about conditions in which it will be possible to rid that region of all WMD and delivery systems.

- We also believe that all States Party—not merely the nuclear weapons states, but naturally including them—should be able to reaffirm their commitment to the disarmament goals expressed in the Preamble and in Article VI of the Treaty. The details of how precisely to fulfill those goals, and when it would be realistic to expect this, may remain subject to some disagreement among reasonable people. But we hope that it will be possible—and believe that it would aid the smooth functioning of the nonproliferation regime—for States Party to reaffirm these commitments publicly and emphatically at the close of this Review Cycle.

These "building blocks," we believe, can be the basis of a strong and constructive but realistic and achievable Final Document in 2010. The discussions in which we engage here over the next two weeks will help provide its substantive foundation. We in the United States look forward to these debates, and relish the chance to contribute to them.

Thank you, Mr. Chairman.

THE WHITE HOUSE
Office of the Press Secretary

FOR IMMEDIATE RELEASE   April 5, 2009

REMARKS BY PRESIDENT BARACK OBAMA
Hradcany Square
Prague, Czech Republic
10:21 A.M. (Local)

PRESIDENT OBAMA: Thank you so much. Thank you for this wonderful welcome. Thank you to the people of Prague. Thank you to the people of the Czech Republic. (Applause.) Today, I'm proud to stand here with you in the middle of this great city, in the center of Europe. (Applause.) And, to paraphrase one of my predecessors, I am also proud to be the man who brought Michelle Obama to Prague. (Applause.)

To Mr. President, Mr. Prime Minister, to all the dignitaries who are here, thank you for your extraordinary hospitality. And to the people of the Czech Republic, thank you for your friendship to the United States. (Applause.)

I've learned over many years to appreciate the good company and the good humor of the Czech people in my hometown of Chicago. (Applause.) Behind me is a statue of a hero of the Czech people—Tomas Masaryk. (Applause.) In 1918, after America had pledged its support for Czech independence, Masaryk spoke to a crowd in Chicago that was estimated to be over 100,000. I don't think I can match his record—(laughter)—but I am honored to follow his footsteps from Chicago to Prague. (Applause.)

For over a thousand years, Prague has set itself apart from any other city in any other place. You've known war and peace. You've seen empires rise and fall. You've led revolutions in the arts and science, in politics and in poetry. Through it all, the people of Prague have insisted on pursuing their own path, and defining their own destiny. And this city—this Golden City which is both ancient and youthful—stands as a living monument to your unconquerable spirit.

When I was born, the world was divided, and our nations were faced with very different circumstances. Few people would have predicted that someone like me would one day become the President of the United States. (Applause.) Few people would have predicted that an American President would one day be permitted to speak to an audience like this in Prague. (Applause.) Few would have imagined that the Czech Republic would become a free nation, a member of NATO, a leader of a united Europe. Those ideas would have been dismissed as dreams.

We are here today because enough people ignored the voices who told them that the world could not change.

We're here today because of the courage of those who stood up and took risks to say that freedom is a right for all people, no matter what side of a wall they live on, and no matter what they look like.

We are here today because of the Prague Spring—because the simple and principled pursuit of liberty and opportunity shamed those who relied on the power of tanks and arms to put down the will of a people.

We are here today because 20 years ago, the people of this city took to the streets to claim the promise of a new day, and the fundamental human rights that had been denied them for far too long. Sametová Revoluce—(applause)—the Velvet Revolution taught us many things. It showed us that peaceful protest could shake the foundations of an empire, and expose the emptiness of an ideology. It showed us that small countries can play a pivotal role in world events, and that young people can lead the way in overcoming old conflicts. (Applause.) And it proved that moral leadership is more powerful than any weapon.

That's why I'm speaking to you in the center of a Europe that is peaceful, united and free—because ordinary people believed that divisions could be bridged, even when their leaders did not. They believed that walls could come down; that peace could prevail.

We are here today because Americans and Czechs believed against all odds that today could be possible. (Applause.)

Now, we share this common history. But now this generation—our generation—cannot stand still. We, too, have a choice to make. As the world has become less divided, it has become more interconnected. And we've seen events move faster than our ability to control them—a global economy in crisis, a changing climate, the persistent dangers of old conflicts, new threats and the spread of catastrophic weapons.

None of these challenges can be solved quickly or easily. But all of them demand that we listen to one another and work together; that we focus on our common interests, not on occasional differences; and that we reaffirm our shared values, which are stronger than any force that could drive us apart. That is the work that we must carry on. That is the work that I have come to Europe to begin. (Applause.)

To renew our prosperity, we need action coordinated across borders. That means investments to create new jobs. That means resisting the walls of protectionism that stand in the way of growth. That means a change in our financial system, with new rules to prevent abuse and future crisis. (Applause.)

And we have an obligation to our common prosperity and our common humanity to extend a hand to those emerging markets and impoverished people who are suffering the most, even though they may have had very little to do with financial crises, which is why we set aside over a trillion dollars for the International Monetary Fund earlier this week, to make sure that everybody—everybody—receives some assistance. (Applause.)

Now, to protect our planet, now is the time to change the way that we use energy. (Applause.) Together, we must confront climate change by ending the world's dependence on fossil fuels, by tapping the power of new sources of energy like the wind and sun, and calling upon all nations to do their part. And I pledge to you that in this global effort, the United States is now ready to lead. (Applause.)

To provide for our common security, we must strengthen our alliance. NATO was founded 60 years ago, after Communism took over Czechoslovakia. That was when the free world learned too late that it could not afford division. So we came together to forge the strongest alliance that the world has ever known. And we should—stood shoulder to shoulder—year after year, decade after decade—until an Iron Curtain was lifted, and freedom spread like flowing water.

This marks the 10th year of NATO membership for the Czech Republic. And I know that many times in the 20th century, decisions were made without you at the table. Great powers let you down, or determined your destiny without your voice being heard. I am here to say that the United States will never turn its back on the people of this nation. (Applause.) We are bound by shared values, shared history—(applause.) We are bound by shared values and shared history and the enduring promise of our alliance. NATO's Article V states it clearly: An attack on one is an attack on all. That is a promise for our time, and for all time.

The people of the Czech Republic kept that promise after America was attacked; thousands were killed on our soil, and NATO responded. NATO's mission in Afghanistan is fundamental to the safety of people on both sides of the Atlantic. We are targeting the same al Qaeda terrorists who have struck from New York to London, and helping the Afghan people take responsibility for their future. We are demonstrating that free nations can make common cause on behalf of our common security. And I want you to know that we honor the sacrifices of the Czech people in this endeavor, and mourn the loss of those you've lost.

But no alliance can afford to stand still. We must work together as NATO members so that we have contingency plans in place to deal with new threats, wherever they may come from. We must strengthen our cooperation with one another, and with other nations and institutions around the world, to confront dangers that recognize no borders. And we must pursue constructive relations with Russia on issues of common concern.

Now, one of those issues that I'll focus on today is fundamental to the security of our nations and to the peace of the world—that's the future of nuclear weapons in the 21st century.

The existence of thousands of nuclear weapons is the most dangerous legacy of the Cold War. No nuclear war was fought between the United States and the Soviet Union, but generations lived with the knowledge that their world could be erased in a single flash of light. Cities like Prague that existed for centuries, that embodied the beauty and the talent of so much of humanity, would have ceased to exist.

Today, the Cold War has disappeared but thousands of those weapons have not. In a strange turn of history, the threat of global nuclear war has gone down, but the risk of a nuclear attack has gone up. More nations have acquired these weapons. Testing has continued. Black market trade in nuclear secrets and nuclear materials abound. The technology to build a bomb has spread. Terrorists are determined to buy, build or steal one. Our efforts to contain these dangers are centered on a global non-proliferation regime, but as more people and nations break the rules, we could reach the point where the center cannot hold.

Now, understand, this matters to people everywhere. One nuclear weapon exploded in one city—be it New York or Moscow, Islamabad or Mumbai, Tokyo or Tel Aviv, Paris or Prague—could kill hundreds of thousands of people. And no matter where it happens, there is no end to what the consequences might be—for our global safety, our security, our society, our economy, to our ultimate survival.

Some argue that the spread of these weapons cannot be stopped, cannot be checked—that we are destined to live in a world where more nations and more people possess the ultimate tools of destruction. Such fatalism is a deadly adversary, for if we believe that the spread of nuclear weapons is inevitable, then in some way we are admitting to ourselves that the use of nuclear weapons is inevitable.

Just as we stood for freedom in the 20th century, we must stand together for the right of people everywhere to live free from fear in the 21st century. (Applause.) And as nuclear power—as a nuclear power, as the only nuclear power to have used a nuclear weapon, the United States has a moral responsibility to act. We cannot succeed in this endeavor alone, but we can lead it, we can start it.

So today, I state clearly and with conviction America's commitment to seek the peace and security of a world without nuclear weapons. (Applause.) I'm not naive. This goal will not be reached quickly—perhaps not in my lifetime. It will take patience and persistence. But now we, too, must ignore the voices who tell us that the world cannot change. We have to insist, "Yes, we can." (Applause.)

Now, let me describe to you the trajectory we need to be on. First, the United States will take concrete steps towards a world without nuclear weapons. To put an end to Cold War thinking, we will reduce the role of nuclear weapons in our national security strategy, and urge others to do the same. Make no mistake: As long as these weapons exist, the United States will maintain a safe, secure and effective arsenal to deter any adversary, and guarantee that defense to our allies—including the Czech Republic. But we will begin the work of reducing our arsenal.

To reduce our warheads and stockpiles, we will negotiate a new Strategic Arms Reduction Treaty with the Russians this year. (Applause.) President Medvedev and I began this process in London, and will seek a new agreement by the end of this year that is legally binding and sufficiently bold. And this will set the stage for further cuts, and we will seek to include all nuclear weapons states in this endeavor.

To achieve a global ban on nuclear testing, my administration will immediately and aggressively pursue U.S. ratification of the Comprehensive Test Ban Treaty. (Applause.) After more than five decades of talks, it is time for the testing of nuclear weapons to finally be banned.

And to cut off the building blocks needed for a bomb, the United States will seek a new treaty that verifiably ends the production of fissile materials intended for use in state nuclear weapons. If we are serious about stopping the spread of these weapons, then we should put an end to the dedicated production of weapons-grade materials that create them. That's the first step.

Second, together we will strengthen the Nuclear Non-Proliferation Treaty as a basis for cooperation.

The basic bargain is sound: Countries with nuclear weapons will move towards disarmament, countries without nuclear weapons will not acquire them, and all countries can access peaceful nuclear energy. To strengthen the treaty, we should embrace several principles. We need more resources and authority to strengthen international inspections. We need real and immediate consequences for countries caught breaking the rules or trying to leave the treaty without cause.

And we should build a new framework for civil nuclear cooperation, including an international fuel bank, so that countries can access peaceful power without increasing the risks of proliferation. That must be the right of every nation that renounces nuclear weapons, especially developing countries embarking on peaceful programs. And no approach will succeed if it's based on the denial of rights to nations that play by the rules. We must harness the power of nuclear energy on behalf of our efforts to combat climate change, and to advance peace opportunity for all people.

But we go forward with no illusions. Some countries will break the rules. That's why we need a structure in place that ensures when any nation does, they will face consequences.

Just this morning, we were reminded again of why we need a new and more rigorous approach to address this threat. North Korea broke the rules once again by testing a rocket that could be used for long-range missiles. This provocation underscores the need for action—not just this afternoon at the U.N. Security Council, but in our determination to prevent the spread of these weapons.

Rules must be binding. Violations must be punished. Words must mean something. The world must stand together to prevent the spread of these weapons. Now is the time for a strong international response—(applause)—now is the time for a strong international response, and North Korea must know that the path to security and respect will never come through threats and illegal weapons. All nations must come together to build a stronger, global regime. And that's why we must stand shoulder to shoulder to pressure the North Koreans to change course.

Iran has yet to build a nuclear weapon. My administration will seek engagement with Iran based on mutual interests and mutual respect. We believe in dialogue. (Applause.) But in that dialogue we will present a clear choice. We want Iran to take its rightful place in the community of nations, politically and economically. We will support Iran's right to peaceful nuclear energy with rigorous inspections. That's a path that the Islamic Republic can take. Or the government can choose increased isolation, international pressure, and a potential nuclear arms race in the region that will increase insecurity for all.

So let me be clear: Iran's nuclear and ballistic missile activity poses a real threat, not just to the United States, but to Iran's neighbors and our allies. The Czech Republic and Poland have been courageous in agreeing to host a defense against these missiles. As long as the threat from Iran persists, we will go forward with a missile defense system that is cost-effective and proven. (Applause.) If the Iranian threat is eliminated, we will have a stronger basis for security, and the driving force for missile defense construction in Europe will be removed. (Applause.)

So, finally, we must ensure that terrorists never acquire a nuclear weapon. This is the most immediate and extreme threat to global security. One terrorist with one nuclear weapon could unleash massive destruction. Al Qaeda has said it seeks a bomb and that it would have no problem with using it. And we know that there is unsecured nuclear material across the globe. To protect our people, we must act with a sense of purpose without delay.

So today I am announcing a new international effort to secure all vulnerable nuclear material around the world within four years. We will set new standards, expand our cooperation with Russia, pursue new partnerships to lock down these sensitive materials.

We must also build on our efforts to break up black markets, detect and intercept materials in transit, and use financial tools to disrupt this dangerous trade. Because this threat will be lasting, we should come together to turn efforts such as the Proliferation Security Initiative and the Global Initiative to Combat Nuclear Terrorism into durable international institutions. And we should start by having a Global Summit on Nuclear Security that the United States will host within the next year. (Applause.)

Now, I know that there are some who will question whether we can act on such a broad agenda. There are those who doubt whether true international cooperation is possible, given inevitable differences among nations. And there are those who hear talk of a world without nuclear weapons and doubt whether it's worth setting a goal that seems impossible to achieve.

But make no mistake: We know where that road leads. When nations and peoples allow themselves to be defined by their differences, the gulf between them widens. When we fail to pursue peace, then it stays forever beyond our grasp. We know the path when we choose fear over hope. To denounce or shrug off a call for cooperation is an easy but also a cowardly thing to do. That's how wars begin. That's where human progress ends.

There is violence and injustice in our world that must be confronted. We must confront it not by splitting apart but by standing together as free nations, as free people. (Applause.) I know that a call to arms can stir the souls of men and women more than a call to lay them down. But that is why the voices for peace and progress must be raised together. (Applause.)

Those are the voices that still echo through the streets of Prague. Those are the ghosts of 1968. Those were the joyful sounds of the Velvet Revolution. Those were the Czechs who helped bring down a nuclear-armed empire without firing a shot.

Human destiny will be what we make of it. And here in Prague, let us honor our past by reaching for a better future. Let us bridge our divisions, build upon our hopes, accept our responsibility to leave this world more prosperous and more peaceful than we found it. (Applause.) Together we can do it.

Thank you very much. Thank you, Prague. (Applause.)

Index

DATE DUE

FEB 1 0 2012	